Narratives in Motion

Remapping Cultural History

General Editor: Jo Labanyi, New York University

This series challenges theoretical paradigms by exploring areas of culture that have previously received little attention. Its volumes discuss parts of the world that do not easily fit within dominant northern European or North American theoretical models, or that make a significant contribution to rethinking the ways in which cultural history is theorized and narrated.

Narratives in Motion

Journalism and Modernist Events in 1920s Portugal

Luís Trindade

berghahn
NEW YORK · OXFORD
www.berghahnbooks.com

First published in 2016 by
Berghahn Books
www.berghahnbooks.com

Library of Congress Cataloging-in-Publication Data

Names: Trindade, Luís, 1971- author.
Title: Narratives in motion: journalism and modernist events in 1920s
    Portugal / Luís Trindade.
Description: New York; Oxford: Berghahn Books, 2016. | Series: Remapping
    cultural history; volume 15 | Includes bibliographical references and
    index.
Identifiers: LCCN 2015046289| ISBN 9781785331039 (hardback: alk. paper) |
    ISBN 9781785331046 (ebook)
Subjects: LCSH: Journalism--Portugal--History--20th century. | Press and
    politics--Portugal--History--20th century. | Reportage literature,
    Portuguese--History and criticism. | Portuguese prose literature--20th
    century--History and criticism. | Modernism (Literature)--Portugal.
Classification: LCC PN5324 .T75 2016 | DDC 076.9/09042--dc23 LC record
available at http://lccn.loc.gov/2015046289

British Library Cataloguing in Publication Data

A catalogue record for this book is available from the British Library

ISBN 978-1-78533-103-9 hardback
ISBN 978-1-80073-218-6 paperback
ISBN 978-1-78533-104-6 ebook

Contents

Figures

Acknowledgements

During my research, I had the chance to discuss some of this book with a number of friends and colleagues whom I would like to thank: Philip Derbyshire, Miguel Cardoso, John Kraniauskas, Pedro Ramos Pinto, Zoltán Biedermann, Rui Lopes, Joana Estorninho de Almeida, Tiago Baptista, José Neves, Nuno Domingos, Alice Samara, Cláudia Figueiredo, Mariana Pinto dos Santos, Pedro Cerejo, Jens Andermann, Dominique Kalifa, António Pedro Pita, Luís Augusto Costa Dias, Bruno Peixe Dias, Rita Luís and Frederico Águas. In different ways, they have all contributed to shaping my ideas more clearly and helped me avoid mistakes and simplifications. Many other colleagues at Birkbeck College, in London, and in particular in the Department of Iberian and Latin American Studies, have provided the perfect research environment for this work: Mari Paz Balibrea, William Rowe, Carmen Fracchia, Luciana Martins, Maria Elena Placencia, Jessamy Harvey, Laura León Llerena and Antônio da Silva. To them, and to their spirit of intellectual resistance over the last few years, I would like to express my admiration and gratitude. Joana, Inês and Francisco gave me everything else.

Introduction

Newspapers and Modernist Events

[I]t is a more difficult thing to write history to make it anything than to make anything
that is anything be anything because in history you have everything, you have newspapers and the conversations and letter writing and the mystery stories and the audience
and in every direction an audience that fits anything in every way in which an audience
can fit itself to be anything.

—Gertrude Stein

One does not have to dig very deep to find references to the press in modernism. The reason for looking for those references, however, may seem
less obvious. In fact, despite the frequency with which modernist writers,
painters and film-makers refer to the news in their plots, use journalists
as characters or images of newspapers, journalism as such is rarely given
a central role in the historical processes that gave rise to modernism in
the first place. It almost seems as if newspapers are too visible for one
to notice how important they were. By being everywhere, they become
banal, and this helps to explain why the press rarely appears at the same
level as other phenomena that usually constitute the core of historical
narratives from the late nineteenth to the first half of the twentieth century: technological revolution, the growth of cities, changes in social
perception with psychoanalysis and cinema – phenomena which are
very close to the transformations occurring in the world of journalism
during the same period, to such an extent that the latter can be seen as the
mediation that gave the former their public configuration. In other words,
we see the period mostly through the pervasive presence of journalistic discourses, and this is probably why the press itself remains largely
unacknowledged.

More than a question of visibility or even of recognition, it seems
that the problem here is one of discrepancy. One cannot say that newspapers are not there, it just seems that what they are shown doing in

novels, for instance, does not match the impact they end up having in plots. Neglecting newspapers and their overwhelming weight in the early twentieth-century public sphere is often used as a device to leave some room for the private, the domestic and the unconscious (and to show these in their permanent state of vulnerability). The press and the most commonsensical tropes around it – sensationalism, noise, reckless-ness – work in these circumstances as an important marker for the limits of what at the time could still be experienced in the realm of individual consciousness. A good example of this can be seen in a very discreet reference by Marcel Proust in *The Guermantes Way*, when the narrator suggests that 'a large number of German café owners, simply by being impressed by a customer or a newspaper when they said that France, England and Russia were "provoking" Germany, made war possible at the time of Agadir' (Proust 2000: 469).[1] *In Search of Lost Time* is not, of course, a novel immediately about its historical context, but the contra-diction between the processes of memory and consciousness in the novel and the incommensurability of what is here discreetly, almost acciden-tally being said – the most terrible events in the period would not have taken place without the pressure of newspapers – may help historians to situate the historical role of journalism, not only politically (as a facilita-tor of wars) but also in the consciousness of contemporaries who, in this sense, would have necessarily been immersed in journalistic discourses. What such reference to the press suggests, in the discrepancy between the impact of newspapers in the historical context of modernism and its seeming insignificance within the novel, is that for contemporaries any affirmation of individual subjectivity would have to be able to resist that same immersion in journalism.

The particular role of the press in the grand narrative of modernity (or at least of modernism) thus seems to be limited primarily to the impact of newspapers in the period's forms of perception. In particular, newspapers are usually seen as a key tool in the formation of mass public opinion and mass politics.[2] This may help explain Proust's reserve in the spe-cific context of *In Search of Lost Time*. Fortunately for us, that is, from the perspective of a historiographical approach to this particular form of discourse, other modern writers were much less discreet. Usually, the image of journalism given by modernists is very harsh, and Karl Kraus, in this context, probably is the most recognizable modernist critic of the press. In his own counter-newspaper *Die Fackel* or in the satirical play *The Last Days of Mankind*, Kraus dissected contemporary journalism, its inclination to be deceitful and the deterioration of language it promoted. The press as a decisive problem in early twentieth-century societies – and a major cause of the First World War – took up much of Kraus's writing and energy, and his critique deserves a study of its own.[3] In particular, such a study would have to track down the comprehensive scrutiny to which Kraus submitted newspapers for decades, especially in *Die Fackel*, a newspaper against newspapers that challenged the daily press in its own terms. However, the distance permitted by literary devices in *The Last Days of Mankind* allows Kraus to take a step further, or better still, beyond the constraints of journalistic routines, and literally stage the inner mechanisms of the press and its impact on Austrian society on the eve of the First World War. The play stages a corrupt triangle formed by politicians putting pressure on journalists, journalists doing favours for politicians, and the journalistic fictions produced by this fraudulent system of information acquiring social existence by being reproduced by a gullible public.

The dialogues in the play prove particularly appropriate to show how discourses shape reality – and not the other way around – how common sense is made out of endless repetition, and how the truth emerges from absurd situations. One particular scene demonstrates both the manipulative power of reporters in transforming fictions into journalistic narratives, and Karl Kraus's literary ability in re-enacting the whole process. The episode describes an interview with Elfriede Ritter, an Austrian actress who had just arrived in Vienna from Russia. While she tries to describe how pleasant her Russian sojourn had been, the two journalists keep distorting her replies in order to instigate the state of belligerency between the two countries:

> ELFRIEDE RITTER: ... the journey home was arduous, but not in the least stressful and ... I am delighted to be in my beloved Vienna.
>
> JOURNALIST 2: An Arduous journey, she admits.
>
> JOURNALIST 1: Stressful – Hang on, I wrote the first part of this in the office – (*writing*) Rescued from the torments of Russian bondage, after the completion of an arduous, stressful journey, actress Elfriede Ritter wept tears of joy at the thought of being, once again, in her beloved Vienna. [...]
>
> ELFRIEDE RITTER: What are you trying to do – I cannot say –
>
> JOURNALIST 1: She hardly dares say it.[4]

The manipulation is very exaggerated, one would almost say grotesque, but as Kraus insists in the appropriation of the actress's discourse by the two reporters, the procedures of journalistic interview are allowed to come forth. In other words, despite the obvious manipulation of the interviewee's declarations and the distance between her answers and how reporters report them, this falsification is nonetheless done in the name of a certain transparency. At the end, she becomes completely caught in a dialogue where her ideas are strangely misrepresented by the literal transcription of her words:

JOURNALIST 2: My dear *Fräulein*, the public wants to read this, you can speak out. Perhaps not in Russia, but here thank God freedom of speech prevails, here you can say anything at all about conditions in Russia! Did any Russian newspaper pay you the kind of attention we are? Exactly! [...]

ELFRIEDE RITTER: But it's not true!

JOURNALIST 1 (*looking up*): Not – true? I'm taking down your every word! Do you suggest our papers would carry something that isn't true?

JOURNALIST 2: The casting committee will be meeting at the Burgtheater on Saturday, for *Faust*, and if I say anything about this to the director it will be Fräulein Berger who ends up playing Gretchen, I promise you! [...]

ELFRIEDE RITTER (*imploringly*): I only – wanted to tell the truth –

JOURNALIST 1 (*angry*): So we're lying, are we?

ELFRIEDE RITTER: As a woman I don't have the correct perspective sometimes – I'm just glad to have escaped from enemy soil – in one piece –

JOURNALIST 2: You see, now you're remembering, bit by bit.

The extract is intriguing at many different levels: in the way it raises issues of gender domination, nationalist consensus and the coercive force (professional, in this case) exerted by the press. But it also raises two other, less evident, issues, on which I would now like to focus. On the one hand, the question of what is true or false depends on the way journalists decide to organize their narrative from a careful selection of the words uttered by the actress. This is why although they are taking what she says completely out of context, their vexed reply ('So we're lying, are we?') is actually difficult to answer. On the other hand, the whole process of manipulation seems to be given a higher rationale when the reporter claims that it is not really he who wants to know the truth about her journey, but the public. This is a decisive aspect as it suggests that journalists respond primarily to the expectations of readers (or to what they imagine those expectations to be) and only afterwards to the events they report about.

The close relation between the two poles of this form of communication – reporters and newspaper readers – was a main point of concern for the modernist critique of newspapers. In *The Man Without Qualities*,

Robert Musil shows that while the reporters of a violent murder of a woman who suffered 'stab wounds in the breast that penetrated the heart ... had expressed their revulsion at this, ... they did not stop until they had counted thirty-five stabs in the belly and explained the deep slash that reached from the navel to the sacrum, continuing up the back in numerous lesser cuts, while the throat showed marks of strangulation' (Musil 1995: 67–68). In the gruesome details of the victim's wounds, Musil replicates the hypocrisy of reporters that simultaneously censor and exploit the crime, but the real problem with this kind of journalistic narrative were those 'thousands of people who deplore the sensationalism of the press' but 'were nevertheless more deeply preoccupied with it than with their own life's work' (Musil 1995: 68). A chain of deceit, one might say: no one, from reporters to readers, seemed to endorse the display of violence, and yet all seemed to indulge in it. But more than sensationalism and the impact of journalistic dramatization on public opinion as such – fueling fear and violence – what seemed truly dangerous from the perspective of most writers was the way journalism, given the short span of the news and the brevity of its narratives, oversimplified reality, reducing politics to Manichean schema, polarizing social conflict and ultimately narrowing the horizons of readership. In other words, if the press was at all able to instigate hatred and drive a whole society into war, this was not only because it spread violence and drama but also because, by doing so, it disabled readers from imagining anything beyond that same violence and drama.

Imagine Plato was alive today, Musil proposes in another moment in his novel. He 'would certainly be ecstatic about a news industry capable of creating, exchanging, refining a new idea every day' (Musil 1995: 352). Conversely, with its inclination to novelties, the press would surely be willing to make a 'tremendous sensation' with him: 'If he were then capable of writing a volume of philosophical travel pieces in three weeks, and a few thousand of his well-known short stories, perhaps even turn one or the other of his older works into a film, he could undoubtedly do very well for himself for a considerable period of time'. However:

> The moment his return had ceased to be news ... and Mr Plato tried to put into practice one of his well-known ideas, which had never quite come into their own, the editor in chief would ask him to submit only a nice little column on the subject now and then for the Life and Leisure section (but in the easiest and most lively style possible, not heavy: remember the readers). (Musil 1995: 352)

The power of newspapers in shaping the ideas of German café owners, manipulating Elfriede Ritter's words, or describing the number of stabs in a victim's body created the predisposition to violence that, to many contemporaries, stood as one of the main causes of the First World War. And yet, tragic as it may have been, this was just a single event amidst the daily impact of the press in the dramatization of social perceptions. The real problem was the way this dramatization took place on a daily basis – and not just on tragic occasions – and how reality itself ultimately became covered by the language of the press. Trouble started with the fact that any perception of reality was created by journalistic discourse, in itself a corrupted form of language at the service of political interests and, even worse, the business of newspapers.[5] One can understand the critique of modernist writers like Karl Kraus and Robert Musil in this context: given the overwhelming presence of the press in society, only literature seemed able to counter the complete blur between reality and the discourses of journalism. Stéphane Mallarmé also suggests this: the corrupted language of the everyday had journalistic origins (it had become 'universal reportage') and human thought was reduced to an exchanged commodity. Only literature could retrieve ideas and their words from total reification:

> Narrate, teach, even describe, that's fine and even if it were enough for each of us perhaps, in order to exchange human thought, to take from or place in the hand of someone else a coin in silence, the elementary use of discourse serves the needs of universal *reportage*, of which, with the exception of literature, all the genres of contemporary writings contain elements. (Mallarmé 1998: 368)[6]

This was more than just hostility towards the press. Language seemed to be under threat and literature the only form capable of preserving it from the corruption of journalism. This is surely an interesting way to approach the study of modernism, in its games with common sense, its struggle against realism and the questioning of language, and also, probably above all else, in the way many modernist novels – *In Search of Lost Time* and *The Man Without Qualities* being good examples – resisted the quick temporality of the daily press. In the insistent inquiry of the past or in the lengthy analysis of the present in all its different aspects, these novels can be seen as desperate efforts to keep something from being lost in the fleeting succession of daily information.

So, if the problem was time, then it necessarily had historical implications. According to Musil, this could be seen in the fact that, though 'much was happening', at least if one believed what came in the press, 'two years or five years earlier there had also been much excitement, everyday had had its sensations' (Musil 1995: 390). In other words, with excitement being delivered on a daily basis, one would lose the sense of the past, as in such circumstances 'it was hard, not to say impossible, to remember what it was that had actually happened' (Musil 1995: 390).

Strangely, then, but as Mallarmé already suspected, newspapers, which were supposed to give their readers the true picture of modernity, were in fact cancelling the ability to perceive time elapsing and thus emptying history as a form of progress:

> What a strange business history was! We could safely say of this or that event that it had already found its place in history, or certainly would find it; but whether this event had actually taken place was not so sure! Because for anything to happen, it has to happen at a certain date and not at some other date or even not at all; also, the thing itself has to happen and not by chance something merely approximating it or something related. But this is precisely what no one can say of history, unless he happens to have written it down at the time, as newspapers do. (Musil 1995: 390)

The modern press was contemporaneous with the birth of historiography, and yet journalism is here shown as an obstacle to historical awareness. According to the modernist critique, the question seems to be: when something happens every day (or, according to the epigraph taken from Gertrude Stein, when 'everything' can now become history), how can we select what is worthy of becoming historical, let alone trust if what was registered in newspapers has happened at all? Our modernist novels can in this sense be seen as a struggle against the press for historical consciousness, or at least for the ability to seize it. The choice of newspapers as one of the main targets in these writers' critique of the times is thus very symptomatic, for it illustrates how deeply historically aware modernism was. More precisely, if modernism can be seen as a response to modernity, itself a form of historical consciousness – rather than a historical period in the strict sense – then whatever threatened the status of history could not fail to become one of its main concerns.

Modernist Events

The two threats posed by journalism – to communication and to the perception of time – suggests that the crisis of modernism can be located simultaneously in the realm of language and in the realm of history. By criticizing the press as an active agent in a generalized deterioration of discourse, modernism situates itself historically as both a critique and a form of regeneration. Furthermore, by treating contemporaneous journalism as a modern experience, rather than just a discourse about modernity, modernism gives the press a new historical density. For the press, unhistorical as it may have been, had a concrete impact on social relations and political events. This is one of the initial problems this book has to come to terms with: newspapers – in particular between the end of the nineteenth century and the first half of the twentieth – were key agents in a historical break within the discursive regime of realism, in which narrative and reality unambiguously played the roles of each other's subject and object.[7] When reality ceased to be readable outside discursive mediation, to give an account of events one has to start considering the circulation of discourses as a fundamental aspect of events materially unfolding through social life. For Hayden White, this is what introduces the possibility to think of modernist events, which would necessarily involve the need of a modernist historiography somehow able to constitute the appropriate narrative of modern life. Following Eric Auerbach's notion of literary figuration, White defines this form of historicism as an account where the fulfilment of a historical event – say, what we traditionally call progress – could be related to previous events in the same way literary fulfilments are related to figures in narratives.[8] Progress would then be the figuration of narrative, rather than historical, causality, whereas historiography would necessarily become metahistory.

However, when White tries to define what a modernist event could look like, he still seems too close to the modernist critique we have been analysing. White starts by pointing out how modern media, rather than a heuristic opening into contemporaneity, constitutes on the contrary what modernist historiography must overcome in order to become the historiographic genre of modernity. Modernist events – figured as 'holocaustal', including the violence of world wars and nuclear weapons, but also 'communications technology' (White 1999: 70) – thus emerge as complex units with 'potentially infinite' details and an 'infinitely extensive' (White 1999: 71) context, whose complexities are simplified, and thus falsified, on a daily basis by the media. 'It is fortunate, therefore, that we have in the work of one of the greatest of modernist writers a theorization of this problem', White (White 1999: 82) tells us: the writer is Gertrude Stein, and the problem – the obstacle to a proper historical narrative of modern life – is the press:

> In real life that is if you like in the newspapers which are not real life but real life with the reality left out, the reality being the inside and the newspapers being the outside and never is the outside inside and never is the inside outside except in the rare and peculiar cases when the outside breaks through to be inside because the outside is so part of some inside that even a description of the outside cannot completely relieve the outside of the inside. (Stein 1998: 347)

We have already seen that Stein, Musil and other modernist writers had common opinions about newspapers. What is new here is the way Hayden White not only incorporates the linguistic challenge of modernism in his historiographical reflection, but also how he embarks on a similar critique of journalism. White's dismissal represents in this sense a decisive challenge to a book like this, trying to come to terms with the historicity of newspapers. The challenge to history posed in my epigraph, on the other hand, may now become clearer: history would have to come to terms with a world covered by newspapers in a pure exteriority where 'everything is happening' so constantly and so visibly as to make 'real life's reality' – the inside of which newspapers would be the outside – invisible. A hierarchy of forms of perception and representation may then come forth: the 'everything' of newspapers from where history must retrieve 'anything' 'is an important enough thing for seeing but it is not an important enough thing for writing' (White 1999: 84). The world experienced through the press is represented as an impoverished experience (here related to the order of images rather than of written words). Against richer forms of experience not subsumed under the transparent immediacy of journalism's image of reality, newspapers could not but deceive. Stein assumes two things: on the one hand, that reality only matches its empty appearance in 'rare and peculiar cases'; and on the other hand, that what journalism lacks in order to faithfully represent reality is the capacity to narrate it, for if reality is an inner process with beginnings and endings, then the punchy images of immediacy[9] produced by newspapers on a daily basis cannot but obstruct understanding.

History would then be the written form capable of transcending the mischievous power of images, an ability which, according to White, could only be attained if historians were willing to somehow 'collapse the distinction' between 'its form and its semantic content' (White 1999: 85) in the same way Gertrude Stein manages to do in her writings. However, even if we accept the highly problematic idea that there is a truer reality waiting to be rescued by proper narratives beyond the disarray of everyday images, something probably much more decisive would still remain overlooked: the extent to which modernity already is materially constituted by the circulation of images and discourses. In other words, whatever the real is, it always happens through the mediation of visibility – those rare and peculiar moments Stein talks about seem the rule rather than the exception. Consequently, I would like to argue, the history of this visibility is in itself what should come forth as the true challenge to modern historians.

This book will take onboard much of modernism's critique of the press – it will pay attention to its temporal brevity and to its ability to 'invent' a reality of its own – and the hypothesis of a modernist event put forward by Hayden White, but it chooses a different path: to work with newspapers rather than against them. This does not mean that the journalistic narratives we are going to analyse will be read literally, at face value, as many modern historians using newspapers as historical sources do. Rather, I will try to look at those narratives as specific forms of experience and, as such, as historical objects in their own right. Paraphrasing White, it is fortunate, therefore, that we have in the work of some of the greatest modernist writers, and artists, a theorization of this problem: authors who also dealt with the press aesthetically by allowing it to contaminate their own narratives, the structure of their canvas and the rhythm of their films (and not only by using it as a sort of character in their plots). At this level, the role of the press becomes much more complex, because, rather than dismissing it along the two lines of the critique we are already familiar with – the temporal chaos of innumerable events and the deteriorated language of mass consensus – these works see the press as a particularly challenging object of representation precisely as a result of the innumerable events and mass production of discourse. In other words, chaos, consensus, manipulation, violence, randomness, brevity and so on do not suddenly disappear from the picture, as if the alternative was a more benign picture of journalism. It just so happens that all those aspects are seen as concrete phenomena that all modern narratives – literary or historical – necessarily have to come to terms with.

At this point, we can make a qualitative move from the reading of discourses about the press in modernist novels to the analysis of some cases where the form of newspapers constituted a model for modernist aesthetic creation. In fact, more than the use of news in plots or the caricature of newspapers and journalists, the press imposed the structural conditions of the period's forms of perception. To start with, with the circulation of newspapers, narratives themselves could be seen as objects in motion. Circulation, on the other hand, necessarily meant that this particular form of narrative was being written and read collectively. Many narratives in circulation, many readers sharing the same news: the first challenge to the history of this object is how to describe the simultaneity of all these disparate, distant things. According to Mikhail Bakhtin, it seems that Dostoevsky shared the same problem: in fact, 'the possibility of simultaneous coexistence' was a key feature in the writer's 'worldview' (Bakhtin 1984: 29). The idea of 'simultaneous coexistence' had implications in the novelist's abstract definition of phenomena – it was, for instance, what allowed him to distinguish 'the essential from the nonessential', according to Bakhtin – but, above all, it was what defined 'his artistic perception of the world: only in the category of coexistence could he see and represent the world' (Bakhtin 1984: 29). Now, this world of simultaneous things, made of many simultaneous voices, was something that only became visible to Dostoevsky on 'the newspaper page as a living reflection of the contradictions of contemporary society in the cross-section of a single day, where the most diverse and contradictory material is laid out, extensively, side by side and one side against the other' (Bakhtin 1984: 30). A 'living reflection': here, newspapers are finally allowed to emerge as privileged sources for the study of modern societies, not by showing how people were led to think (as Proust seemed to suggest, in his advice to modern historians), but, on the contrary, by showing the many different thoughts in circulation in societies immersed in journalistic discourses.

Rosalind Kraus recovers 'the polyphony that Bakhtin sees in Dostoewsky [*sic*]' in her own analysis of Picasso's use of newspaper fragments in his cubist collages. Kraus goes to great lengths to counter the usual interpretations that try to read the painting's meaning in the particular news one can read in Picasso's newspaper clippings. Instead, what she sees in the combination of pieces of newspaper with other objects is a true 'whirl of signifiers' in which the press becomes a sign in circulation, rather than a particular meaning or even a symbol:

> The polyphony that Bakhtin sees in Dostoewsky ... is what we have seen happen characterizing Picasso's circulation of the sign. And this whirl of signifiers reforming in relation to each other and reorganizing their meanings seemingly out of nothing, in an almost magical disjunction from reality, this manipulation at the level of the structure, can also be appreciated ... at the level of the textual representation of the 'voice'. Each voice, in dialogue at least with itself, is doubled and dramatized by becoming the voice of another. (Kraus 1999: 47–48)

This proves particularly challenging, as it seems to imply that words, or written objects, have to be treated like images, or at least handled in their visual form. Understandably, the temptation to read the words and take the meaning from them is almost irresistible. However, if one manages, even if briefly, to treat those clippings as signs, rather than news proper, it may then become possible to picture a multiplicity of polyphonic voices where, rather than 'the object who speaks' – that is, newspapers – we move 'to the object who is journalistically spoken': a whole system of circulation where the news can be seen beyond the chaos of events or normative consensus. In these circumstances, the press becomes an object in circulation – a very special object, to be sure, as in it discourse and the material presence in the world coincide. But this is precisely what allows for these 'signifiers' to enter 'in vivid enough circulation to trigger the constellation of signifieds' (Kraus 1999: 85). In conclusion, only circulation can produce meaning, or, in other words, meaning can only emerge in 'the conversation that circulates in [a] polyphonic space' (Kraus 1999: 85).[10]

My suggestion at this point is that the 'constellation of signifieds', something newspapers are able to encapsulate with the proviso that one treats them as narratives in motion, has become, not exactly a model, but indeed the infrastructure of many modernist works. At this level, the impact of newspapers must be grasped in formal aspects like the temporality of James Joyce's *Ulysses* (1922) or the rhythm of Walter Ruttmann's *Berlin: Symphony of a Great City* (1927) and Dziga Vertov's *The Man with a Movie Camera* (1929). To start with, this is because these works seem to find it hard to conceive of human experience outside the daily unit organized by the press. Even more decisively, the whole synthesis of many different voices and disparate objects in circulation juxtaposed within the space of the city throughout the twenty-four hours of a single day (and both the day and the city constitute the spatio-temporal structure of the newspaper) produce the perfect setting to re-enact the polyphonic voices Rosalind Kraus identified in Picasso's collages. Moreover, the language of montage as the appropriate narrative technique to render simultaneity – something those urban symphonies skillfully demonstrate – may also prove a productive tool with which to think about newspapers: the multiplicity of news in a single edition and the circulation of that same edition's many different copies throughout the day.

In this context, John Dos Passos's *USA* probably constitutes the best example of a modernist work where the circulation of voices triggered by the press is ostensibly embodied by the structure of the narrative. The novel can in this sense be seen as a piece of montage where different characters are shown in parallel (sometimes intersecting) with a series of different discourses and events in the background setting the conditions in which those characters not only experienced the historical period, but were indeed able to perceive it. The fact that these discourses and events are presented through the terminology of film – in sections titled 'Newsreel' and 'The Camera Eye' – should not be seen to contradict my hypothesis, for, as I will be insisting throughout this book, cinema itself participated in the whole journalistic structure of perception. 'Newsreel 35' (Dos Passos 2001: 618) can be seen as a good example of this:

the Grand Prix de La Victoire run yesterday for fifty-second time was an event that will long remain in the memories of those present, for never in the history of the classic race has Longchamps presented such a glorious scene

Keep the home fires burning
Till the boys come home

LEVIATHAN UNABLE TO PUT TO SEA
BOLSHEVIKS ABOLISH POSTAGE STAMPS
ARTIST TAKES GAS IN NEW HAVEN
FIND BLOOD ON $1 BILL

While our hearts are yearning

POTASH CAUSE A BREAK IN PARLEY
MAJOR DIES OF POISONING
TOOK ROACH SALTS BY MISTAKE

riot and robbery developed into the most awful pogrom ever heard of. Within two or three days the Lemberg Ghetto was turned into heaps of smoking debris. Eyewitnesses estimate that the Polish soldiers killed more than a thousand Jewish men and women and children

LENIN SHOT BY TROTSKY IN DRUNKEN BRAWL

you know where I stand on beer, said Brisbane in seeking assistance
Though the boys are far away
They long for home
There's a silver lining
Through the dark clouds shining

Some of these pieces of news evoke our initial critiques of the press, in the way *everything* is treated at the same level, or when things are just made up (Trotsky never shot Lenin). And yet, it should be clear by now that this is not how one should read newspapers from a historical per-spective. For the meaning being produced here is whatever emerges from the juxtaposition of different forms, the random succession of discourse (one could even ask whether it is a question of meaning in the strict sense, or something closer to the idea of rhythm or even atmosphere). Newspapers thus seem to encapsulate the whole of social experience not because they systematize everything, but precisely to the extent in which modern reality is perceived as random and inarticulate. Tristan Tzara's 'To Make a Dadaist Poem' can in this sense be presented as the ultimate modernist account of the journalistic structure of the modern world:

> Take a newspaper / Take some scissors / Choose from this paper an article of the length you want to make your poem / Cut out the article / Next carefully cut out each of the words that makes up this article and put them all in a bag / Shake gently / Next take out each cutting one after the other / Copy conscientiously in the order in which they left the bag / The poem will resemble you. (Lewis 2007: 107).

'The poem will resemble you': and yet, there is a limit to the arbitrari-ness with which the image of this particular subject – the poet whose work was a collection of newspaper clippings – is produced. For those words would not have been reassembled in the poem by themselves. The image of the poet was the outcome of a process of cutting, shaking, alignment, copying and, eventually, reading. It may seem a minor detail in the poem, but the consequences to the apprehension of what newspa-pers do to the world (and to the way the historical status of newspapers is analysed in this book) are decisive: both the random circulation of words and the emergence of meaning are produced in a negotiation between journalists and readers. In other words, if circulation really plays such a central role in the way newspapers work, then we have to take the image of polyphonic voices to its ultimate consequence and include the public, that is, virtually everyone, in the process of production of this particular cultural object.

Narratives in Motion

Like Hayden White, several other authors have asked historians to shift the structure of their narratives from realism, still seen as the literary paradigm of most historiography, to modernism. The reasoning, as we have seen, is simple and, apparently, fair: if modernity represents a specific historical situation with its own problems and challenges, then historiographic discourse should keep up and adapt its narrative forms to historic change (just as modernist literature had done, and precisely for the same reason).[11] I am afraid this book will not match these expectations. However, I would like to argue, it will try to do something equally challenging. In the chapters that follow, journalistic narratives will be exposed to other literary forms and confronted with their own context of circulation, from production to reception. In this sense, the book will try to estrange the logic of the news and, hopefully, bring forth, not exactly what newspapers said, but the meaning they were allowed to produce in specific circumstances.

'Estrangement' is of course a procedure with a Brechtian resonance. Georges Didi-Huberman (2009) has recently analysed Bertolt Brecht's journals, in which the German author assembled newspaper clippings and other images and texts in order to unveil historical contradictions (in the context of the Second World War).[12] By tracking down the whole information process and, even more decisively, by confronting several journalistic narratives with each other and with other literary forms, my aim is, just like in Didi-Huberman, 'to *break up* the falsifying configuration of newspapers and to recompose or *reassemble* the factual elements released by the illustrated press and filmic newsreel on their own terms' (Didi-Huberman 2009: 19). The combination of text and image, or of narratives and other narratives, corresponds, according to Didi-Huberman, to the technique of montage. This relationship with cinema at the level of method – both in Didi-Huberman and Brecht – is important as it evokes the form of confrontation I find most productive in the analysis of this particular object: that between the press and film. Each chapter in this book can in this sense be seen as an attempt to short-circuit the linearity of the news by breaking up the latter's different elements and reassembling them in my own narrative. And yet, as we will see later, journalists themselves thought their work had strong affinities with that of film-makers. We thus have to emphasize the constructivist aspect of the method, to make sure these relationships are not seen as reproducing discourses that already existed in the past, as if waiting for us to reassemble them. In other words, to contrast different objects comes here as a historiographic move, a narrative technique to disclose the contradictions hidden beneath the discourses of the press and, as such, allow history to appear, as Fredric Jameson would put it:

> We must therefore retain this violence and negativity in any concept of intersection, in order for this dissonant conjunction to count as an Event, and in particular as that Event which is the ephemeral rising up and coming to appearance of Time and History as such. Nor is this a purely textual or philosophical matter: for *it is the same* discordant conjuncture that constitutes the emergence of time and of history in the real world. (Jameson 2009: 544)

Each chapter in this book in this sense focuses on journalistic reportage in relation to both other narrative forms and the historical context. The only chapter that does not focus on a specific event and its journalistic reporting analyses a silent film made in 1928 about the making of a newspaper, thus reversing the usual order of the narratives –reassembling events from journalistic reports – and transforming the process of production of a daily edition into an event in its own right. But before moving on to short presentations of the different chapters, three clarifications are in order. The first has to do with the book's periodization. Although Chapters 1 and 7 establish the narrative's temporal markers (a front page from 1890 and a cultural process unfolding from the mid 1920s until the late 1930s, respectively), the book's main focus is on the 1920s, here understood as an identifiable period, at least from the perspective of the history of the press and of reportage as a journalistic genre. The order of chapters is not, in this sense, organized chronologically, but accordingly to the evolution of my own argument about the impact of reportage as a narrative technique.[13]

The second clarification concerns the book's geographical and historical setting. All events described in this book took place in Portugal, and every newspaper and journalist here mentioned is Portuguese. And yet, Portuguese history as such is not what is most relevant here, as the events under analysis – a flight, a football match, a film, a crime and a strike – could have taken place in any other country or society, at least the ones undergoing similar processes of modernization. The book's 'country', so to speak, is that of journalism and modernity, or, better still, of the development of specific forms of narrative and perception in the context of urbanization and cultural industrialization. However, the reader unfamiliar with Portugal will of course be better equipped to contextualize those events if they have a general sense of the broader history of the country between the late nineteenth and the early twentieth century.

As in other contemporary European nations, in Portugal this was a period of dramatic political breaks and social transformations. The book starts with a crisis in 1890 that would trigger a profound questioning of the country's institutions and historical narratives, particularly its imperial vocation. The impact of 1890 (in many ways similar to the 1898 Spanish–American War, which led to the loss of colonies and a moral and intellectual crisis in Spain) would resonate well into twentieth century Portugal: the fall of the monarchy and the creation of a republican regime in 1910, the country's participation in the First World War from 1916 onwards, or even the fall of the Portuguese Republic and the beginning of the long period of authoritarian rule in 1926 (that would last until 1974) can be seen as after-effects of that initial crisis. In short, all these events were part of the crisis of political liberalism and liberal institutions that drove so many other countries to adopt fascism.

However, none of these political breaks are truly comprehensible outside the context of the deeper social transformations occurring at the same time. In fact, the succession of political regimes – from monarchy to republic and fascism – can to a large extent be seen as the consequence of the pressure exerted on the political system by industrialization, urbanization and social and cultural massification. The emergence of an industrial working class and the mass participation of new social strata in the public sphere – proletarians, lower middle classes and women, for example – will render the country's politics more dramatic and more polarized, especially in the context of the 1920s, when the postwar economic crisis and working class struggles (with the formation of a strong anarcho-syndicalist movement) would coalesce in the fall of the Republic. Ultimately, the nationalist revolution of 1926 and later (from 1933) the Estado Novo – the dictatorial regime led by António de Oliveira Salazar – can be seen as conservative responses to the challenges all the new social actors and political events posed to the historical perception of the country's elites.

This is where journalism becomes so decisive not only as a privileged document of contemporary phenomena, but as a key social actor in its own right, a mass cultural form contributing both to the democratization of the public sphere and, later, to the hegemony of authoritarian ideas. In other words, democratization can be equated with the growth of newspaper readership whereas authoritarianism can be read as a journalistic narrative. In this sense, the press allows us to analyse the historical process beyond political history as such (monarchy, republic, dictatorship) and reverse the usual relation between political events and journalistic discourses (where the latter are treated as a consequence of the former). Accordingly, the different political regimes can here be seen as a consequence of transformations in the orders of discourse established by the press and of the impact of journalistic styles in the political sphere throughout the historical period in question.

My final clarification stems directly from the historicity that will guide my analysis of journalism in 1920s Portugal. For, in the same way that the chronology of events and the role of newspapers will be autonomous from the chronology and protagonists of political history, so were the authors the reader will meet throughout this book chosen according to their visibility in the public sphere organized around journalism. In this regard, the reader unfamiliar with Portuguese culture will not be at a disadvantage, for these writers and journalists, in most cases, have been forgotten, and do not form part of the literary canon. Their disappearance from the country's cultural memory tends, in this sense, to be inversely proportional to their renown in Portuguese public life during the 1920s.

Chapter 1 works as a methodological introduction to my reading of newspapers. It provides a close reading of a newspaper edition reporting on a major political event in Portuguese modern history (the British Ultimatum of 1890) and shows how the coverage of that specific event was not in fact the most spectacular piece of news the newspaper reported on that day. The front page contained another story, that of the suicide of one of the newspaper's most important feuilletonists – popular authors of feuilletons, a section of fictional or critical texts that was easily distinguishable from the information section in newspapers. A comparison of these two stories allows me to reflect upon questions of circulation and visibility as two key aspects of the reading of newspapers, and to mobilize categories from art history and visual studies as the tools for my analysis of newspaper narratives as protagonists in modern experience.

This first attempt to read a newspaper edition in detail (and taking into account the different aspects involved in the production of the news) proves useful in the following analyses. Chapter 2 focuses on the circulation of news concerning the first flight across the South Atlantic by Gago Coutinho and Sacadura Cabral in 1922, and the public reaction to the event in Lisbon. Journalists had to base their reports on a constant but unreliable flow of telegraphic information coming from several islands, as well as from ships crossing the Atlantic Ocean. Readers, on the other hand, attempted to experience the event simultaneously by following telegraphic information as it was updated and displayed on newspaper billboards. The chapter also identifies aviation and the figure of the aviator as an important topic of Portuguese modernist fiction, especially in novels and short stories published by modernist journalists.

The figure of the aviator as a kind of sportsman – and especially the public image of Sacadura Cabral produced by the press – introduces the body and its visual representation as a key feature of early twentieth-century journalism. In Chapter 3, the history of modern sport is told in parallel with an account of the proliferation of printed images in newspapers and other publications, as they feed on each other. A specific sporting event, a football match between the national teams of Spain and Portugal in 1925, will show how, on the one hand, sport had become a journalistic spectacle, and on the other how journalism struggled, in the 1920s, to produce narratives of events whose visual nature and mobility seemed more suitable to filmic representation.

The efforts made by reporters to provide a written account of moving images had a counterpart in a film produced in 1928 on the making of an edition of *Diário de Notícias*, one of Portugal's leading newspapers. This is the main object of Chapter 4. Organizing its narrative around twenty-four hours in the life of a city – like so many other urban symphonies of contemporary cinema – the film's editing enables it to reconstitute the different layers of journalism: reporters searching for events, machines printing newspapers, peddlers and trains distributing the newspaper, and readers simultaneously being informed of the news. The film represents the power of modern art to materialize narratives in everyday life. This form of power can also be seen in modernist feuilletons, where journalists insistently deployed the imaginary of film in the representation of women and their bodies (reporters as lenses focusing on filmic bodies) to not only dramatize the narration of the historical context, but also to enhance the material impact of narratives.

The reporting of a murder of an actress by her lover in 1925 described in Chapter 5 shows how the female body became an object of literary exploitation – that is, one of its principal resources – and journalistic sensationalism. The book takes a political turn here, in two ways: on the one hand, the representation of women in newspapers in both the news and feuilletons enacts a system of power that reproduces in written form the 'split between [the] active/male [gaze] and passive/female [body]' as identified by Laura Mulvey in film (Mulvey 1975: 11). On the other hand, the fictional representation of the female body defined a social division of labour between an elite of modernist journalists who wrote feuilletons and a lower class of professionals who published erotic pulp fiction.

In Chapter 6 the social and cultural gap separating modernist journalists from an intellectual proletariat formed by typesetters and the lower ranks of journalism is interpreted through the analysis of a number of fictional utopias and dystopias written by journalists in the 1920s, in which the political horizon of expectations of the period is represented. This allows me to introduce my last modernist event: a strike by journalists and typesetters. The lack of newspapers in Lisbon for a period of several months in 1921 triggered a near-revolutionary situation. If, as the book's narrative demonstrates, modern reality was mediated and perceived through the movement and image of events produced by newspapers, the strike gave rise to a feeling of social collapse.

Lastly, Chapter 7 reflects upon newspaper articles and pictures produced on the subject of their own role in not only producing the perception of modern reality, but also in organizing social and political life. The press, I argue, presents itself as an industrial accumulation of events and, as such, as a modern archive of reality. In a final twist of the narrative, I will try to show how this form of accumulation was the origin of a new idea of culture in the 1930s, which, despite its activism against authoritarianism, can also be seen as the emergence of a new intellectual norm and cultural discipline. In conclusion, I will discuss Friedrich Kittler's notions of information storage and discourse network (Kittler 1990) to argue that newspapers are prime historical examples of both these ideas.

Notes

1. Proust continues, with a recommendation to historians: 'Historians, if they have not been wrong to abandon the practice of attributing the actions of peoples to the will of kings, ought to substitute for the latter the psychology of the individual, the inferior individual at that' (Proust 2000: 469).
2. Antonio Gramsci identified a key philosophical event in this: 'for a mass of people to be led to think coherently and in the same coherent fashion about the real present world, is a "philosophical" event far more important and "original" than the discovery by some philosophical "genius" of a truth which remains the property of small groups of intellectuals' (Gramsci 1971: 327).
3. One of the best analyses of Kraus's 'great battle' against the press is that of Bouveresse (2001); see also Reitter (2008).
4. All quoted passages from *The Last Days of Mankind* come from Act 1, Scene 14 (see Kraus 2013).
5. Although modern newspapers always had a commercial component (both as a product to be sold and a vehicle for advertising), the relation between the press and business was frequently criticized, as if its commercial aspect was incompatible with the neutrality of information. Walter Benjamin, in his Arcades project, saw this relation as a key aspect of the nineteenth-century need for novelties: 'Just as in the seventeenth century it is allegory that becomes the canon of dialectical images, in the nineteenth century it is novelty. Newspapers flourish, along with *magasins de nouveautés*.

The press organizes the market in spiritual values, in which at first there is a boom' (Benjamin 2002: 11).

6. Here too, the key issue was of course the way in which universal reportage was undermining the ability of readers to focus on things: 'I prefer, in the face of this aggression, to respond that some contemporaries do not know how to read – Except newspapers; of course these provide the advantage of not interrupting the chorus of [daily] distractions' (Mallarmé 1998: 386).

7. Hayden White situates this break – championed by modernism – in the crisis of the nineteenth-century historical novel, when the model based on 'the presumed capacity of the reader to distinguish between real and imaginary events', 'fact and fiction', and 'life and literature', was put into question (White 1999: 67).

8. 'In this respect, then, to say, for example, that a given historical event is a fulfillment of an earlier one is not to say that the prior event caused or determined the later event or that the later event is the actualization or effect of the prior one. It is to say that historical events can be related to one another in the way that a figure is related to its fulfillment in a narrative or a poem' (White 1999: 89).

9. 'Therefore in real life it is the crime and as the newspaper has to feel about as if it were in the act of seeing or doing it, they cannot really take on detecting they can only take on the crime, they cannot take on anything that makes on beginning and ending and in the detecting end of detective stories there is nothing but going on beginning and ending' (Stein 1998: 42).

10. 'From the subject who speaks, to the object who is journalistically "spoken", Picasso joins the conversation that circulates in the polyphonic space of the collages. But his is only one voice, itself bifurcated. Many other voices attach to these speakers, all of them doubling or tripling from within. A small amount of text will do it … [T]he collages have just enough meaning for the circulation of the sign, while the signifiers are in vivid enough circulation to trigger the constellation of the signified' (Kraus 1999: 85).

11. Eric Auerbach, Hayden White, Fredric Jameson and Jacques Rancière seem to agree about the modernist writer who should become the model for historians: Virginia Woolf. Despite their differences about the historical situation modernist historiography responds to (the modernist event, in White; 'the surging of countless millions of new subjects', in Jameson; or 'democratic disorder', in Rancière), all recognize in the narrative structures of *To the Lighthouse* or *Mrs Dalloway* the expression of 'the random contingency of real phenomena', as Auerbach puts it (White 1999; Auerbach 1953: 538; Jameson 2009: 515; Rancière 1994: 100).

12. 'The key and most powerful form of estrangement in his *ABC of War* involves establishing a link (*tirer un trait d'union*), quick as a lightening strike, between images of the crime and poetry texts' (Didi-Huberman 2009: 44).

13. In *In 1926*, Hans Ulrich Gumbrecht identified a series of figures, events and narratives that contemporaries would recognize as typical traces of the 1920s – reporters were of course among them. To focus comprehensively on a specific year allowed the author to treat it as a synecdoche of the larger period (Gumbrecht 1997).

Chapter 1

Glancing over Newspapers

Ultimatum and Suicide

Historians generally assume that the Portuguese twentieth-century in fact begins with the episode of the 1890 British Ultimatum. On 11 January, Lord Salisbury, the British prime minister, sent a memorandum to Lisbon urging the withdrawal of Portuguese troops under the command of Major Serpa Pinto, then stationed in territories claimed by the British Empire (in what is now Zimbabwe). The note in itself was rather laconic. It demanded clear instructions be sent by the Portuguese government to the governor of Mozambique to ensure Serpa Pinto's evacuation of the disputed regions, in the absence of which the British ambassador in Lisbon would receive orders to leave the city. In nineteenth-century diplomatic language, however, this brevity was clear enough: it meant a military ultimatum.[1]

The event would later become the synecdoche of a national crisis largely transcending the diplomatic episode. Its historical meaning now stands not only for a deeply felt political crisis, but also the country's late nineteenth-century financial collapse and a major break in its cultural and intellectual self-consciousness. All together, the various dimensions of the event, or the different events now combined in the crisis of the Ultimatum, gave way to an acute awareness of Portugal's vulnerability as a historic empire – a central feature in the country's national narrative – and its subordinate role in European history. Internally, this was the moment when both republicanism and nationalism established themselves as the two dominant political cultures of the following decades. Despite the discrepancy between the historical significance and the sobriety of the diplomatic note, the event was immediately experienced as having both deep and wide-ranging consequences. Demonstrations of all kinds followed and something decisive happened to the sense of national identity. What would become the republican national anthem,

'A Portuguesa', was composed at the time as an anti-British protest. Patriotism was displayed with an intensity that came close to the consistency of twentieth-century nationalism. In other words, perhaps the diplomatic note was less discreet than we were initially led to believe. Its impact, however, was not due to the indiscretion of the politicians and diplomats concerned but to the media, through whom the note emerged into intense public visibility.

The regime of this visibility is, in itself, our problem. By looking at the reaction of *Diário de Notícias* – Portugal's leading newspaper in 1890

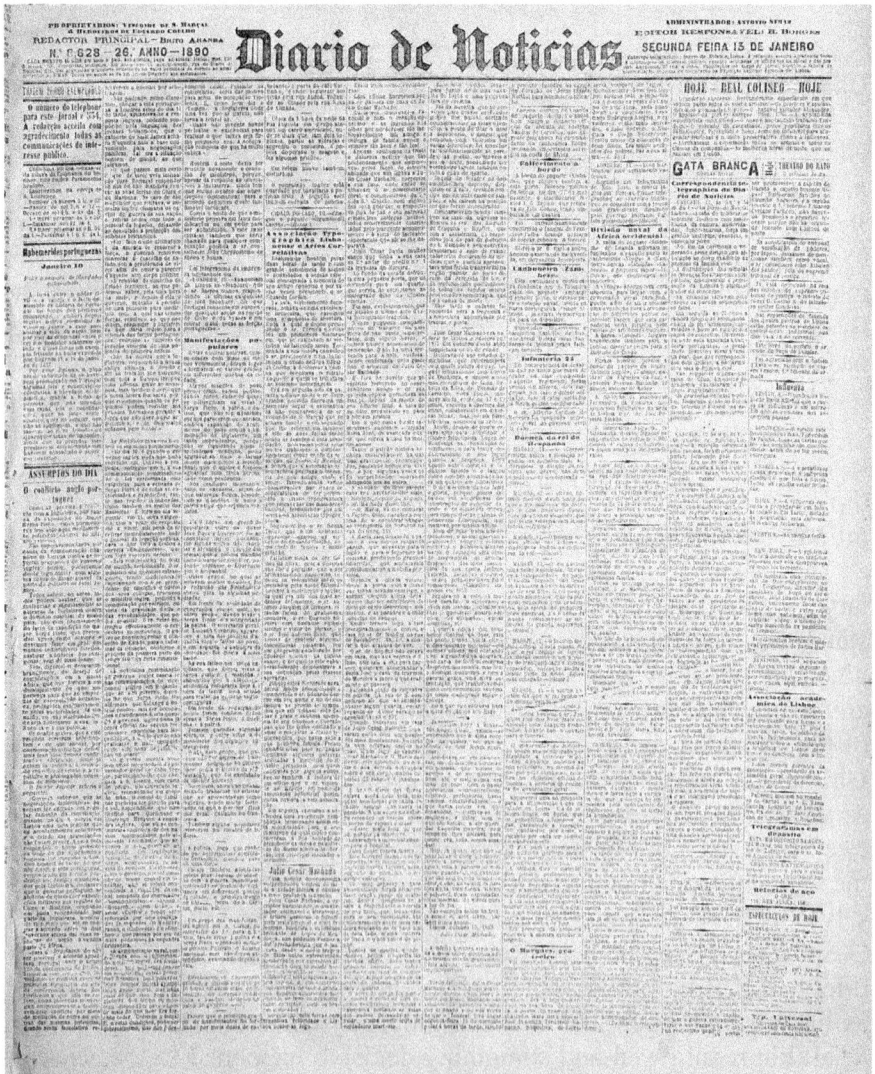

Figure 1.1: Front page of *Diário de Notícias*, 13 January 1890. Archive of *Diário de Notícias*.

– to the event on its front page on 13 January (Figure 1.1), we can see that such visibility was not based on images. There were no pictures or headlines about the Ultimatum, just a heavy block of text. At first sight, then, the newspaper did not keep pace with the importance of the historic event. But this impression may be biased. After more than a century of visual information, we may tend to identify journalistic sensationalism with images, whereas the report about the Ultimatum, occupying more than three columns of the paper's front page, was entirely textual. Apparently, then, the event's visibility must be read through the ways in which this written narrative is organized – as if what is being shown can be seen in the words.[2] Only then will we be able to unveil what really happened between London, Lisbon and the African regions over which the two governments were in dispute.

The article's discreet heading, 'The Anglo–Portuguese Conflict', did not promise much drama. Moreover, the text started with an almost casual 'as anticipated', later reinforced, at the beginning of the second paragraph, with a reassuring 'as everyone knows, or at least can imagine'.[3] The outcome of the diplomatic tension between the two countries was what, according to the newspaper, could easily be 'anticipated' by the reader, who was also supposed to 'know', or at least 'imagine', the brutality of Britain's display of power. It thus seemed that while the events were taking place, as they should, between ministerial cabinets and diplomatic chancelleries, part of the information was on the loose, circulating in the form of 'serious rumours' and leaving the newspaper with the pacifying – although secondary – role of confirming what 'the readers already know'.

In these circumstances, one could ask: what was the use of journalism? Why should anyone buy, and read, a newspaper with information easy to anticipate, and an account of events that everyone already knew or at least could easily imagine? The answer to this question must be able to clarify the true object in the report of *Diário de Notícias*, or better still, the ways the newspaper transformed the information at its disposal into a narrative. On that particular Monday, the reader could not only recreate the entire exchange of telegrams between the two governments but also reconstruct the whole process through which Lisbon's newspapers in general (the piece includes excerpts taken from *Novidades* and *Diário Popular*) organized the public perception of what was going on.

The event had started more than a week earlier, on Sunday 5 January, with the arrival of the first note sent by the British government, to which Lisbon replied on Wednesday 8 January. Taking into account the time it took, in 1890, for communications to be transmitted between the two countries, a second note from London could not have been received in

Lisbon before Saturday 11 January. The anxiety was evident in newspaper reports. That day's issue of *Diário Popular* (quoted by *Diário de Notícias*) seemed to believe that, 'considering the language used by British newspapers, the Court of Saint James [is] expected to take [the reply sent by the Portuguese government] as an appropriate basis for peaceful negotiations'. However, according to the edition of 12 January of *Novidades* (once again quoted by *Diário de Notícias*), not only was the reply that had arrived on 11 January remarkably violent, but this had been anticipated the previous day by a first verbal demand for Serpa Pinto's withdrawal, which did not even take into account the Portuguese reply on 8 January.

In short, what seemed to count as journalistic information was less the content of the diplomatic exchange than the form of its circulation. The event was somehow transformed in the production of information about it, and everything happened as if the news were reporting what had already been constituted as news. This may look like an impoverishment of the political event, as if there were nothing but its text, a metanarrative with no material dimension. But things were not that simple. For that same political event itself – that is, a political crisis between two governments – had been initially triggered by a network of information – a flow of discourses – circulating between London, Lisbon and several other interconnected positions in Europe and Africa:

> Yesterday the government received a telegraphic warning from the governor-general of Cape Verde, informing them that an English battleship with secret instructions had arrived in S. Vicente. The possibility of an attack was creating anxiety. Zanzibar's consul notifies that the English fleet that had concentrated there with ten ships, left towards the south, supposedly heading to Quelimane or Lourenço Marques ... Finally, the [Portuguese] government knew, from information received from our consul in Gibraltar, that a fleet formed by the battleships Northumberland, Anson, Monarch, Iron Duke, was concentrated at the canal ... being meanwhile reinforced by two battleships from the Mediterranean fleet, the Colossus and the Benbow, recognised as the most powerful of the British fleet.[4]

The newspaper thus took part in this intense network, where the constant communication between distant places produced political events that became news, which further transformed into new events.[5] The last section of the report described the impact the news had had on the streets of Lisbon: 'this and other news, discussed with more or less passion, gave rise to several demonstrations in different areas of the city'.[6] In fact, Sunday 12 January was tense. Several groups of people walked the streets cheering Serpa Pinto and shouting slogans against England – 'which', the reporter added, 'we will not reproduce, as it could make matters even worse in the present situation'.[7] The British consulate and the Portuguese Foreign Office were stoned and several windows were

broken, theatres were invaded and orchestras forced to play patriotic an-
thems. The crowds invariably ended up gathering in front of newspaper
offices, as if the press was the last reliable institution. These people had
responded to the news, and their response was bound to become news.

The reader thus had good reasons to buy the newspaper on Monday
13 January, after all. They might have known the diplomatic memorandum's content beforehand and even imagined its political consequences,
but the newspaper gave more. Namely, a narrative where that particular
piece of information was organized in a continuous chain of events, as
both the consequence of previous information and the cause of subsequent events. Our reader – especially if from Lisbon – might even read
about episodes in which he had himself participated (the reader's gender
must be specified when readership concerns the street, for, if a given
newspaper's readership was constituted by men and women, only the
former were expected to participate in public demonstrations). In that
case, to read the newspaper widened the scope of participation by making readers aware of the circulating network they were part of.[8]

This also meant that the reader of *Diário de Notícias* on 13 January
1890 was able to make her own narrative by adding that day's information to what she already knew after reading the issue of the previous day,
and resuming it with the news published on the next. These consider-
ations seem to assume that the same readers bought the newspaper every
day, which is of course something we cannot be entirely sure of. More
likely, that same reader did not stop reading her paper after the story of
the Ultimatum but kept browsing for more information in the following
columns. After all, there was still more than two thirds of the newspaper
left to read. If we follow this imaginary reader as she moved forward,
we can almost imagine her disbelief on discovering that the news of the
British Ultimatum was not even the most dramatic piece of information
that issue of *Diário de Notícias* had in store for her. For the day when
the streets of Lisbon erupted in protest against the British, the city also
witnessed the suicide of the popular writer Júlio César Machado and his
wife.

Machado was none other than one of the newspaper's main feuilletonists, writers who contributed fictional or critical texts to the feuilletons, a special section of the newspaper separate from that which
contained the news. Machado had been a regular presence in the same
pages that now announced his death, which made the news even more
tragic, both from the perspective of the reporter – a colleague – and the
reader – someone certainly familiar with Machado's writings. His career
as a feuilletonist was inseparable from the evolution of feuilletons in
Portuguese newspapers: the popularity of both – feuilletons as a literary

genre and César Machado as author – grew hand in hand from the 1850s (De Marchis 2009). Throughout the second half of the nineteenth century, readers became increasingly used to reading these special sections where fiction and opinion went loosely together without the journalistic constraints of the news proper. This combination of different styles within feuilletons constituted a site of intense creativity where the relations between fictional and journalistic discourses opened new ways of representing reality: by the end of the century, feuilletons were closely entangled with literary realism.

In this sense, the genre occupied a unique space where the authority and legitimacy of journalism as a transparent discourse between reality and its readers had to negotiate with the more nuanced relation with the world proper to literature. Júlio César Machado was thus at the centre of a literary system where newspapers functioned as mediators in the permanent negotiation between fiction and reality. Feuilletons often showed a sharp awareness of their own concrete situation – narratives regularly published side by side with quotidian information – and reflected upon it. The young bohemians of *A vida em Lisboa* (Life in Lisbon), one of Machado's first and most popular dramas, showed how ambivalent this negotiation could be. If, on the one hand, they complained about the dullness of everyday life in the Portuguese capital – on the grounds that 'life in Lisbon wouldn't even yield a feuilleton' (Machado and Hogan 1861: 2) – on the other, however, they seemed to accuse that same reality of being too dramatic because of its close resemblance with the content of dramas: 'My dear friend, usually it is not the theatre that depicts society: it is society that copies the characters in plays!' (Machado and Hogan 1861: 38). Any contradiction between these representations of the relation between fiction and reality is only an appearance, for they ultimately showed how deeply both types of narrative were related. Lisbon's life might lack what it took to make good drama or have too much of it. In any case, reality seemed unthinkable without its fictional counterpart as much as – if not more – fiction seemed unthinkable without its referent.

The trope of modern reality imitating popular literature has been identified as one of the most recognizable stereotypes in feuilletons (Thiesse 1984). More than a literary trope, however, this insistent image may be read as a kind of realistic common sense. For, as we have seen with the discursive origins of the Ultimatum, realism in 1890 had to focus on a reality already organized by the circulation of information. The challenge was thus twofold. On the one hand, the distinction between events and news became harder to maintain with the proliferation and interpenetration of events based on discourses and discourses that constituted events in their own right. On the other, fiction and reality were constantly blurred by the coexistence of literary and journalistic narratives within the same newspaper pages.

The most shocking thing about César Machado's suicide was the way in which in its crudity it resembled a scene from a realist novel. Contrary to the British Ultimatum's journalistic narrative, everything in this second event was unexpected and occurred away from public visibility. The reporter of *Diário de Notícias* himself had trouble getting hold of it. After all, the 'painful news took the whole city by surprise',[9] and he was as shocked as his readers. When the 'bad news spread' ('with amazing speed'), he was in no privileged position and had to run to César Machado's house like everyone else did 'as soon as we knew about this sad and painful news'. 'Bad', 'sad' and 'painful news': the reporter's troubles were more than just the obstacles standing between him and the information. The death of Júlio César Machado had a personal, intimate, dimension that made it much more difficult to endure, and thus to narrate, than the Ultimatum itself. Half way through the report, however, the reporter suddenly seemed to gain the upper hand. The same emotional reservations initially blocking the narrative became a sign that, unlike everyone else except the police, he had been able to enter the house and see what happened with his own eyes: 'It is hard to describe. We do so with a heavy heart and tears in our eyes'. The scene was tragic enough, but the reporter does not hesitate adding a little creativity: 'it was obviously there that the last episode of this frightening drama occurred ... [T]here is not a shadow of a doubt that the deranged spirits of our unfortunate friend and his wife had been occupied by the idea and willingness to commit suicide for some time'.[10]

At this point, the observed facts and the reporter's presuppositions become hard to distinguish. It seemed that the writer and his wife were unable to cope with the recent death of their only son, thus deciding to take their own lives as well. But neither husband nor wife left any explanation. The whole report thus becomes an assumption based on the few elements that remained visible. In this sense, whereas the Ultimatum was recreated through the assemblage and articulation of public communications, the narrative of the suicide involved what happened in the invisible realm of private life, being somehow brought to public visibility. What the reporter could see – the traces left behind – matched what the police (the only other people allowed on the scene) used as clues to solve the mystery: a still picture from which all motion had been extinguished, of walls and floor covered in blood, dead bodies lying inanimate and several other signs of disorder.[11] The difference between the police report and the report in *Diário de Notícias* was that, in the latter, the reporter employed all his available literary resources to dramatize the story:

> This terrible drama, carried out by mutual agreement, presumably had, without any doubt, the following plot: the loving couple started by praying by the altar, then proceeded to the living room where they removed the son's picture from the wall and took it to the office. There, they put it on a chair around which the parents sat in an Italian chair and on a pine stool. After many affectionate kisses of that beloved image, Júlio tried to commit suicide first, by hanging himself with a small rope, which he hung on a nail on the door connecting the stairs and the room. The weight of his body broke the rope, which made the couple decide to terminate their lives by cutting the veins in their wrists and letting themselves bleed painfully to death, as in martyrdom. To do this, they had taken a barber's razor and a small kitchen knife. It was the barber's razor they used to produce deep cuts in the wrists, which opened up the veins and tendons, to such an extent that the bones themselves became visible. The blood spurted violently in all directions in an extraordinary way, staining wall, doors, furniture, and even the ceiling, and producing a veritable carpet in the bedroom floor as well. Wounded, the loving couple went to the living room, leaving an enormous trail of blood, and there fell down into the positions in which they were later found.[12]

'This terrible drama, carried out by mutual agreement, presumably had, without any doubt, the following plot': to treat a mere presumption as something about which no doubts should remain paradoxically summarizes the rhetorical power of visibility in this report. By blurring the distinctions between the things that could be seen – the cutting of the veins, the bones showing through, the spurting blood – the things that had to be inferred – the removal of the picture to the office, Júlio's first attempt to commit suicide, the passage of the wounded couple from the office to the living room – and the things that could only be presupposed – the prayer by the altar, the affectionate kisses – the reporter made use of the elementary tools of fictional narrative to plot (as he himself assumes) a real event. Next day, the reader would get a single plane with both the reporter's privileged perspective on the event (from inside the couple's home) and a fictional supplement to what not even the reporter was able to see, but was, somehow, able to show.

Circulation, Visibility, Simultaneity

The problem, as we know, was a question of visibility, a question that can now be articulated as follows: How did newspapers fill the gap between what they could, and could not, see, and what they actually showed? What happened in the production of the news that gave the reader a wider perspective than the reporter's initial viewpoint? The episodes of the British Ultimatum and the suicide of Júlio César Machado presented a double challenge to journalism. At first sight, both events seem to exceed the spatio-temporal scope and point of view of a single newspaper edition. The Ultimatum circulated over a week or more and involved very distant countries and regions on two different continents.

The suicide of Júlio César Machado and his wife was committed at home, far from public view.

Despite these obvious constraints on reportage, the narratives of *Diário de Notícias* managed to overcome the manifest limits of the newspaper form and stage the whole communication that led to Lord Salisbury's memorandum and to penetrate the intimacy of the suicides of César Machado and his wife and disclose the moment when they took their lives. Historians may be right after all when they identify something completely new in the events reported in *Diário de Notícias* on 13 January 1890. The flow of information and the retrieval of what was concealed seemed to transcend all recognizable forms of conventional representation. However, events like a diplomatic crisis between two countries and the suicide of a celebrity, sensational as they may have been, were not unfamiliar to a nineteenth-century reader of newspapers. In other words, nothing in the two events entailed a historic break or was perceived as particularly modern. Moreover, the first impact of the Ultimatum immediately referred to the past: it meant the decay of a certain idea of Portugal, not necessarily the beginning of a new era. As for César Machado's death, it did not seem to be read as the expression of any new type of disturbance, but rather as a manifestation of an excessive romanticism. And yet, the intense circulation and visibility at play in *Diário de Notícias*'s front page that day indicates a new form of experience at the opposite end of journalistic communication. So, even if there was nothing radically new about what reporters had witnessed, the whole composition of their narratives seemed to require from readers a level of literary engagement that can be seen as a truly modern experience, that is, an experience only modernism could fully retrieve.

We can try to grasp the form of this experience by looking at the way in which the word 'ultimatum' suffered a dramatic evolution in literary modernism itself. A few decades after the British diplomatic note, two of the most prominent poets of Portuguese modernism, Fernando Pessoa and José de Almada Negreiros, marked their appearance on the literary scene with their own loud ultimatums. They did this simultaneously and in the same place: the magazine *Portugal Futurista*, published in 1917 as a second attempt (after *Orpheu*, in 1915) to announce the new literature – hence a new world – to their contemporaries. The use of the word 'ultimatum' (instead of 'manifesto', as futurists traditionally had since Marinetti in 1909) showed how familiar it had become in the country's political culture. The violence of the futurist ultimatums was a sign that from Lord Salisbury to Almada Negreiros and Fernando Pessoa the word had been established as an expression of change and marking the foundation of a new era – and a more intense one as well: Pessoa wanted to perform nothing less than 'an act of sociological surgery' (Pessoa 2001: 81) with his text. Fernando Pessoa's 'Ultimatum' (signed as Álvaro de Campos, his futurist heteronym)[13] and Almada Negreiros's 'Ultimatum futurista às gerações portuguesas do século XX' ('Futurist ultimatum to the twentieth-century Portuguese generations'), manifested, in that sense, a very acute perception of time.

Both were explicitly conceived as interventions in the context of an event, the First World War, which, as we already know, immediately took on an indisputable status as a historic break for its contemporaries, both in general and for modernist writers in particular. It could thus be said, even at the risk of making the whole process overdetermined, that these literary ultimatums tried to change history because they used the British Ultimatum – which had, in fact, changed it – as their initial model. To periodize Portuguese modernism in this way – relating it back to events in 1890 – is a delicate move, as it grounds literature in a political event. It may, in any case, be an appropriate way of thinking its temporality, or more specifically, to think an act that by intervening in its present simultaneously classified and transcended it: from this perspective, these ultimatums can be seen, to use the words of Peter Osborne, as 'an aes-theticization of modernity' (Osborne 1995: 12).[14] If by modernity we understand a form of temporal experience, rather than a period or an era, then modernism may appear as 'a term identifying the immanent histori-cal logic of a particular dynamic of artistic development' (Osborne 1995: 207), an aesthetics committed to the expression of its own time. In this sense, what was modern in the British Ultimatum was less the political event itself than the way in which it was journalistically constructed and eventually transformed into a historical event. Or, to put it very simply, what was modern in it was its form, the modernist form given to it by newspapers.

Which brings us back to the ways in which *Diário de Notícias* staged the Ultimatum's circulation and the suicide's visibility. For circulation and visibility are the foundation of two of the most recognizable tropes of the modern: speed and surfaces.[15] In our case, the reconstitution of the connections of a modern political event enabled the reader to follow it, whereas the ability to read the signs of the visible gave that same reader an insight into the core of things hidden behind its superficial manifestations.[16] So, if what the paper's reporters allowed readers to at-tain that day was a modern form of experience, this was because read-ers had the possibility of grasping speed and seeing beyond the surface of the socially visible through a specific journalistic narrative. Such an experience was thus intrinsically a narrative one, even if the narratives that triggered it were not necessarily modernist. After all, those pieces of reportage still lacked the historical awareness needed to satisfy the modernist demands of temporal classification and transcendence mentioned by Peter Osborne. But in a sense, what they did was even more decisive, for by rendering the complex spatiality of the modern (the evanescence of movements and surfaces) they can be said to have offered readers the possibility of engaging with modernity proper, rather than just representing it.

It might be interesting, then, to think of what a properly modernist account of these same modern tropes could look like. For if modernism became whatever form of representation succeeded in coming to grips with the challenges of modern life,[17] then surely the forms of managing circulation and visibility must have been at the core of the modernist undertaking. Ideally, we should be able to find moments when reality posited the modernist writer in the face of the same kind of obstacles the reporters of *Diário de Notícias* of 13 January 1890 had to deal with. And this is, I believe, what we can find in two different moments in the work of Fernando Pessoa. The first is a passage of Álvaro de Campos's struggle and engagement with modern forms of mechanization and violence in 'Ode triunfal' ('Triumphal ode'). Throughout the poem, the intensity of the experience narrated by Campos seems unconstrained. At the particular moment when the poet faces the rules of social visibility, however, his entire endeavour reaches a frustrating limit:

> Ah, what complex lives, what things inside their homes!/ Ah, to know all about them, their financial troubles,/ their domestic quarrels, their unsuspected depravities,/ Their thoughts when all alone in their bedrooms,/ and their gestures when no one can see them!/ Not to know these things is to be ignorant of everything, O rage/ O rage that like a fever or a hunger or a mad lust/ makes my face haggard and my hands prone to shaking …! (Pessoa 2006: 158)

Álvaro de Campos, unlike the reporter of the suicide, was forced to stand still in the presence of the laws of private life. This comes as a shock, even to the reader, by then already familiar with the poet's total fusion with modernity. Campos had embodied the whole mechanization of modern life, but whatever people did in the privacy of their rooms was out of his reach. On the other hand, in what seems like a paradox, Fernando Pessoa's more passive literary self, Bernardo Soares, is able to cast his gaze beyond the surface of what was immediately visible in the everyday life of his 'factless autobiography', *Livro do desassossego* ('Book of disquiet'). Here, the poet is sitting on a tram, quietly looking for details – 'details, for me, are things, voices, letters' – in the people around him. When he focuses on the dress of the girl sitting in front of him, he notices that suddenly 'the whole of social life lies in my eyes':

And immediately, as in a textbook of basic economics, factories and jobs unfold before me: the factory where the cloth was made; the factory where the darker-colored silk was spun to trim with curlicues its place around the neck; the factories' various divisions, the machines, the workers, the seamstresses. My inwardly turned eyes penetrate into the offices, where I see the managers trying to stay calm, and I watch everything being recorded in the account books. But that's not all: I see beyond all this to the private lives of those who live their social existence in these factories and offices. The whole world opens before my eyes merely because in front of me – on the nape of a dark-skinned neck whose other side has I don't know what face – I see a regularly irregular dark-green embroidery on a light-green dress. (Pessoa 2002: 253)

What is most remarkable here is not just the way in which Soares was able to reconstitute the circulation of the fabric in the girl's shirt. Truly decisive was how such a narrative, the narrative of the industrial mode of production, found a way out of the factory into the offices and then into the domestic lives of everyone involved. More than the ability of Bernardo Soares (or the reporters of *Diário de Notícias*) to see more than Álvaro de Campos, what is really at stake here is the status of the gaze in capitalism. Only the perspective of production could give the modernist *flâneur* Soares the chance of seeing the whole world unfolding before his eyes.[18] If the workers' privacy could be included in his point of view, that was because private life was yet another product of capitalism: from the perspective of production – the perspective of Bernardo Soares gazing at his fellow commuter's shirt – the whole circulation of commodities was made to appear, from the factory machines to the bedrooms hidden from Álvaro de Campos. In other words, the differences between what Álvaro de Campos and Bernardo Soares were able to see reveal the true character of the break in modern life between public (production) and private (intimacy). When Soares managed to incorporate the latter into the narrative of the former he unveiled the hidden secret of this social law: intimacy is the private form of reification, the production of individuals' lives as commodities, which become publicly visible as such.

The fact that the reporter of *Diário de Notícias* managed to break that law – just as Bernardo Soares did – poses a difficult challenge to the analysis of newspapers, and particularly to our front page. In fact, Soares and the reporter seemed able to track down the intimate lives of the workers in the factory where the cloth was produced and the events of the suicide of César Machado in exactly the same way. In the poet's case, we already know that what made this possible was the all-encompassing character of production in capitalism. And now I would like to argue that the same can be said about the report of *Diário de Notícias*: what allowed the newspaper to fix the flow of information and reconstitute what was hidden was a narrative based on its own mode of production. The self-reflective character of the reporter's work – reportage as a

description of how information was assembled and how the gaze overcame the obstacles in its way – incorporated production within journalistic narrative. In short, the journalistic stories of the British Ultimatum
and the suicide were both about Lord Salisbury's memorandum and the
death of Júlio César Machado and his wife, on the one hand, and the
ways in which the reporters managed to narrate them, on the other. By
taking what happened the day(s) before as its referent, the newspaper set
itself the difficult task not only of reconstituting the events but also of
showing how plausible that reconstitution was. Newspaper stories were,
in this sense, a hybrid narrative of an event and the efforts to narrate
it. This particular engagement of reportage with the world's dynamic is
what made journalism a narrative in motion, a narrative of circulation.

Before being the object of this narrative, movement was already its
structure. This was what allowed the reporter to see and, therefore, to
show. Journalistic circulation and visibility are in this sense coextensive.
Visibility here means the ability both to see and to make oneself seen;
it refers to what both reporters and readers were able to see, for readers
were both shown what reporters had seen and the conditions in which
they had transformed it into news. This is why, whatever the journalistic
narrative may be, we can never limit it to the relation between the event
and the journalist. The circulation of the newspaper moves beyond this
and, in fact, in a rather obvious sense, it only begins after that relation
is transformed into a narrative that then circulates once again in printed
form among readers. Only then can we say that the experience of journalism's circulation has reached full circle.

At this point, events, reporters, newspapers and readers constitute the
historical unity with which we must come to terms. The stories this book
will try to narrate thus focus on the world according to the press in a very
specific way: it is not so much a narrative that follows what the press
said, but one that tries to reconstitute its production of reality through
narrative and, as such, the ways in which it constituted itself as a tangible protagonist of the modern world. For the form of newspapers was,
as our edition of *Diário de Notícias* illustrates, a complex process in its
own right. The journalistic representation of modernity as, simultaneously, a form and its perception, based in tropes like speed and surface
challenging both representation and the senses, required a specific form
of perception.

Newspapers, as places of intense concentration of fast discourses and
glittering images (even without pictures in the strict sense), opened up
perception to singular experiences of simultaneity (and immediacy).
On the page, events seemed to have happened at the same time and to
have produced their own representation at the exact moment of their

occurrence. This is not how things worked, of course, but to say that events not only did not necessarily happen simultaneously, but also did not happen on the pages of the newspaper, is less useful as a warning against the spell the press might cast over its readership than to emphasize the central role readers must necessarily have in the whole process.[19] In fact, when represented in the form of news, events become experiences to be performed by readers. Simultaneity and immediacy lay in written representations as a potential, unable to stand on their own. They need to be activated by readers who somehow reenact the simultaneity of all the disparate events on the page and their immediacy in the act of reading. Newspapers may indeed be poor representations or even falsifications of reality, as Gertrude Stein and others have claimed. But the moment when the whole process of making a newspaper edition converges on the act of reading, a unique experience takes place where multiple times and places intersect in front of the reader's gaze. It was previously suggested that our readers ended up with a wider perspective than the reporter's initial purview. If so, this was less because the reporter showed more than what he himself had seen, but because the reader activated the entire constellation of visibilities circulating through the newspaper.

We should in this sense emphasize that he reader actually saw. Not that they did not read the reports and understand – with more or less suspicion – the meaning of what was narrated. I am not suggesting that newspaper readers necessarily rushed through their daily newspaper – although representations of reading tended to describe it as something habitual and rushed in the everyday life of busy citizens – as in fact there was a lot to read in the edition we are talking about, and many readers surely read it all. However, the experience I am trying to reconstitute here consisted in seeing what was not given in the form of information, but nonetheless composed an opening to perception emerging through the clues with which the making of the news was disclosed by the newspaper. In other words, to the extent that each piece of the report showed what the reporter saw, and the page's layout unified – even if discreetly – what was separated, the work of synthesizing all the disparate elements that were assembled there depended entirely on the reader.

The discrepancy between the conventional act of reading a newspaper's front page and the demand to reconstitute the multiple times and spaces converging on it involved an ability somehow to distance oneself from the content of the news proper and grasp the fleeting circulation that had been assembled there, utilizing something that seems to belong to the realm of vision rather than, or as much as, reading in the strict sense. It was as if the reader were able to absorb the content of a newspaper front page by glancing at it and reconstitute circulation and visibility through a figuration of simultaneity and immediacy, thus experiencing the modern world at its fullest. However, this reader did not have to possess one of those modern superpowers overcoming the limits of time and space that so many vitalisms proliferating around 1900 announced. The most decisive thing about this experience was that it was accessible to virtually every literate person through the daily act of reading newspapers: complex as it might be, it was something that happened constantly, a break in the empirical experience of urban daily life becoming simultaneously modern and banal.

It might be argued that there was nothing banal about the contents of *Diário de Notícias* that day. After all, this was supposedly the first day of a new era in the country's history (further dramatized by a public tragedy). Readers surely knew that they were experiencing a unique moment. And yet, apart from their interpretation of what had happened the day before, what they were required to do with the Ultimatum and the suicide was identical to what they did on the days without such spectacular events: they had to synthesize the circulation of information and the reporter's visibility. This means that what became banal with the reading of the newspaper, merely routine for everyone who read daily newspapers, was whatever the awareness of that circulation and visibility made appear. For these categories of time and space functioned as the raw materials with which the reporter worked. When readers activated simultaneity and immediacy, by reenacting, in the act of reading, the circulation of information and the reporter's visibility, what they ultimately glimpsed, even if only momentarily, was nothing less than the material structures organizing modern life.

So, on the one hand, the experience of simultaneity rigorously corresponds to those intersections of different temporalities Fredric Jameson (2009) identifies with the way capitalism works.[20] Reconstituting circulation between different places through time could thus be seen, not exactly as a representation, but more radically as the mobilization of capitalism's spatial and temporal structures themselves. On the other hand, immediacy as perception of both space (contiguity) and time (instantaneity) suggests something very close to the status of modern visibility T.J. Clark identifies in Cézanne: here, modernity is something that can be mastered by looking at it, a 'world ... present *in seeing, strictly and narrowly conceived*' (Clark 1999: 17, original emphasis).[21] If the world is image, or at least something waiting to be seen, it can be literally said that readers saw the world by looking at newspapers. Readers perceived the form of newspapers, and the form of that perception was what empowered them to see the world. And yet there remains a feeling of discomfort (perhaps reinforced after more than one century of visual information). Gertrude Stein's accusation – that 'in real life that is if you like in the newspapers which are not real life but real life with the reality left out' (Stein 1998: 347) – cannot just be dismissed without further thought. Unlike the published report, there are no traces left of the reading (a key aspect of 'real life'), which makes it almost impossi- ble to carry this history through: we will never know exactly how these stories were read. There is, however, something else that can be done. By staging the ways in which newspapers appeared as visible artifacts, we may try to hint at the conditions in which perception responded to them. One proviso: modernity in newspapers cannot be reproduced by the collapse of form into semantic content as in Hayden White's reading of modernism in Gertrude Stein. It is rather something that works like Cézanne's paintings as the site in which T. J. Clark observed a shift in modern visibility.

Cézanne, rather than Gertrude Stein, that is, a perception whose worldly manifestation occurred through images. This is not so much the idea that the world was made of images – this is, after all, and in news- papers more so than anywhere else, a world of words as well – but that the perception of the world seemed better understood through concepts used to analyse images. In this sense, the modern experience of newspa- per reading as a gaze over modernity becomes something similar to, or at least analysable in the same terms as, the gaze over Cézanne's work. Jonathan Crary's archaeology of modern forms of perception will help define my own point of departure. Crary argues that modern life, that is, 'capitalism, as accelerated exchange and circulation' (Crary 2000: 30), is primarily recognizable through a multiplication of stimuli to attention. Here, however, attention should not be seen as the traditional 'attention to something' (Crary 2000: 45), but an interaction between subjects and objects caught in an exteriority that seems appropriate to describe the en- gagement of readers in the same world they themselves activated when facing a newspaper. In this sense, if, on the one hand, this interaction seemed to enable modern observers to see both what is visible as well as 'what is not perceived, or only dimly perceived' (Crary 2000: 40), on the other hand it engulfed them as figures of a regime where everything exists to be seen.[22] The ultimate form of this process would be achieved precisely where visibility and movement converge: in the new visual art of cinema as the presupposition of a world based in movement and shap- ing both how modern perceptions work and how they appear.[23]

Crary sees in the paintings of Cézanne's last phase – when the painter reached the peak of his abstraction – a moment when all the forms of visibility that would be imposed on cinema's spectators were already in place. I would add, and this is key to my argument here, that newspapers had done something similar to their readers. Cézanne's paintings present an image where the synthesis of disparate fragments forces the viewer to apprehend many different but simultaneous things, an apprehension that finally constitutes an experience of flux.[24] This is where our effort to recreate a phenomenology of newspaper reading seems to find a rigorous method for conceptualizing the experience by which readers perceive the form of newspapers, rather than the world given in newspapers.[25] Crary's description of the material conditions in which this took place shows a remarkable similarity to the physical situation of a newspaper reader: this experience emerges from a fixed attention to the paper whose duration enables the reader to dissolve the page's unity and allows them to activate reality's fluidity:

> the idea of the fixed … eye has been posed as a formative element of classical systems of representation, functioning to arrest duration and change in order to achieve a conceptual mastery of phenomena. However, I am suggesting the problematic and contrary notion that the fixed, immobile eye … is what annihilates the seeming 'naturalness' of the world and discloses the provisional and fluid nature of visual experience, whereas the mobile glancing eye is what preserves the pre-constructed character of the world. (Crary 2000: 300)

Crary has good reason to stress how problematic the new function he attributes to the fixed eye is, for with it he seems to challenge the very modern idea proposed by Bergson and others, that the supposition that 'we can think the unstable by means of the stable' and 'the moving by means of the immobile' (Bergson 2007: 297) is illusory. To think and represent a world of speed and surfaces would entail a certain number of faculties enabling perception to engage with flow. Crary, on the other hand, casts a critical eye, not exactly on Bergson, but on a historical moment (in which both Bergson and our newspapers coexisted) that strongly believed in instantaneity as a coincidence between perception and phenomena. The extremes of this belief are familiar enough, from the many vitalisms that traverse modernism as a total experience (of which fascism would constitute the most recognizable political form) to the dystopian immersion of modern subjects in societies of spectacle (which is maybe the ultimate form of capitalism).

What Crary does, then, is to conceive of a point of resistance through which the apparent passivity of reading is suddenly empowered with a decisive capacity to perceive. On the one hand, the way he sees immobility, not as an interruption of phenomena but as an estrangement of the viewer's position in relation to the world, seems to constitute a precondition for the kind of interpretive intelligibility traditionally associated with the act of reading. On the other hand, however, the act of glancing seems to emerge in close connection to the kind of immediate experience we were just talking about, which, under the appearance of an active engagement with the world's mobility, in fact institutes a passive relation between readers and a world already given in the form of circulation. In this case, the reader's wandering from report to report on the page could end up being just that kind of spontaneity that permeates the ideology of modernity in its most uncritical moments.[26] By combining the two sides of the experience – the fixed gaze and the mobile glance – the reader was put in a position where they negotiated the limits of what could be done with newspapers. Drawing on Crary's own words, reading a newspaper combined the fixation that annihilated any naturalness in the reporter's narrative with a new mobilization of glance from narrative to narrative. In any case, the result – the belief in or resistance to what was published – was neither given in advance nor stable.

Such a position should be rigorously described in its spatiality. I referred to the issue of *Diário de Notícias* of 13 January 1890 as a piece within a dense network of communication. It should now be stressed how that front page synthesized the whole process unfolding from the event to its reading as news. From this perspective, the front page's intensity stems from it being a synthesis of syntheses. On the one hand, there is the world (the previous day) brought together in the newspaper through a first synthesis composed by the sum of all reports. This meant that the reader, when looking at the front page, was actually seeing two things: each piece of report, whose reading reenacted its circulation and visibility, and the front page as a whole. Moreover, they had to perform a second synthesis between the two opposite experiences described by Crary, for in both the fixed reading of a single report and in the wandering through the ensemble of reports that constitute the front page, the reader was forced to glance.

The reader thus glanced both at each story and through the ensemble of stories. However, glancing here should be given a different status to the act of perception of a painting. The use of visual tropes to describe this experience plays between the two senses of glance as a brief look and a quick reading, less to question the verbal structure of journalism than to try to represent the particularities of its presence in the modern world. This is my final point in this chapter: we will never know what readers thought while reading the news, which means this history cannot be directly about them. However, if we treat newspapers as products conceived as a response to a specific form of perception, it may then be suggested that journalistic production and its forms of representation matched the reader's ability to perceive things.[27] In this sense, readership may not be what a history of newspaper narratives narrates, but their role is even more decisive, for they were the absent cause of these narratives, and, as such, the true historical background – rather than the events filling its content – of journalism.

Newspapers as the historical events that this book engages with intersect three moments: that of the event proper, the production of news and its reading. However, only the second moment is left for us to see and analyse. We will have to consider the events mediated by the news and reading as something established by the form by which that same news was produced. Glancing over newspapers, in this sense, will refer less to the particular ways reading was performed, than to the image with which newspapers represented themselves as machines of visibility that were made to be seen.

In 1922, reporters from six Portuguese newspapers were filmed while sitting on the deck of a ship (see Figure 1.2). Most of them sat still as if they were posing to be photographed. Norberto Lopes, one of the youngest, however, already showed an acute perception of what it meant to be filmed. He acted for the camera and his performance shows how he wanted his profession to be seen: sitting on the right hand side of the image, he began by focusing on an imaginary object and then started writing about it in his notebook, after which he raised his eyes as if to confirm what he had already seen or in search of some unnoticed detail.

Figure 1.2: Still from *O raid aéreo Lisboa–Rio de Janeiro pelos heróicos aviadores Gago Coutinho e Sacadura Cabral,* dir. Henrique Alegria (Invicta Film, 1922). ANIM/Cinemateca Portuguesa.

His gesture resembled that of the painter glancing for a detail in the landscape, or that of the cameraman, grasping movement and transformation. Either way, he was writing images, capturing images through writing, as if there was a coincidence between him and the machine capturing his gesture.

Lopes was a contemporary of Fernando Pessoa and the industrialization of cinema, rather than the Ultimatum and Júlio César Machado, living in a period when journalism often represented itself as film and reporters as cameramen. But Lopes's gesture in front of the camera also represented something else: by pretending his writing was somehow able to express the visibility of circulation – as in cinema's moving images – he necessarily assumed that his report would be read through the fluidity of a glance. It is of course just a representation, almost a fiction, but precisely as such it seemed to rely on a recognition by the viewer, who might also be his reader, as if they all shared a common horizon of what was expected from each other's showing and writing, seeing and reading.

Notes

1. The full version of the memorandum reads as follows: 'What Her Majesty's Government require and insist upon is the following: that telegraphic instructions shall be sent to the governor of Mozambique at once to the effect that all and any Portuguese military forces which are actually on the Shire or in the Makololo or in the Mashona territory are to be withdrawn. Her Majesty's Government considers that without this the assurances given by the Portuguese Government are illusory. Mr Petre [the English ambassador in Lisbon] is compelled by his instruction to leave Lisbon at once with all the members of his legation unless a satisfactory answer to this foregoing intimation is received by him in the course of this evening, and Her Majesty's ship Enchantress is now at Vigo waiting for his orders.' The memorandum can be read in Coelho (1990).
2. The tension between images and words is key to my argument, as I will try to demonstrate throughout this book. What is important to stress at this stage is how this relationship was historically situated. As Gerry Beegan has suggested, the close relationship between journalism and photography was redefining not only the general perception of late nineteenth-century readers of newspapers (even when images were still rare in their pages), but the sheer act of reading itself: 'In this respect it seems hardly possible to over-estimate the importance of the silent teaching of the photograph' (Beegan 2008: 154).
3. *Diário de Notícias*, 13 January 1890, p.1.
4. *Diário de Notícias*, 13 January 1890, p.1.
5. This may allow us to introduce newspapers as a particularly complex form of communication in an era deeply conscious of the importance of circulation, according to Wolfgang Schivelbusch: 'The nineteenth century was very aware of this achievement, the conquest of space; this can be seen in the relatively high value it assigned to the

means of communication and transportation in its official self-perception: the triad of the rail-road, steamship, telegraph, was evoked time and again as representative of industrial progress' (Schivelbusch 1986: 194).

6. *Diário de Notícias*, 13 January 1890, p.1.
7. *Diário de Notícias*, 13 January 1890, p.1.
8. We can recognize here a familiar image of journalism as an active participant, rather than just a narrator, of modern city life: 'Newspapers benefited from the experience of city life as spectacle, and they contributed to it' (Schudson 1978: 105).
9. *Diário de Notícias*, 13 January 1890, p.1.
10. *Diário de Notícias*, 13 January 1890, p.1.
11. Carlo Ginzburg shows how 'the model of medical semiotics or symptomatology' spread through different forms of knowledge and discourse, such as the history of art, psychoanalysis and detective fiction, and became, 'toward the end of the nineteenth century', 'a paradigm or model based on the interpretation of clues' (Ginzburg 1980: 12). The episode in the house of Júlio César Machado suggests that we could easily add the discourse of journalism to the list.
12. *Diário de Notícias*, 13 January 1890, p.1.
13. Heteronym was a figure created by Fernando Pessoa in his literary 'programme', in which the poet experimented with different genres – futurism, classicism and so on – under different names, imaginary writers to whom Pessoa gave a set of psychological and biographical traits (while simultaneously establishing literary and personal relationships between them).
14. According to Peter Osborne, modernity, 'as a form of historical consciousness and its transformation into a general model of social experience' not only 'designates the contemporaneity of an epoch to the time of its classification', but it also 'registers this contemporaneity in terms of a qualitatively new, self-transcending temporality which has the simultaneous effect of distancing the present from even that most recent past with which it is thus identified' (Osborne 1995: 14).
15. A particularly interesting discussion about recognizable tropes of modernity, and most notably the relationship between the two I mention here – and the role of the arts in capturing surfaces in the age of speed – can be found in Clark (1999: XIX–XXX).
16. Following Ginzburg, it can even be said that the world of public circulation and the world of private invisibility are not really distinct, but two aspects of a single world where precisely the uncontrolled speed of the former is what marks the limits through which knowledge must depart from discreet manifestations taken from superficial signs: 'In a social structure of ever-increasing complexity like that of advanced capitalism, befogged by ideological murk, any claim to systematic knowledge appears as a flight of foolish fancy. To acknowledge this is not to abandon the idea of totality. On the contrary, the existence of a deep connection which explains superficial phenomena can be confirmed when it is acknowledged that direct knowledge of such a connection is impossible. Reality is opaque; but there are certain points – clues, symptoms – which allow us to decipher it' (Ginzburg 1980: 27).
17. Eric Auerbach goes as far as to suggest in a discussion of Virginia Woolf that modernism produced 'the realistic novel of the era between the two great wars' for, among other things, its 'disintegration of the continuity of exterior events' and the 'shifting of the narrative viewpoint' (Auerbach 1953: 546).
18. In his presentation of the *flâneur*, Walter Benjamin specifies that 'once a writer had entered the marketplace, he looked around as in a diorama' (Benjamin 1983: 35).
19. I here distance myself from Richard Terdiman's image of nineteenth-century newspapers as random collections of texts, of no use to the ways readers made sense of

the world. According to Terdiman, newspapers presented a 'random disposition of unrelated articles which … induced in the reader a tolerance for inorganic confusion which served much more the needs of the layout editor than it did the reader's own' (Terdiman 1985: 137).

20. As we have seen, Jameson explores this idea and also stresses that simultaneity as the 'intersection of several different temporalities' (Jameson 2009: 494) is what opens space for the formation of imagined communities, groups which Benedict Anderson to a large extent had already attributed to the readership of newspapers (see also Anderson 1991).

21. In Clark, this experience of visibility, where modern life already appears itself as image, makes the viewer vacillate between absolute certainty and doubt, not so much in relation to the thing seen as to the act of seeing. Unstableness thus seems to be not an obstacle but the condition for the subject's self-awareness: '"seeing" … believes that it *has* the world, in all its fullness and articulation, and that the world is present *in seeing, strictly and narrowly conceived*. Yet at the same time it seems to grow progressively uncertain as to how its procedures give rise to the separateness and connection of things. Thus the task of representation comes to be twofold; to demonstrate the fixity and substance of the world out there, but also to admit that the seer does not know – most probably cannot know – how his or her own sight makes objects possible. The more one looks, the more one attends to interruptions and paradoxes in perception' (Clark 1999: 17, original emphasis).

22. Guy Debord's notion of spectacle would be the extreme point of this process, where the subject is undermined as an observer to become a pure object of spectacle (Debord 1977). See also Crary (2000: 74).

23. Gilles Deleuze situates the impact of cinema in this same world both philosophically and historically: '[H]ow can a movement be prevented from already being at least a virtual image, and the image from already being at least possible movement? What appeared finally to be a dead end was the confrontation of materialism and idealism, the one wishing to reconstitute the order of consciousness with pure material movements, the other the order of the universe with pure images in consciousness. It was necessary, at any cost, to overcome this duality of image and movement, of consciousness and thing. Two very different authors were to undertake this task at about the same time: Bergson and Husserl. Each had his own cry: all consciousness is consciousness *of* something (Husserl), or more strongly, all consciousness *is* something (Bergson). Undoubtedly many factors external to philosophy explain why the old position had become impossible. These were social and scientific factors which placed more and more movement into conscious life, and more and more images into the material world' (Deleuze 1986: 58).

24. 'Cézanne's work poses the idea of an attentive fixation, a subjective immobilization that, instead of holding together the contents of the perceived world, seeks to enter into its ceaseless movements of destabilization' (Crary 2000: 297).

25. Leo Charney's account of the film spectator's apprehension of movement is not far from the experience of newspaper readership as I am trying to describe it. The following quotation shows how close both are, especially in the articulation between the fragment (the frame, the individual news) and continuity (the moving image, 'glancing over newspapers'), and in this sense how useful early film analysis can be to the study of *fin-de-siècle* and early twentieth-century newspapers: 'The fissures between the separate moments [in the photographs of Eadweard Muybridge] remind us that we are seeing something that simply replicates a continuous movement but can never

be one. We have, that is, entered the zone of representation, with which the bond to the real introduced by photography became re-presentation. The difference of the re-presentation is inscribed in the representation of motion by the gaps that render it discontinuous and fragmentary, whereas the original motion – the present motion – was seemingly continuous' (Charney and Schwartz 1995: 291).

26. Here I am thinking of those debates about the nature of the relation between modernity, modernism and social change. Perry Anderson, for example, famously warned against an idealized notion of modernity in Marshall Berman's *All That is Solid Dissolves into Air*, in which, according to Anderson, modernity appears as sheer flow detached from the social, political and historical frames with which it confronted itself and in relation to which it should be defined. Terry Eagleton, on the other hand, identified a particularly uncritical discourse on modernity in Peter Conrad's *Modern Times, Modern Spaces*, where the spell of 'fragmentation, a sense of space shrunken and time accelerated, giddying technological advance, the crumbling of moral certitudes, the rise of the faceless masses, the human individual as fractured, estranged, disorientated' (Eagleton 2003: 146) has taken modernity out of its context and turned it into a set of stereotypes (Eagleton 2003; Anderson 1984).

27. In this context, Hans Robert Jauss's theory of literary reception may constitute a useful frame for thinking about the reception of newspapers as narrative forms circulating amidst other narratives and forms of representation: 'The analysis of the literary experience of the reader avoids the threatening pitfalls of psychology if it describes the reception and the influence of a work within the objectifiable system of expectations that arises for each work in the historical moment of its appearance, from a pre-understanding of the genre, from the form and themes of already familiar works, and from the opposition between poetic and practical language' (Jauss 1982: 22).

Chapter 2

Travelling News

Norberto Lopes, the reporter who played the role of 'onboard camer-aman', was in fact engaged in reportage (see Chapter 1). He and his colleagues had been sent by their newspapers to cover the first attempt to fly the South Atlantic from Lisbon to Rio de Janeiro in the spring of 1922. The ship they were travelling on also carried an aeroplane for Gago Coutinho and Sacadura Cabral, the heroes of this adventure, who were by then safe on the Brazilian islands of Fernando Noronha after an accident. Their first plane had sunk after a forced landing at sea, but the public enthusiasm around the flight persuaded the Portuguese authorities to send them another one. Lopes and the other reporters were thus about to witness an event they had helped to create back in Lisbon by extensive journalistic coverage.

Lopes's own form of involvement in the event would become clear in the style of his reports, where the desire to make sure that readers would share his own experience of the flight – 'I'll try to reconstruct the journey as if I was inside the plane myself' (Lopes 1923: 125) – was formulated through the use of metaphors related to cinema: 'I still have the aston-ishing film of the arrival imprinted on the screen of my memory as sharp as an impeccably accurate and splendidly luminous movie' (Lopes 1923: 157). By 1922, this image had become commonplace: cinema appeared as the ultimate model for the clarity the reporter espoused. Clarity, how-ever, was not the only thing Lopes found useful in the new technology, for to reconstruct the journey as if he was inside the plane also involved the ability to express the movement of aviation.[1]

This is what made that particular event so exciting to the reporter: the plane was not only an image in the landscape, but moved through it. In this sense, aviation matched cinema's challenge to the traditional perception of time and space. Both responded to what Walter Benjamin identified as 'a heightened need for ever-changing impressions' (Benjamin 2008: 316).[2] Accordingly, whereas aviation constituted the most challenging object for filmic representation, cinema would conversely be the only form capable of rendering the motion of flying machines. The reporter was then faced with the need to think, and represent, a phenomenon happening 'in less time than it took to think of it' (Lopes 1923: 92), something apparently beyond the scope of his pencil and notebook.

We can now understand Lopes's restless gaze over the seascape on deck a little better. The filmic metaphor gives us the measure of the challenge. Planes, as the most pioneering technological invention of the early twentieth century (possibly only matched by cinema itself), stood metonymically for what was modern and sophisticated. To a certain extent, aeroplanes played the same symbolic role as cars (and if planes were not an everyday presence like motor vehicles, their achievement was much more spectacular). They were expressions of those same features that marked the era: speed, circulation and movement. The discourses (journalistic and literary) of aviation indicated quite clearly how its implications transcended issues related to science and transportation. Planes were a pretext to revive the classics (Icarus and Prometheus) and helped define the aesthetics of modernism (as we will see later in this chapter). They were used both to narrate modern experiences and to emphasize – especially around episodes like the flight to Brazil – continuities in national heroism, and seemed to revolutionize the bodily experience of space.

By 1922, the general enthusiasm for aviation had already been present for more than a decade. The expectations around the new technology were so high that the creation of an aero club in Portugal anticipated by a year the first flight on national territory, in April 1910, only six months before the republican revolution of 5 October. The uproar associated with the end of the monarchy did not diminish the enthusiasm for aviation. On the contrary, the first aircraft were purchased by public subscription organized by some of the most politically interventionist newspapers (*O Século* and *Comércio do Porto*) and the Republican Party itself, as if to reinforce the spirit of change embodied by the new regime.

The First World War, in which Portugal participated between 1916 and 1918, could not but intensify this interest, dramatizing it with a sense of urgency. After 1918, what had up to then been mostly a question of science and technology (the apogee of modern civilization) became a military problem with decisive implications for the future of national autonomy. In fact, from 1919 onwards, the country began to witness – especially through newspapers – a permanent competition between aviators trying to achieve the most daring feats of flight. The Paris–Lisbon and Lisbon–Porto–Lisbon routes were flown in 1919, but in 1920 there took place the even more impressive flights (because of the sea crossings involved) from Lisbon to London (by Sacadura Cabral, one of the two aviators involved in the 1922 attempt to reach Brazil) and from Lisbon to Madeira. The latter was particularly spectacular, as the young officers who made it disobeyed their superiors' orders forbidding the project, and used a plane built out of scraps of older aircraft – without floats, they landed in the shallows off Madeira with their wheels down. Aviation, in a word, had become the epoch's ultimate adventure, and aviators its greatest heroes.

This is why the flight to Brazil became such an enormous challenge for both aviators and whoever was narrating it. As we already know, Norberto Lopes and his fellow reporters travelled with cameras and a cameraman. Their reports thus had to compete with a medium that was still not considered to be a form of journalism, but which nonetheless seemed capable of showing what newspapers could not. But if this is fundamental for an understanding of the new challenges posed to the reporter's work – Lopes's metaphors were, in this sense, filled with anxiety – nevertheless the whole event was still completely dominated by the written press.

The Flight from Lisbon to Rio de Janeiro

As soon as the prospective flight was made public, it was headline news. The idea of flying to Brazil had been around for a while, but doubts about its feasibility – given the long stretches of ocean that had to be crossed with no recognizable landmarks – caused some scepticism among the military authorities on whom the whole initiative depended. By the end of March 1922, however, everything was settled: the Portuguese navy had granted officers Cabral and Coutinho permission and, anticipating newspapers' interest, put in place an information service for journalists to facilitate their work. On 28 March, Sacadura Cabral himself published an article in the most influential newspapers, *Diário de Notícias* and *O Século*, explaining the difficulties of the enterprise and warning against excessive enthusiasm. Among other things, it became clear that the journey had to be divided into several stages. The section between the Cape Verde archipelago, off the West African coast, and the Brazilian island of Fernando Noronha, in particular, was potentially insurmountable.

This did not cool journalistic enthusiasm, however, and when the moment of the departure arrived, on 31 March, a whole epic narrative was already in place in the pages of the newspapers. According to this, even though the country was poor and its aviation deficient, Portugal's 'human material' was more than enough to overcome any obstacles, or so

O Século would claim.[3] The flight thus became something much more decisive than a simple military or sporting event. According to *Diário de Notícias*, the meaning of what was at stake was 'immense, spiritually huge, [coming] from our past and our future, from our eternal civilizing hegemony, from our splendid Latin immortality'.[4] In an image that was both easily understandable and hugely appealing, what was at stake was the 'genius of the race' guiding the aviators, who, as such, were a modern version of sixteenth-century navigators now travelling in a 'small aerial caravel, sister of the caravels of the [maritime] discoveries'.[5]

So, when the plane left for South America – via Africa – newspapers tried to convince readers that the 'glorious' episodes of discovery and navigation from the nation's past were somehow being repeated. The success of the two first sections of the flight – from Lisbon to the Canary Islands and from there to Cape Verde – contributed to reinforce this feeling and tone. The difficulties, however, were just beginning. By mid April, everyone already knew that the stage from Cape Verde onwards would necessarily be different. This would in fact prove to be the most difficult part of the journey. And, as we know since we have already met Norberto Lopes on the ship carrying a second plane, an accident occurred on the journey. What we still do not know is that a second accident would destroy the second plane as well, and that the continuation of the journey to Brazil would have to wait for a third craft. This chapter's narrative will thus focus on what caused those two accidents, and on the ways journalistic coverage evolved from the first to the second.

As the fuel that the first seaplane, the *Lusitânia*, carried was not enough to allow it to reach South America in one go, the aviators had to find a way to refuel. This was difficult, for two reasons. Firstly, there was a lack of reference points on the high seas as the Portuguese navy did not have the resources needed to provide the flyers with a convoy of ships, as had been the case in other famous flights. The solution was found in two solitary rocks, Saint Peter and Saint Paul, whose position was more or less equidistant from Cape Verde and Fernando Noronha. To choose the rocks as the meeting point for the *Lusitânia* and the *República* (the ship sent to accompany the crossing) may have seemed the only alternative, but it raised a second problem: as Saint Peter and Saint Paul were too small to land on and did not even provide a harbour, the plane would be forced to perform the very risky manoeuvre of landing just off the coast.

Despite the risks involved, Lisbon's optimism on 18 April (the day the flyers left Cape Verde) seemed unshaken. According to the following day's edition of *O Século*, 'yesterday, in the streets, in the cafés, in the trams, in the theatres, everywhere, the glorious enterprise of the two Portuguese aviators was enthusiastically discussed'.[6] That morning's edition of *Diário de Notícias* confirmed that 'nothing else could be of interest, there was no other topic of conversation'; 'What happened … is not easy to describe', the reporter would add, 'an enormous crowd was gathered all night long in front of the billboards that belonged to our paper and to our rivals'.[7] Newspapermen may indeed have felt it hard to describe the city's excitement, but it was not something very difficult to explain: newspapers not only focused their narratives on the crowd back in Lisbon, rather than on the flyers out in the Atlantic, but what they stressed above all was their own role in creating public enthusiasm.

As soon as news of the departure from Cape Verde for Saint Peter and Saint Paul was broadcast at 9 A.M., *O Século* ordered fireworks to be set off in several locations, as a pre-established sign for its readers. After that, information was posted on the many billboards the newspaper had throughout the city, while telegrams were sent to the provinces carrying the good news. Correspondents around the country posted the content of the telegrams on local billboards as well. The centre of all this excitement was the main billboards in Lisbon's central squares Rossio and Terreiro do Paço, where the most important newspapers constantly updated information. Hundreds of people gathered there, discussing what they already knew, and waiting for any new information to arrive.

According to *O Século*, the day was marked by demonstrations of patriotic fervour, with cheers for the republic, the navy and the newspaper itself. There seemed little room for doubt with regard to the flight's success. And yet, all the newspapers had told the public was that the seaplane had left Praia, in Cape Verde, en route to the two rocks of St Peter and St Paul. At this stage, then, something other than concrete journalistic information had to be used in order to keep up the enthusiasm. Reporters had to infer what was supposed to be happening from whatever knowledge they had about the flight. 'According to our rigorous calculations, based on average speeds reached on previous journeys, the distance between Praia and the rocks cannot be covered in less than 12 hours', was the prudent approach of *Diário de Notícias*.[8] *O Século* made a less prudent claim: 'The two great Portuguese men Sacadura Cabral and Gago Coutinho left Praia and arrived at Saint Paul's rocks at precisely the time previously estimated'.[9] To *O Século*, the combination of technological resources and scientific knowledge seemed sufficient for the achievement to be taken for granted.

In these circumstances, the news coverage resembled something like a mere confirmation of a pre-established mechanical procedure, a modern chronicle of technological times. According to *Diário de Notícias*'s calculations, having left Cape Verde at 8 A.M., the plane should have reached the rocks at 8 P.M., Portuguese time. At sunset, any attention focused elsewhere turned exclusively to the aviators, and those who had been otherwise engaged began to congregate around the main billboards in Lisbon's city centre:

> At 11pm, Rossio was absolutely crowded. Thousands of people obsessively looking at the billboards [were] waiting to see the liberating news. The same picture, maybe even bigger, could be seen in front of the central post office in Terreiro do Paço. It was clear to everyone that none of those electrified Portuguese would leave the square before the arrival of news about the aviators … Midnight. 1 A.M.. A city burning with fever. The crowd shivers with emotion. No one speaks.[10]

As the emotion, or at least its journalistic representation, started to become unbearable, a telegram finally arrived at 1.15 A.M. with the news everyone wanted to hear: 'the seaplane arrived at the rocks of Saint Peter and Saint Paul at 10 P.M. local time'.[11] The narrative could finally reach its apotheosis: 'and now the reporter must give up trying to describe what went on downtown when the firecrackers started exploding in the air. An enormous roar burst out from the crowd. Strangers hugged each other. In a few minutes, the whole city was alive with firecrackers. Automobiles joined the happy celebration with the noise of their horns'.[12]

The papers were immediately printed: 'Another Victorious Journey' was *O Século*'s triumphant headline on the morning of 19 April. However, while Lisbon enjoyed its euphoria and the journalists, accordingly, experimented with their exuberant literary talents, Gago Coutinho, Sacadura Cabral and the sailors onboard the *República* were still struggling against the waves in the middle of the Atlantic. Shortly after the plane's arrival at the rocks, and after just enough time for the ship to send a message containing the news of the landing, a sudden wave broke off one of the plane's wings, and the aircraft sank. A second message was sent immediately, but its arrival in Lisbon was delayed because of its routing through several transmission stations, which made it impossible to stop the newspapers being distributed. When this second message finally arrived, *Diário de Notícias* decided to post the sad update on its billboards and print a special supplement immediately after the morning edition. Through it, the public was reassured that the aviators were fine, and that the government had already decided to provide a second aircraft, making sure that the crossing could continue.

O Século, however, reacted very differently to the failure of its triumphant headline. Not only did the newspaper not acknowledge that the plane had sunk after landing at the rocks, but it also decided to follow another lead, based on a radio message received from a British steam packet, the *Avon*, and transmitted by Reuters, claiming that the aviators had already arrived to Fernando Noronha and were off to the Brazilian coast – a sheer impossibility at that moment, even if everything had gone well at the rocks (presumably, the messenger mistook the rocks for Fernando Noronha). For several hours on the morning of 19 April, billboard readers in central Lisbon had to decide between contradictory accounts: the news of the accident and the consequent interruption of the journey, as *Diário de Notícias* had it, or the arrival of the *Lusitânia* at the Brazilian islands of Fernando Noronha and its departure for Pernambuco on the Brazilian coast, as claimed by *O Século*.

The decision to release the supplement of *Diário de Notícias* was a response to this impasse. Given the temporal gap between the two sequences of events (the aviators' adventures in the South Atlantic and the enthusiasm in Lisbon) and their reporting in the morning editions of the newspapers (the journey on April 18, the reception of the news and public reaction to it on April 19), that week's most exciting editions were the ones published on 20 April, when both *O Século* and *Diário de Notícias* explained their attitude and commented upon their rival's editorial choices the day before. *Diário de Notícias*'s rationale for the supplement implied a harsh critique of *O Século*'s insistence in maintaining the news of the arrival at Fernando Noronha on its billboards:

> Through our supplement, the public could ascertain that the aviators had not arrived at Fernando Noronha simply because they were kept at the rocks by a technical problem with the plane. The priority was to reassure the public about the well-being of our beloved countrymen. That is why we congratulate ourselves for having only told our readers the truth.[13]

This seemed reasonable. However, *O Século*'s view on the subject was radically different. In the second page of the paper's edition that day, a facsimile of the rival's supplement was printed under the heading 'Ao povo' ('To the people').[14] The caption was a fierce attack on *Diário de Notícias*, levelling against it the worst charge imaginable at a moment of such patriotic passion: defeatism. Obviously, *O Século* did not try to deny that an accident had occurred and the journey interrupted. But apart from a brief apology (after all, the newspaper was merely using official sources), the newspaper's edition on 20 April seemed pleased with choosing to keep false information on its billboards.

We should try to avoid posing the conflict between *O Século* and *Diário de Notícias* in the same terms they used against each other: that of ethical conduct versus patriotism. Instead, *O Século*'s editorial option should be interpreted as the logical outcome of the close relation between an event that had been completely taken over by nationalist passion and its journalistic coverage. In fact, even when the flight's success was still uncertain, the level of euphoria around it was such that newspapers like

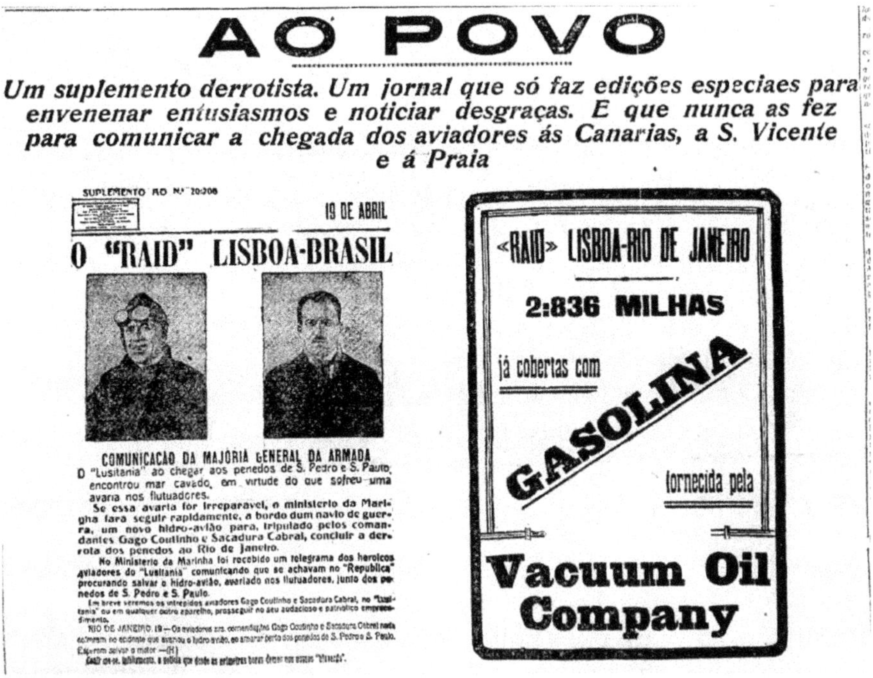
AO POVO

Um suplemento derrotista. Um jornal que só faz edições especiaes para envenenar entusiasmos e noticiar desgraças. E que nunca as fez para comunicar a chegada dos aviadores ás Canarias, a S. Vicente e á Praia

SUPLEMENTO AO N.º 20:206

19 DE ABRIL

O "RAID" LISBOA-BRASIL

COMUNICACAO DA MAJORIA GENERAL DA ARMADA

O "Lusitania" ao chegar aos penedos de S. Pedro e S. Paulo, encontrou mar cavado, em virtude do que sofreu uma avaria nos flutuadores.

Se essa avaria fôr irreparavel, o ministerio da Marinha fará seguir rapidamente, a bordo dum navio de guerra, um novo hidro-avião para, tripulado pelos comandantes Gago Coutinho e Sacadura Cabral, concluir a derrota dos penedos ao Rio de Janeiro.

No Ministerio da Marinha foi recebido um telegrama dos heroicos aviadores do "Lusitania" comunicando que se achavam no "Republica" procurando salvar o hidro-avião, averiado nos flutuadores, junto dos penedos de S. Pedro e S. Paulo.

Em breve veremos os intrepidos aviadores Gago Coutinho e Sacadura Cabral, no "Lusitania" ou em qualquer outro aparelho, prosseguir no seu audacioso e patriotico empreendimento.

RIO DE JANEIRO, 19 — Os aviadores srs. comendadores Gago Coutinho e Sacadura Cabral nada sofreram no acidente que avariou o hidro-avião, ao amarar perto dos penedos de S. Pedro e S. Paulo. Esperam salvar o motor —(H)

«RAID» LISBOA-RIO DE JANEIRO

2:836 MILHAS

já cobertas com

GASOLINA

fornecida pela

Vacuum Oil Company

Figure 2.1: Facsimile of *Diário de Notícias* supplement published by *O Século*, 20 April 1922. Biblioteca Nacional de Portugal.

O Século immediately perceived it as an irreversible process of 'national regeneration', conceivable only through an 'intense, sweet, pure and sincere communion and affection', the 'alliance of every heart and every will' that had been mobilized by, and organized around, newspapers in the first place.[15]

We are thus facing a true dialectic: *O Século*'s option to persist in the publication of false news can be understood as a compromise with public pressure and enthusiasm. And yet, to a large extent that enthusiasm had a journalistic origin. The flight was a good opportunity to mobilize all the resources available within the network of information in order to attract public attention, but its immense impact was also a direct consequence of the strong symbolism the event had for public opinion. *O Século*'s final response to the critique of the dubious criteria it had used in its coverage sums up the ways in which newspaper mediation had become a central element in the event's mobilization:

> And so, as we let off the firecrackers, we took the good news to every corner of the city, where it had been anxiously expected … we also guaranteed the cooperation of our local councils; through our correspondents, we informed the most remote areas of the country of the seaplane's course; we also asked our correspondents to organize local committees

to celebrate; we encouraged the Church to toll its bells and thus join in with the nation's happiness; it was also our idea ... that all military bands should give public concerts at the Lusitânia's arrival in Rio de Janeiro; we stressed how good it would be to have the flag flying everywhere (*embandeiramento geral*) and houses and streets to be lit up throughout the day; we asked our greatest poet, Guerra Junqueiro, to compose a message to be sent in the name of all the Portuguese, a message that already bears the President's signature; our pages reminded us that ... the names of Gago Coutinho and Sacadura Cabral, should be engraved on the most appropriate monument, the Tower of Belém, in order to perpetuate their heroism... And so we are at ease with our conscience.[16]

This extract performs one of those syntheses mentioned in the first chapter. Here the paper acted as an intersection between something happening far away – in motion and with no identifiable location – and public expectations that had been transformed into journalistic events. Norberto Lopes's initial filmic gesture, in this sense, embodied the whole process: he showed himself seeing, and thus participating, in the event he was trying to narrate. With it, he tried to reassure his readers that he could observe as well and as efficiently as a movie camera while simultaneously making himself observed, somehow situating himself in the narrative.

When Lopes travelled with the second plane, the journey could then be scrutinized from a position of greater proximity. A camera and six reporters joined the aviators, who, after some weeks of enforced leisure in Fernando Noronha, could now resume their adventure in another plane. In the meantime, for almost a month, interest in the event had been kept alive in Lisbon with daily reports of technical details about planes and anecdotes about the pilots' stay on the islands. A new plan was meanwhile prepared. In order to fly over the full extent of the Atlantic, Coutinho and Cabral decided to go back to the rocks by air and then fly back to Fernando Noronha.

The new flight was scheduled for 11 May. The presence of reporters on the islands made little difference to the way in which Lisbon experienced the second long night from May 11 to 12. As before, the gap between event and information about it could lead to despair, and despite their proximity to what was going on, the reporters could do little to change matters. But unlike the first attempt on 18 April, everyone now seemed better able to deal with the uncertainty surrounding the flight. Still, as night fell on 11 May with no news about the aviators, the silence would prove almost unbearable, just as it had before. This time, however, no last-minute telegram with the hoped for news was to rescue the newspapers. In fact, there was no news at all that night. As a result, the headline of *O Século* on 12 May was very different to the triumphant tone of April, and barely announced anything at all: 'The whole country is anxious' was something the public – the whole country – already knew. The echo of the first accident gave this second flight – and the second accident – a sense of repetition that will allow us to see the ambiguous status of the whole event – in between a flight, its journalistic coverage and the public's response to the first through the second – more clearly.

The editorial that night could not but reinforce the gloomy tone of the headline: 'little is known and there is tremendous anxiety. It is as if the country's heart had stopped beating and its life was only sustained by the hope of receiving the news … Only one thing is certain: everyone lives in anxiety, everyone is afraid, everyone is shaking, everyone desires, everyone suffers'.[17] Clearly written under pressure, which explains its dramatic insistence, the text may be read as hinting at the stressful conditions in which the reporter worked during that particular night: 'the crowd asked our agents for news. Day and night, in great distress, our telephones had to reply to the same vast phone call made by thousands of voices, the inner voice of thousands of souls, the spontaneous cry in every heart'.[18] We can of course imagine how anxious the public must have been, but it might be suggested that at that moment the journalist was more anxious than anyone else.[19] His editorial is truly remarkable in the way it shows how *O Século* seemed better equipped to deal with the false news of the first accident than with the absence of news altogether during the second. The initial enthusiasm of the first night – which was kept alive even through the hours of uncertainty before the news of the arrival at the rocks – seemed completely lost. The absence of news, made worse by the recent memory of 18 April – which reminded everyone that accidents could happen – made it impossible for the journalist to conclude his piece. His anxiety was thus twofold: he ran the risk of having to go to press before the story was over, while the threat of bad news hung over his head.

The pathetic insistence on everyone's feelings suggests that the journalist was buying time, postponing the full stop. Towards the end, however, he did give something away: 'If, for any reason, the cause of the accident was solely due to a failure on the plane, the entire nation burns with the desire that the crossing be concluded anyway'.[20] The journalist's discreet assumption that an accident had taken place showed, here too, a tacit compact with the readers. Even though the episode in April when *O Século*'s billboards carried erroneous news was still fresh in everyone's minds, people nevertheless expected the journalist, and the dailies more generally, to provide full accounts of what happened the day before. It was an explosive mixture: what was worse than bad news was having the suspicion that something bad had happened without being able to transform it into news. So, if 'the country's heart had stopped beating' because 'its life was only sustained by the hope of receiving the news', then the whole country's anxiety was somehow the responsibility of the journalist. His own anxiety was the consequence of the incapacity to mitigate a general distress provoked by the lack of what, at the moment of going to press, he could not give: the news. A title like 'The whole country is anxious', in this sense, reveals the extent to which the main event had already moved, not only from the flight to journalism, but farther away to its public reception.

And yet, what was more disquieting at that moment was not exactly the complete absence of information as such, but rather the absence of news about the aviators despite the intense communication taking place about the flight. In fact, communication arrived all night long at the offices of the newspapers. Telegrams and radio transmissions went back and forth between Europe, Africa and America and the Atlantic – and the plane – at the centre of the triangle. The drama could thus be said to be the consequence of expectations created by this permanent flow. For the technical resources available through radio and the telegraph already made possible an aspiration to simultaneous communication that fell very short of the experience of a truly live transmission.[21]

The way the structure of *Diário de Notícias*'s front page was composed that night illustrates this rather well. Through it, the morning reader could follow the exact sequence of information as it arrived at the office by telegram and radio. Reading the page from top to bottom that day took the public through a frantic series of communications between Lisbon, Paris, Brest, Dakar, Praia, Pernambuco and several Portuguese, French and British ships in the Atlantic. It really looked as if the whole world were connected through the event. To guarantee that 'we know that all telegraphic stations are on permanent call' was of course promising, but all the information the reader would get was a succession – hour by hour, at 8, 9, 10, 11 P.M. and after – of the same desperate void, or of a void made desperate through insistence: 'there is no news from the plane'.[22]

The repetitiveness of *O Século*'s editorial was, then, a direct consequence of this hectic traffic. Nothing happened, yet communication kept flowing. According to the list of telegrams on the front page of *Diário de Notícias*, at 1 A.M. 'there is still no news. The crowd, in Terreiro do Paço is huge and restless'; at 1:30 A.M., 'from Paris comes the news via Brest, in communication with Fernando Noronha, that at 4 P.M., Brazilian time, nothing was known about the aviators'. At 4 A.M., the journalist had to stop: 'we must close this report. We still haven't heard anything from our glorious aviators'.[23] A form without content, one might say. A whole apparatus set up to render the flow of information emptied out by the invisibility of what was happening far away.

The succession of items of 'news' that were read in the morning followed the sequence of their arrival at the newspapers' offices the night

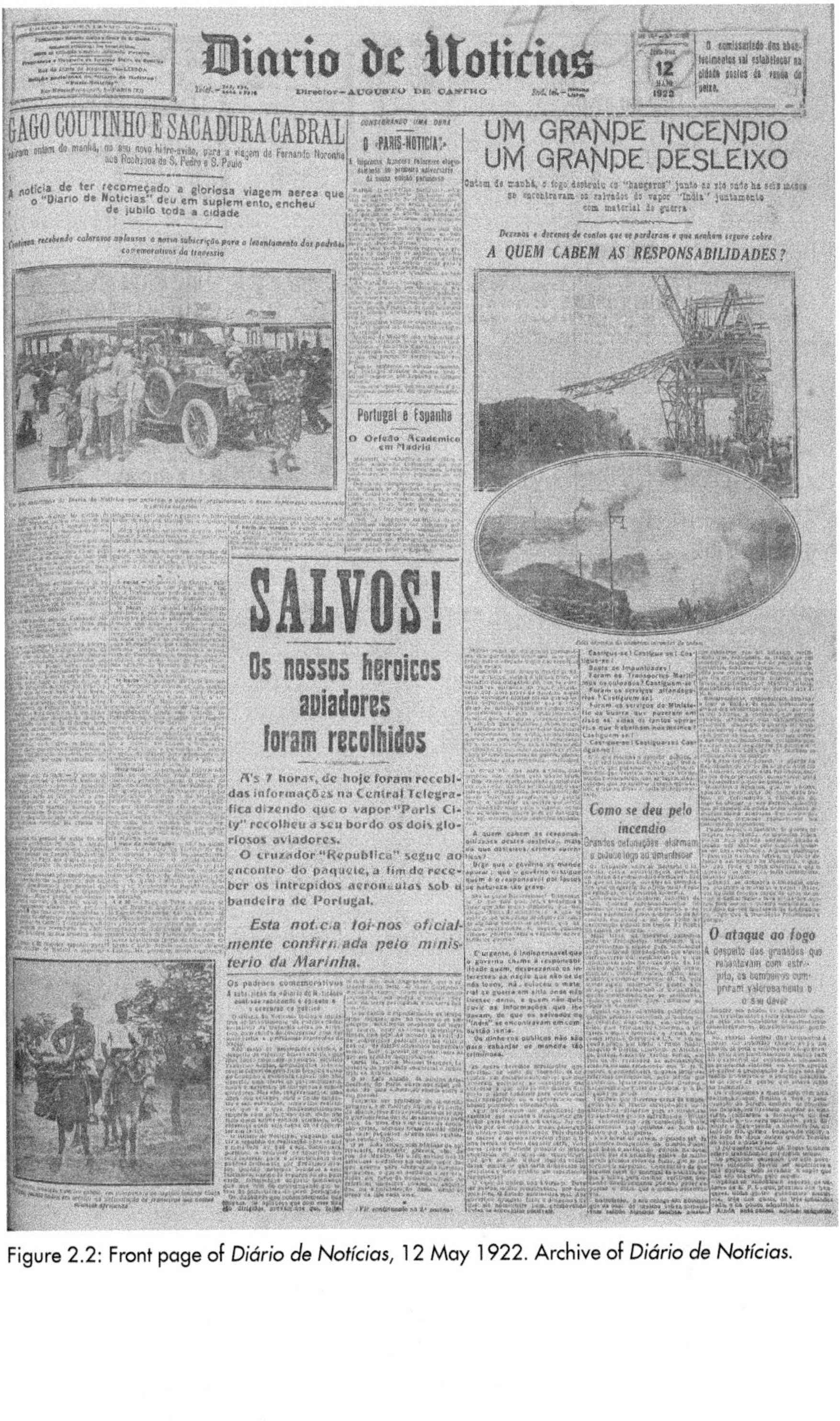
Diario de Noticias

Director—AUGUSTO DE CASTRO

12 1922

GAGO COUTINHO E SACADURA CABRAL

A noticia de ter recomeçado a gloriosa viagem aerea que o "Diario de Noticias" deu em suplemento, encheu de jubilo toda a cidade

O «PARIS-NOTICIAS»

UM GRANDE INCENDIO UM GRANDE DESLEIXO

Dezenas e dezenas de contos que se perderam e que nenhum seguro cobre

A QUEM CABEM AS RESPONSABILIDADES?

Portugal e Espanha

O Orfeão Academico em Madrid

SALVOS!

Os nossos heroicos aviadores foram recolhidos

A's 7 horas, de hoje foram recebidas informações na Central Telegrafica dizendo que o vapor "Paris City" recolheu a seu bordo os dois gloriosos aviadores.

O cruzador "Republica" segue ao encontro do paquete, a fim de receber os intrepidos aeronautas sob a bandeira de Portugal.

Esta noticia foi-nos oficialmente confirmada pelo ministerio da Marinha.

Como se deu pelo incendio

O ataque ao fogo

Figure 2.2: Front page of *Diário de Notícias*, 12 May 1922. Archive of *Diário de Notícias*.

before and thus could be seen to resemble a simulacrum. It seemed to give the reader the impression that they were able to experience the events as they succeeded in real time, as if they could re-enact the journalist's frustrating experience and thus simulate a live transmission. However, the rigidity of the newspaper form, that is, the need to have a finished edition ready to print and distribute in the morning, necessarily interrupted that incantatory moment. The people who bought Portugal's most popular newspapers on 12 May could read nothing but the void felt at 4 A.M., which, some hours later, might already be obsolete.

In fact, in the gap between its going to press and *Diário de Notícias* arriving at the newsagents, one piece of news finally did become known. In a later edition that day, a box in block capitals placed right after the journalist's final note at 4 A.M. announced the news that allayed everyone's concerns: 'Today at 7 A.M., the Central Station was informed that the steam-ship *Paris-City* had rescued the two glorious aviators'. No one could be entirely sure what had happened. Only later, when further information arrived, did readers finally find out that the plane, already on its way back from Saint Peter and Saint Paul to Fernando Noronha, had to make an emergency landing due to a mechanical problem. The fuel tanks were almost empty and the pontoon floats started leaking. The aviators managed to take off and approach the standard route for South Atlantic maritime navigation, hoping to find a ship. Meanwhile, they were once again forced to land. The plane was damaged beyond repair. When the *Paris-City* spotted them, Gago Coutinho and Sacadura Cabral had been in the water, their plane slowly sinking, for several hours.

That was not the hoped for outcome. But as we already know, after reading the front pages of the morning editions, it was probably the best news one could expect at 7 A.M., after the night's vigil shared by both leader writer and readers. This is why we cannot just shift our attention from the aviators to the reporters. As it had become obvious in the nocturnal vigils that surrounded the accidents, the real event to which the journalists and editorials were somehow trying to respond was happening in the main squares of Lisbon, where the crowds anxiously stood in front of the billboards of the national newspapers.

If we take a look at the 12 May edition of *O Século*, we can read another list of telegraphic messages displaying the constant arrival of information at the office the night before, though there is one difference: whereas *Diário de Notícias* printed the succession of telegrams with no further clarification, *O Século* explained that the list they had printed matched the information available that night on the newspaper's billboards.[24] In other words, what seemed just a mere simulacrum of simultaneity, produced by reading the morning paper, suddenly becomes a true simultaneous experience if seen from the perspective of readers who watched their newspapers' billboards being updated with the content of telegrams as they arrived.

We can reinforce this idea by looking a bit further at the many accounts of the city's reaction to the news as it arrived and circulated. On 13 May, for example, according to *Diário de Notícias*, when the rescue of the two pilots became known, 'in Lisbon, the good news spread like a bullet. As well as its fourth edition, *Diário de Notícias* immediately printed a placard that was distributed and posted by journalists and other staff at the busiest spots'.[25] Anyone in Lisbon could thus have had contact with the news by hearing newsvendors announcing the headlines, or by looking at a placard or billboard, or simply by hearing it from someone before buying the latest edition. In any case, the journalistic dialectic I mentioned earlier could be experienced by everyone involved: the circulation of information mobilized the public, but only the public's mobility within that information network allowed it to circulate, thus transforming journalistic events into something absolutely interiorized through everyday urban experience.

According to a standard definition of journalism, newspaper stories of what happened on those two dramatic nights may seem displaced. The narratives either describe a concrete enthusiasm precipitated by something that did not take place, or an intense anxiety provoked by the firm belief that something unspeakable was happening at that same moment – something almost, but not quite, within reach. 'Our billboards', one could read in *O Século* on 20 April, after the first accident, 'posted the good news that unfortunately could not be confirmed'.[26] On the same day, not even *Diário de Notícias*, which, as we know, had tried to avoid spreading unconfirmed 'good news', could fail to depict the city being taken over by a euphoric crowd surrounded by the noise of firecrackers and horns, all because some 'good news that, unfortunately, we must repeat, was only a false alarm'.[27]

And yet, this displacement, the felt discrepancy between the event and the reaction to it, may be seen as what a true modernist event looked like, when the narrative object of the news had become the flow of information itself, a metanarrative that, because of newspapers' material circulation, was experienced as a reality in its own right. When *O Século* described a city where everything 'was suffused by the cheerful atmosphere of all great moments',[28] that was because it was indeed a great moment, one in which the enthusiasm was as authentic as if what had caused it had really happened. The report of *Diário de Notícias* of the reactions to the false accounts of the aviators' arrival at Fernando Noronha finished with an amusing episode. In order to celebrate the achievement, the directors of a bank had given their staff the day off on full pay. These directors may have felt deceived. But from the staff's point of view, the 'success' of the flight was a concrete reality with material consequences.[29]

Eventually, Gago Coutinho and Sacadura Cabral arrived in Rio de Janeiro in a third plane, on 17 June. The actual flying time required to cross the South Atlantic from Portugal to Brazil was only a couple of days. The journey, however, with all its technical setbacks and unexpected accidents, lasted from the end of March to mid June. For two and a half months, then, newspapers kept the event alive by addressing every imaginable detail about seaplanes, the two heroes and the importance of aviation to human civilization, but also, and fundamentally, by exploring the nationalist significance of the journey: after discovering Brazil with the most sophisticated technology available in the fifteenth century, Portugal was now capable of leading the most recent technological revolution, repeating the feat of Pedro Álvares Cabral in 1500, but this time by air.[30]

This was, of course, a fiction. But precisely in that sense it captures the essence of what really happened: a plot through which newspapers managed to attract public attention to a good story and its efficient emplotment. The spectacular supplement distributed gratis by *Diário de Notícias* on 17 June showed an image with a figure of the republic opening her arms to Rio de Janeiro's Sugarloaf Mountain (Figure 2.3). So with the city's most recognizable symbol as backdrop, the union between Portugal and Brazil was sealed by the flight, the latter's most significant outcome. 'The most epic adventure of the last centuries glorifying the immortal Portuguese race is now completed!', Augusto de Castro, *Diário de Notícias*'s editor, claimed. However, his final words would turn, almost inevitably, to the narrative of the event as if to make sure that everything would be properly remembered through its journalistic dramatization:

> Two and a half months was the duration of this wonderful spectacle. And these were two and a half months of ecstasy, two and a half months of feverish shiver (*tremulando*), two and a half months of ever growing enthusiasm … The play includes tragic scenes that Aeschylus and Shakespeare would not dare dream of … Our aviators finally arrived at Rio de Janeiro. The curtain slowly descends.[31]

Aviation and Modernism

It would be clearly overstating things to suggest that the journey would not have been possible without the press. And yet, the active contribution of narrative to the unfolding of the event was publicly perceived at, at

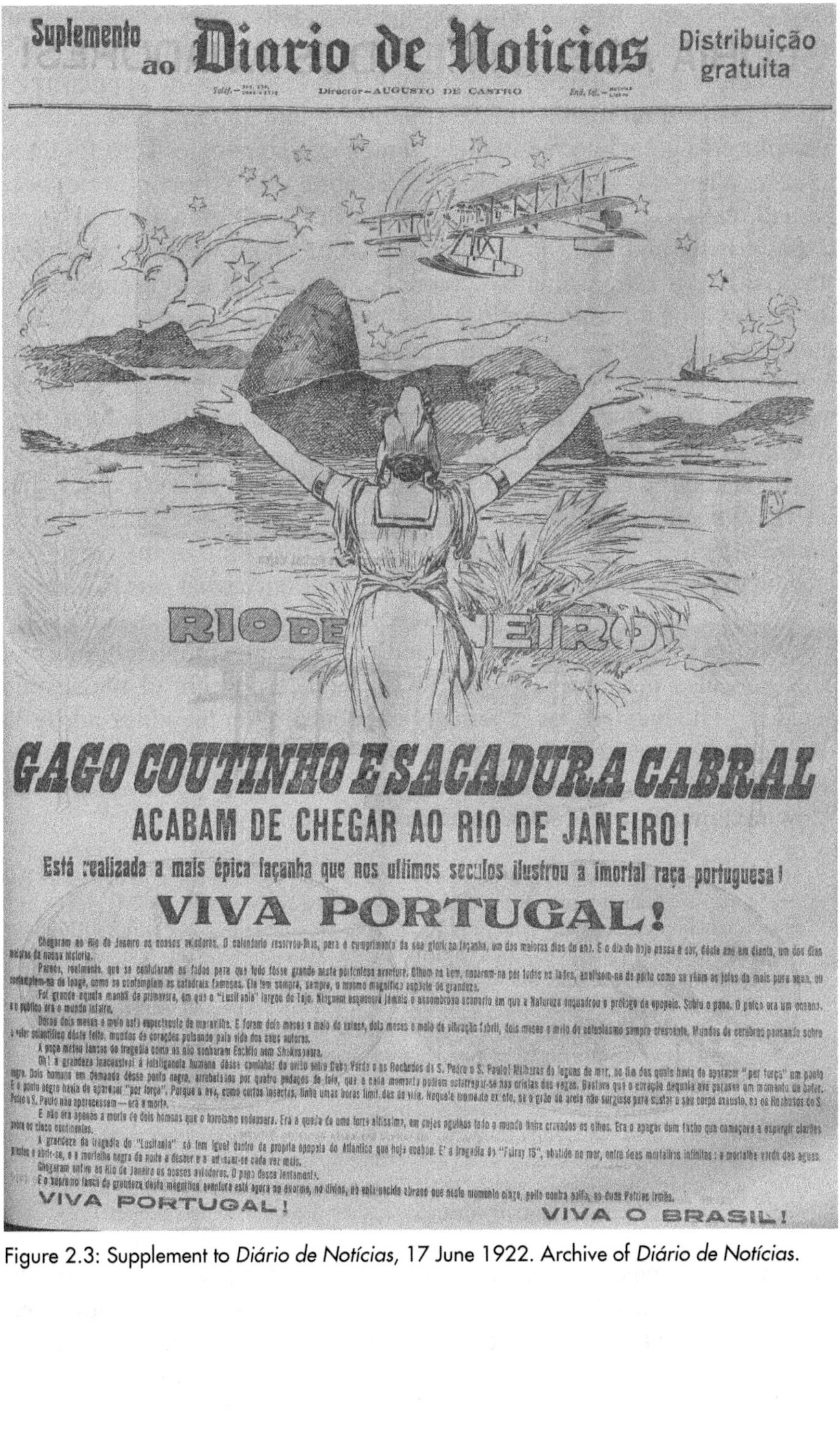

Suplemento ao **Diario de Noticias** Distribuição gratuita

Director—AUGUSTO DE CASTRO

GAGO COUTINHO E SACADURA CABRAL

ACABAM DE CHEGAR AO RIO DE JANEIRO!

Está realizada a mais épica façanha que nos ultimos seculos ilustrou a imortal raça portuguesa!

VIVA PORTUGAL!

Chegaram ao Rio de Janeiro os nossos aviadores. O calendario reservou-lhes, para o cumprimento da sua gloriosa façanha, um dos maiores dias do ano. E o dia de hoje passa a ser, dêste ano em diante, um dos dias maiores da nossa historia.

Parece, realmente, que se conjuraram os fados para que tudo fôsse grande nesta portentosa aventura. Olhem-na bem, encarem-na por todos os lados, analisem-na de perto como se vêem as joias da mais pura agua, ou contemplem-na de longe, como se contemplam as catedrais famosas. Ela tem sempre, sempre, o mesmo magnifico aspecto de grandeza.

Foi grande aquela manhã de primavera, em que o "Lusitania" largou do Tejo. Ninguem esquecerá jamais o assombroso scenario em que a Natureza enquadrou o prólogo da epopeia. Subiu o pano. O palco era um oceano, e o publico era o mundo inteiro.

Durou dois meses e meio êste espectaculo de maravilha. E foram dois meses e meio de extase, dois meses e meio de vibração febril, dois meses e meio de entusiasmo sempre crescente. Mundos de cerebros pensando sobre o valor scientifico dêste feito, mundos de corações pulsando pela vida dos seus autores.

A peça meteu lances de tragedia como os não sonharam Eschilo nem Shakespeare.

Oh! a grandeza inacessivel à inteligencia humana dêsse caminhar do avião entre Cabo Verde e os Rochedos de S. Pedro e S. Paulo! Milhares de leguas de mar, ao fim das quais havia de aparecer "por força" um ponto negro. Dois homens em demanda dêsse ponto negro, arrebatados por quatro pedaços de tela, que a cada momento podiam estatelar-se nas cristas das vagas. Bastava que o coração daquela ave parasse um momento de bater. E o ponto negro havia de aparecer "por força". Porque a ave, como certos insectos, tinha umas horas limitadas de vida. Naquele momento exacto, se o grão de areia não surgisse para sustar o seu corpo exausto, se os Rochedos de S. Pedro e S. Paulo não aparecessem — era a morte.

E não era apenas a morte de dois homens que o heroismo endeusara. Era a queda de uma torre altissima, em cujas agulhas todo o mundo tinha cravados os olhos. Era o apagar dum facho que começava a espargir clarões sobre os cinco continentes.

A grandeza da tragedia do "Lusitania" só tem igual dentro da propria epopeia do Atlantico que hoje acabou. E' a tragedia do "Fairey 16", abatido no mar, entre duas mortalhas infinitas: a mortalha verde das aguas [illegible] a abrir-se, e a mortalha negra da noite a descer e a adensar-se cada vez mais.

Chegaram enfim ao Rio de Janeiro os nossos aviadores. O pano desce lentamente.

E o supremo lance de grandeza desta magnifica aventura está agora no enorme, no divino, no enternecido abraço que neste momento cinge, peito contra peito, as duas Patrias irmãs.

VIVA PORTUGAL! VIVA O BRASIL!

Figure 2.3: Supplement to *Diário de Notícias*, 17 June 1922. Archive of *Diário de Notícias*.

least, two levels. To start with, the insistent daily coverage throughout the two and a half months kept public attention focused on the flight, and gave it the status of a national priority.[32] This enhanced the popularity of the airmen and ultimately transformed them into national heroes, but it also placed a great burden on them, which was sometimes hard for them to bear. When it was all over, Sacadura Cabral told Norberto Lopes how he had realized, as early as when he was at Cape Verde, that the flight to Saint Peter and Saint Paul depended so much on weather conditions (that is, on an extraordinarily favourable wind) that giving up seemed the only reasonable thing to do. When the journalist asked why they had gone on anyway, the answer was 'because you gentlemen [the reporters] had already made a lot of noise' (Lopes 1923: 115). This led to an extraordinary confession: the flyers set off for the rocks convinced that they would not reach their destination.

The second contribution of journalism to the event was equally decisive. Whereas headlines and billboards – what Cabral referred to as 'noise' – helped drive the flight on, the dramatic tone of the narratives created the form in which readers would experience what was to happen. Sometimes, as we have seen in the reports of Júlio César Machado's suicide, the frontiers between fiction and reality were completely blurred. This was also the case in Norberto Lopes's description of the second accident. The incident, as it actually happened, with the plane adrift on the high seas, was dramatic enough, but the reporter somehow managed to turn it into a tragedy by imagining the worst-case scenario, and thus showing how close to death the airmen had been:

> After the *Fairey-16* [the name of the second plane] had come down, and the pilots had spent long, uncertain hours drifting, caught between sea and sky, waiting to be saved by a distant light appearing on the horizon, Commander Sacadura turned to Admiral Coutinho – a ship officer told me this – and with the utmost tranquillity asked him what should they do when the plane sank and all hopes were gone. Let the waves do the rest? Shoot themselves in the head and get it over with? Do you know what Admiral Gago Coutinho replied? Only this, in thought, because the words were lost in the immensity of the ocean and nobody heard them, nobody; Commander Sacadura could barely hear them because they were pronounced with a gesture, with a look, rather than with the lips; they looked at each other, calmly assessed the danger, figured out how long it would be before the plane sank and then – it is impossible to write this without an extreme emotion; without feeling a shiver down the spine; without stopping for a moment to fantasize what might have happened – they simply, tacitly, decided to go down with the aircraft, shrouded by its white wings, covered in glory by them, deified by the white wings. (Lopes 1923: 109)

Fortunately, Lopes's fantasy did not become reality, and the aviators survived to tell their tale and enjoy all the tributes they were about to receive. But the ways in which the concrete situation that the airmen faced at that difficult moment became entangled with what was on the verge of happening but did not produced an overlap of reality and imagination and, in doing so, endowed the former with the (tragic) appearance of the latter. So, it was not just that Lopes was working at the borders of journalism and fiction. By treating what did not happen journalistically, he somehow incorporated imaginary events (the courageous death of the two airmen) into reality (their glorification) itself.

The flight could then be seen as an adventure to the exact extent that narrative treated it as such. While the press kept the story in the spotlight, the aviators and their achievement entered into all sorts of representations. Among these, the most insistent trope used to give meaning to the voyage was, as we have seen, nationalism. Predictably, the parallels with the discovery of Brazil in 1500 were made to the point of exhaustion: not only was the destination the same, but both were also pioneering attempts to utilize the most up to date technologies of the time. And of course, one of the aviators even had the same surname as the navigator Pedro Álvares Cabral. The literary dimension of an event so burdened with its own narrative was not forgotten, and parallels were also drawn between the journey and Camões's *The Lusiads* (a sixteenth-century epic of maritime discoveries and the ultimate classic of Portuguese literature), with Sacadura Cabral and Gago Coutinho as the protagonists of a modern epic. It was suggested that the aviators took a copy of Camões's text with them, enhancing the parallel even further, for it evoked the author's own rescue of the manuscript of *The Lusiads* after a shipwreck.

If airmen were given the role of modern navigators, reporters should accordingly be treated as modern chroniclers. In his preface to the volume in which Norberto Lopes assembled his reports of the flight, Gago Coutinho went so far as to compare the author with Pêro Vaz de Caminha, who chronicled the arrival of the Portuguese in Brazil: 'he [Norberto Lopes] gives everyone the impression that, if Pedro Álvares Cabral discovered the land of Brazil by sea, we, twentieth-century Portuguese, went to modern Brazil by air ... So says Norberto Lopes, a Caminha for today, one of our most gifted chroniclers, or journalists, as we now say' (Coutinho, in Lopes 1923: 12). This is where journalism and literature most clearly intersect in the narrative of the flight. As we will see in what remains of this chapter, if aviation represented such a challenge, and opportunity, to journalism, then its impact would necessarily be felt in literature as well.

The fact that the flight coincided with a moment marked by a particular nationalist consensus contributed to its immediate appropriation by both national literature and history. Ironically, the modern world of aircraft was suddenly bathed in nostalgia, or at least a form of revivalism. One of the most popular and influential writers of the period, Júlio

Dantas, set his point of evocation of the plane's arrival in Rio de Janeiro in a monastery, surrounded by the tombs of medieval monarchs, which he experienced as a mystical moment synthesizing tradition and modernity (Dantas n.d.: 95). However, the contradiction involved in celebrating modern technology with romantic images was soon exposed. At a conference in Rio de Janeiro, António Ferro, a young reporter and modernist writer, reacted against Dantas's historicism and complained about the use of skeletons from the past 'to praise an airplane' (Ferro 1987: 240). Just like the reporters who saw the flight as a challenge to their ability to render movement, young modernists – many of them reporters themselves – immediately perceived it as a test of their sense of modernity.

In May, while the journey was still in process, a new magazine, *Contemporânea*, marked the beginning of a new phase in Portuguese modernism, after the iconoclasm of *Orpheu* and *Portugal Futurista* in the 1910s. Some tropes of modernism had since become familiar, not to say banal, through their recurrent use in journalistic narratives. In this context, 1922 saw the emergence of a new generation of modernist journalists like Norberto Lopes and António Ferro, whose ambition as writers was to become the reporters of modern life, which they tried to express by adopting a style deeply marked by sensationalism (in both reportage and fictional short stories). *Contemporânea*'s editorial was written by one of these modernist reporters, Afonso de Bragança, and took the flight's momentum to mark a distance from older generations and literary institutions. His main target seemed to be the same as Ferro's: Júlio Dantas, or any of the other writers who let 'romantic emotions' capture the moment by equating the flight with the departure of a caravel. Those were accused of living in the past, whereas the new generation was committed to the difficult task of living in the present and being 'contemporaneous'. It was not so much that romanticism was doomed as a literary form in the twentieth century. Rather, the problem was that the older generation's dependence on old-fashioned ideals of beauty and order did not allow them to see, let alone represent, the modern world as 'something always so inventive, so strange, so inexplicable, so tumultuous, [and] so contradictory' (Bragança 1922a: 2). However, apart from a certain rhythmic frenzy – of which the previous sentence is a good example – the distinction between romantics and these moderns was less a literary one than an existential one.

According to Bragança, only an unconditional engagement with the times could allow writers to feel and thus express the 'mathematical' beauty of modernity. This did not mean abandoning the nationalist horizon. On the contrary, from now on it was Portugal itself that had to be 'lived with wings, with engines, with movement', that is, 'with other eyes, other paints, another soul' (Bragança 1922a: 3). But the obvious authority of such a discourse had moved from the spiritual isolation of traditional literature to the material engagement with the world proper to journalism. The young were not only more prone to understand, but also to get involved. The stress on experience rather than literary form drew the writer into the object of representation in much the same way as the reporter was drawn into the event – or Álvaro de Campos into machines in 'Ode triunfal'. The new life of this generation – Bragança starts his text by saying that all he wants is 'to live the life of his own generation' (Bragança 1922a: 1) – would then be an embodiment, in the form of narrative, of all the modern technologies of movement.

Flying and aeroplanes thus presented a particular challenge to this literature. We can recognize this by identifying the attributes of modernity – like speed or superficiality – that are present in numerous modernist narratives of aviation. António Ferro, for instance, drew a comparison between women and aeroplanes on the grounds of their common evanescence: both planes made of 'screen and aluminium' and women with their 'epidermis and silk' were equally 'fragile and light' (Ferro 1987: 243). The comparison was then further explored when both women and planes were pictured 'in the hands of a good pilot', which would allow them to 'overcome enormous distances'. The plane could here become a sign of modernity, but the image of the female body as an object in men's hands was of course old school – in fact, it was one of Júlio Dantas's favourite subjects, which may explain why António Ferro would replace him as the dominant figure in the literary field (Trindade 2008).

More significant is the impact of speed on syntax, which becomes apparent in, for example, the depiction of a plane crash in 'Asas trágicas' ('Tragic wings'), a short story written by Artur Portela (who worked as a reporter with Norberto Lopes, António Ferro and Afonso de Bragança on *Diário de Lisboa*, an evening paper launched in 1921), where every paragraph in the last three pages begins with the (decreasing) altitude of the plane: 'One hundred and fifty metres! … One hundred metres! … Ninety metres! … Eighty metres! … Forty-five metres! … Twenty metres! … Last instant!' (Portela n.d.: 24–26). This structure resembles the sequence of telegrams we saw on the front page of *Diário de Notícias* on the night of the second accident. The written expression of motion had to fragment narrative: motion could only be imagined by isolating each segment and then placing it in filmic succession. Both *Diário de Notícias*'s telegrams and Artur Portela's paragraphs function, in this sense, as frames.

The different role of planes and images of flight in António Ferro and Artur Portela was no accident. The proximity of the end of 'Asas trágicas' to the structure of reportage illustrates the way in which modernism was affected by journalism. Rather than a literary form degraded by the speed and rhythm of the press, modernism, in this case, would constitute a spatio-temporal experience enabling modern narratives to go further in their expression of modern tropes. Ferro's comparison between women and planes, by contrast, remained much closer to conventional models. Paradoxically, the more these writers distanced themselves from the journalistic style of their profession – that is, from the style of reportage proper, as Ferro did in his effort to become more of a writer than a journalist – the less they were able to distance their fiction from the very traditional literature they attacked. This struggle between the urge of modernism to represent flight and the resistance of established tropes within it can be easily observed in what probably constituted the group's most important attempt to create a modern epic of aviation: João Ameal's *A religião do espaço* ('The religion of space').

Written in 1922, thus clearly participating in the general enthusiasm triggered by Gago Coutinho and Sacadura Cabral, the novel is a self-proclaimed Nietzschean epic. Its epigraph (taken from one of Ameal's previous books) invited the reader to see the author and his art in the context of the same spirit of vitalism that led the protagonist, Parsifal – in an obvious reference to Wagner – through the novel: 'to reduce the crowd to transfigured ciphers and perfect lines represents the major victory an artist can achieve in the epic glory of his work' (Ameal 1922: v). Parsifal was of course an aviator, a modern hero elevated above the rest (especially women and the crowd, here representing the two most frequent types of subalternity in this literature) and whose achievements in the First World War had entitled him to 'the exclusive selfishness of all Nietzscheans' (Ameal 1922: 24).

The plot itself was remarkably simple, not to say schematic. Exclusively dedicated to aviation, which for him represented a mystical, almost religious experience, Parsifal lived isolated from the rest of the world. His seclusion meanwhile enticed Eva, a femme fatale who, used to seducing every man she came across, found his lack of interest in her irresistible. The whole narrative will then be organized around Eva's pursuit of him while its climax comes when her 'fervent sexuality' 'intoxicates him like an overwhelming dose of cocaine' (Ameal 1922: 136). At the end, Parsifal finds the strength to resist her moves and flies away in his white plane into space. More than schematic, the limits of the narrative become apparent when the exaggerated use of adjectives and hyperbole fail to conceal the most conventional motif under the appearance of modern sophistication: women reduced to pure matter seducing men away from higher intellectual or heroic aspirations.

The novel's interest is thus not in its literary merits. Parsifal's heroism, however, is remarkably suggestive of the possible meanings of aviation and aviators in the ideology of these modernists. In this sense, Parsifal's personality shared the attributes that contemporary journalism used to transform Sacadura Cabral – but not Gago Coutinho – into a hero. In a way, this is surprising: what was most innovative about the 1922 crossing of the South Atlantic was Coutinho's adaptation of the standard nautical sextant which enabled the airmen to produce an artificial horizon which served as the reference point in aerial navigation. Without this, their flight over an ocean devoid of visible reference points would have been impossible. But whereas Coutinho represented the scientific aspect of the adventure, Cabral was a true flyer, and as such a much more palatable figure to modernist narratives.

Cabral died in a plane accident in 1924, just two years after the journey to Brazil. His plane disappeared in the North Sea as he was flying from Amsterdam to Lisbon, and his body was never found. A myth was immediately constructed around him, in which he embodied the higher form of existence proper to modern times. Maria Feio's *A alma de Sacadura Cabral* ('The soul of Sacadura Cabral') was the first in a long line of literary variations on the subject – which probably reached its climax in a poem by Fernando Pessoa himself.[33] Using supernatural references and making parallels between Cabral and other acknowledged symbols of contemporary heroism – in the tradition of Gabrielle D'Annunzio's proto-fascist vitalism – Feio pictured Cabral as a leader whose superiority was defined both in relation to the other men he was born to guide and the women he was bound to seduce:

> He had the profile of men who were born to command, who are used to command, who know how to command, calmly, dispassionately, with no sudden moves, outbursts or enthusiasms. Someone who was intimate with him said that his secret, the reason he was destined to ride in a car while other people walked, was the careless, cold and sober way he dealt with men and the excessive gallantry he displayed to women. (Feio 1924: 247)

Cabral's death was of course decisive in the making of this legend. But it must be said that the process of his heroization began whilst he was still alive. Norberto Lopes, for instance, almost seemed to forget Coutinho's existence when the plane arrived in Rio. Rather his attention was focused on the way Brazilian women were waiting for Cabral's arrival, their eyes anxiously scanning the sky. While the sparse references to Coutinho dealt with scientific matters and his intellectual achievements, Cabral was featured as the 'bareheaded' protagonist with 'his face burnt by the equatorial sun, his sharp silhouette, well defined lines, and the cigarette in his mouth, always the cigarette in his mouth' (Lopes

1923: 88). He did not say a word but looked around the crowd as if to 'gauge the degree of enthusiasm, the temperature of the cheers and the intensity of the clapping' (Lopes 1923: 164). Whether Norberto Lopes really managed to project a film-like representation through his report, as he initially promised, is open to question, but his description of the protagonist did resemble that of a movie star.

The most distinctive thing about Cabral was not his elegance, beauty or impeccable outfit. According to Lopes's journalistic depiction, unlike the clothes of the literary dandies strolling through Chiado, Lisbon's smart literary district, Cabral's uniform looked worn: crossing the Atlantic was no stroll and the pilot wore the marks of the adventure on his own physical appearance. Lopes was able to transform him into a modern hero – he even named 1922 the year of *sacadurismo* – to the extent that he appeared as a body in movement. Or, to use one the epoch's most suggestive images, because he was a sportsman – a figure that only this literature at the borders between journalism and fiction, that is, in the intersection between modernism and modern experience, could express.

Notes

1. Both challenges, that of clarity and that of movement, were not new to journalism, as photography had already been in place for a while. In his (unfortunately) unpublished PhD dissertation, André Gunthert shows how the pressure coming from the mechanical reproduction of images was contemporaneous with the birth of modern journalism: 'But image's growing importance will in turn change the content and the style of written journalism. As contemporaries, the two forms are inextricably linked. If the search for sensationalism pre-existed the use of photography, the latter will give it a powerful edge. Reports will become increasingly shorter to give room to illustrations, and the popular press will be lead to privilege some topics according to the iconography they generate: sporting activities, for example, will from the beginning of the twentieth century occupy a space equivalent to the development of illustration' (Gunthert 1999: 333).
2. One of the most famous equations between cinema and aviation is still Edgar Morin's 'L'avion, le cinéma' (Morin 1978: 13–19).
3. *O Século*, 2 April 1922, p.1.
4. *Diário de Notícias*, 7 April 1922, p.1.
5. *Diário de Notícias*, 7 April 1922, p.1.
6. *O Século*, 19 April 1922, p.1.
7. *Diário de Notícias*, 19 April 1922, p.1.
8. *Diário de Notícias*, 19 April 1922, p.1.
9. *O Século*, 19 April 1922, p.1.
10. *Diário de Notícias*, 19 April 1922, p.1.
11. *Diário de Notícias*, 19 April 1922, p.1.
12. *Diário de Notícias*, 19 April 1922, p.1.
13. *Diário de Notícias*, 20 April 1922, p.1.

14. *O Século*, 20 April 1922, p.2.
15. Quotes from *O Século*, 20 April 1922, p.2. The gathering of crowds in these circumstances becomes the true journalistic event. Peter Fritzsche describes a similar moment – the flight of a Zeppelin in Berlin – in which 'Berlin has only one single neck today … one cheering mouth, one eye, one heart'. Here too, what united the crowd around the journalistic event was an acute sense of national enthusiasm: 'The masses of Berliners assembled under the zeppelin symbolized a new Germany, a nation that was technologically advanced and oriented toward the future. What newspapers celebrated was the formation of a popular, patriotic entity beyond the confines of class and the hierarchies of the monarchy' (Fritzsche 1996: 229).
16. *O Século*, 20 April 1922, p.2.
17. *O Século*, 12 May 1922, p.1.
18. *O Século*, 12 May 1922, p.1.
19. In fact, it can be said that both anxieties (that of the public and that of the editorialist) were tied together. Michael Schudson gives us an example of an editor of *The Times* whose writings apparently also shared readers' emotions: 'He, with a newspaper, is like the orator. Both of them address a crowd, with an understanding of its emotions, or rather, with a likeness of emotions, and as the orator and the crowd react to each other, so Mr. O. and the *Times* readers react on each other' (Schudson 1978: 116).
20. *O Século*, 12 May 1922, p.1.
21. The sinking of the Titanic gives us another good example of how the period's expectations about permanent and comprehensive information through wireless communication were already high, but also how the medium's ability to respond sometimes fell short of those same expectations: 'Press reports noted that if one or two nearby ships had had its wireless working and its operator on duty (instead of its engines off and its operator asleep), it could have saved all the lives that were lost' (Starr 2004: 218).
22. *Diário de Notícias*, 12 May 1922, p.1.
23. *Diário de Notícias*, 12 May 1922, p.1.
24. See *O Século*, 12 May 1922, p.2.
25. *Diário de Notícias*, 13 May 1922, p.1.
26. *O Século*, 20 April 1922, p.2. The Portuguese original – *a boa nova que, infelizmente, não se confirmou* – could almost be read as 'the good news that unfortunately did not take place'.
27. *Diário de Notícias*, 20 April 1922, p.1.
28. *O Século*, 20 April 1922, p.2.
29. See *Diário de Notícias*, 20 April 1922, p.1.
30. Peter Fritzsche shows the role of aviation in the making of twentieth-century national consciousness and the importance of modern mass media in the process. See esp. his discussion of 'modernist visions' and 'national dreams' (Fritzsche 1992: 133–184).
31. *Diário de Notícias*, 17 June 1922, p.1. Walter Benjamin, commenting on Charles Lindbergh's flight from the United States to France in 1927, could well be speaking of Augusto de Castro and *Diário de Notícias* on the occasion of the flight to Brazil: 'Among the medieval Scholastics, there was a school that described God's omnipotence by saying: He could alter even the past, unmake what had really happened, and make real what had never happened. As we can see, in the case of enlightened newspapers editors, God is not needed for this task; a bureaucrat is all that is required' (Benjamin 2008: 353).
32. Modris Eksteins describes the role of the press in Lindbergh's flight along the same lines: 'Was Lindbergh in any sense a creation of the press? The press was at its apogee

in the 1920s. Never before or since have there been as many newspapers or as many readers of the printed word. The press was the source of news, information, and entertainment. Every European capital had dozens of newspapers. Many editors, moreover, did judge the Lindbergh flight to be the biggest news story since the war' (Eksteins 1989: 249).

33. The poem about Sacadura Cabral was initially thought to be part of Pessoa's *Mensagem* ('Message'), Pessoa's own national epic, first published in 1934 and the only book of his work published in his lifetime. The poem on Cabral was left out, however. If it had been included, Cabral would have been the only modern figure in the poet's gallery of heroes of national history.

Chapter 3

The Spectacle of Sport

We have seen in the previous chapter how the enthusiasm for aviation was a challenge to representation. This challenge had two meanings: on the one hand, that narratives (journalistic, literary or filmic) had to come to terms with the movement of aeroplanes; but also, given the necessary involvement of representation in its referent, that the narrative forms themselves would become part of the general movement of things. This physicality on the two sides of the narrative (both aviators and reporters had to be present in events) goes a long way to explain the importance of sport, and the figure of the sportsman, in early twentieth-century mass culture.[1] Aviation, in particular, was included in the branch of sport connected with the technologies of movement: bicycles, motorcycles, cars, gliders and balloons were in this sense all part of the same sporting experience. Unlike other sports, these involved mechanical – usually motorized – motion, which propelled the body to superhuman speeds and distances. Aviation could thus be seen as 'the greatest sport of our times', as a 1923 auto magazine would describe it,[2] because airplanes took human beings faster and longer than any other vehicle.

Profiles of sportsmen – some of them aviators – frequently published in the press reveal some of the most common tropes of what it meant to be modern in the early twentieth century. According to his biography published in 1929, sportsman Luís de Noronha's enthusiasm for physical activity in the 1910s led him to dance (the tango) and to participate in sports like rowing and swimming. Flying, however, was his passion. His first flight was in France where, over Paris, he could see 'the City of Light passing like a film beneath his ecstatic eye' (Conceição 1929: 11). The relation between aviation and film is by now familiar, but the terms are here reversed: the movement of aeroplanes could only be rendered by movie cameras, as we saw in Norberto Lopes's metaphors, but what was seen from a plane already seemed to resemble the motion of images on screen. It was being a sportsman that made

Luís de Noronha modern. His travels and leisure pursuits were seen as sophisticated and cosmopolitan, and sport also turned him into another image of visibility, someone who showed himself seeing, just like the reporter posing onboard ship. And yet, this was not just a question of technological sophistication and cosmopolitanism. Noronha needed something more than just his physical and intellectual attributes in order to indulge in his favourite sports; he needed wealth. In fact, although Amadeu de Vasconcelos, one of the first authors to write about aviation in Portugal, could still write nonchalantly in its early years that aviation 'was just a matter of money' (Vasconcelos 1909: 159), the truth was that these activities were far too expensive for most people. This was very obvious in a new genre of illustrated magazines dedicated to sport, showing images of sportsmen, which proliferated at the beginning of the century.

There was for instance João Luiz da Veiga, another famous sportsman who, according to an article published in the shooting magazine *Tiro Civil* in 1903, seemed at first sight just a modern adventurer: 'Because of his restless and acute spirit, movement, novelty and the uncanny electrify, attract and dominate him; however, his sensations are ephemeral, for his soul is eager for new thrills'.[3] Be that as it may, it is impossible not to think about the costs involved in his sporting activities: after flying a balloon in Paris, he travelled in the Orient Express before exploring the North Sea. As a cyclist, he imported the most sophisticated French bicycles, yet his most significant expenses had recently concerned his newest passion: motor sports. After buying an 8 horsepower Peugeot, with which he was able to make some interesting but short excursions, he posed for the magazine's Kodak camera with the maker's latest model, sporting a potent 18 horsepower engine that could take him anywhere in the country.

This type of activity was thus reserved for society's upper levels, the middle classes and the aristocracy. Guilherme Ferreira Pinto Basto, a renowned entrepreneur, took part in an impressive number of sports: tennis, golf, football (which he introduced into Portugal), rally-paper [paper-chase], cross-country running, rowing, yachting, cycling and bullfighting. As a man educated in France and England, sport – according to *Tiro Civil*'s profile of him – was seen as one of the most defining aspects of his excellent upbringing and noble character:

> Exquisite spirit and polished good taste, connoisseur, in his frequent visits to Europe's main centres, of the most distinguished sports, his enthusiasm is so serious that he is capable of travelling to Wimbledon and Henley just to watch the most important tournaments of tennis and [rowing] regattas. Furthermore, this gentleman is the proprietor of what probably is the most important collection of photographs related to tennis and yachting.

Some reproductions of his numerous images (*clichés*) are available to be seen in the rooms of many clubs both in Portugal and abroad.[4]

Once again, the distinctive features of a sportsman were related to the lifestyle of the upper classes: the frequent travelling and the familiarity with photography were more than just a sign of the leisure only pursued by the wealthy, but a true modern ethos whereby being part of events, as in the case of reporters and aviators, meant both participating in and representing it (and thus becoming part of the representation – especially through photography). So much distinction, the reporter concluded, could not fail to guarantee Pinto Basto a particular place in the king's 'esteem and trust'.

These articles were of course published before 1910, the year of the republican revolution. In other words, bourgeois sportsmen like Pinto Basto represented the new aristocracy, and sport was the new form of symbolic merit used to distinguish the happy few in the modern symbolic order. A questionnaire published by *Tiro Civil* in 1906 containing the questions 'What is Sport?' and 'What is a sportsman?' already revealed a strong consensus around the idea that sport depended on a rare aesthetic intuition and ethics and, accordingly, that even if virtually everyone could practice it, only a minority could be treated as sportsmen. Within this logic, the monarch – by then the throne was occupied by Carlos I, who was famously interested in several sports – should be seen as the nation's first sportsman.

This apparently symbolic idea – sportsmanship as aristocratic distinctiveness – entailed a very tangible material consequence: any competitions involving money and professionals should not be treated as sport.[5] This was yet another way of saying that sport was a privilege for those who could practice it in their leisure time as amateurs - in other words, with no interest in it apart from the physical, intellectual and moral virtues involved. All respondents to the magazine's questionnaire insisted on this.[6] This consensus, however, concealed concrete social disparities. In fact, by the beginning of the century, the status of the aristocratic sportsman was under threat (as was the monarchy itself). The more these sportsmen were defined as noble and aristocratic, the more sport was becoming popular; the more magazines like *Tiro Civil* championed disinterested amateurship, the more sport was becoming a business. The press and its images played a key role in this process, to such an extent that the gap between aristocratic and popular sport was produced by the types of publication concerned with it. In this sense, I will be speaking of a 'magazine' sport and 'newspaper' sport, the distinction between which I shall now discuss.

From Magazines to Newspapers: The Sport of Attractions

O Tiro Civil was probably the most visible magazine dedicated to sport in early twentieth-century Portugal, but to say this is not enough, for sport itself had become a decisive aspect of the new regime of public visibility, making the country's elites more visible. In this sense, the type of image in the magazine was not that different from those published in *Ilustração Portuguesa*, the most influential paradigm of this new visual culture, a photographic record of the habits, rituals and ceremonies of the official nation and its upper social strata. The choice of sport as an appropriate activity for the privileged to make themselves visible in public – especially to the lower middle classes, who also had access to this type of magazine – is easily understandable: through sport, the leisure class could combine the higher values of the traditional aristocracy with the utilitarian habits of the bourgeoisie. Cascais, a seaside resort near Lisbon, was the perfect environment to show, especially in the summer, how the Portuguese aristocracy spent their free time. It was the place where it

> can be seen unfolding, as in a kaleidoscope with magic effects, the entire range of fashionable entertainments with which the most distinctive section of society occupies its leisure hours while vigorously maintaining the vital strength of its precious existence through activity: because it not only contributes powerfully to the development of sport in general and man's physical development in particular, it also counters the negative effects produced by a sedentary and unattractive life.[7]

Sportsmen, it seems, were not just having fun. Physical activity was both a sign that the best part of society had a strong sense of self-preservation and, as such, that they were able to keep their role as exemplar citizens. This was particularly important at a moment when, with the new technologies of photographic reproduction, illustrated magazines were able to give unprecedented visibility to the upper classes. Suddenly, what they did became public, which turned the status of their representation into a modern concern.

In general, the issue was treated lightly, or even enthusiastically, as in the 'kaleidoscopic magic effects' reported by *Tiro Civil* in Cascais. In 1910, only a few months before the republican revolution, a reporter from *Ilustração Portuguesa* at an equestrian festival in Lisbon's hippodrome paid even more attention to the 'striking effect' with which 'the most beautiful and elegant ladies of our first society ornamented' the occasion with their '*toilettes*' than to the horses and their riders.[8] Some of these ladies were 'photographic amateurs' themselves. In this sense, their public image was still another example of those typically modern figures that both registered and participated in events, being shown while seeing.[9] Soon, however, the regime of visibility guiding these social events was bound to raise its own problems. The question had already been posed in *Tiro Civil*'s piece on Pinto Basto, where the sportsman's profile was contrasted with what seemed to be a new phenomenon: some people – the French word *parvenus* was used by the journalist – started to dress as sportsmen, thus pretending to practise some kind of sport but just for effect. Sheer exhibitionism would turn into farce with fake competitions where every team won a cup and everyone took medals home became the usual practice.

This was of course the complete denial of sport as we have been describing it. Sport's transformation into a vanity fair did not only affect its social status, that is, the nobility with which it was usually associated. It also put its mission in danger, for sport depended on its public image as the embodiment of values that were essentially symbolic. To fake sport, by appearing in movement just for the sake of appearances, did not only have physical consequences but moral ones too. In fact, in the context of late nineteenth-century hygienism, the notion of health synthesized both moral and physical virtues. This is why the status of the sportsman was a combination of social distinction and personal well-being. Conversely, falsifications had to be exposed through negative representations of physical and intellectual vitality and vigour. In the period's order of representations, this was partly the function of a very specific social type: the dandy.

In 1888, Frederico Avellar, a pioneering promoter of gymnastics in Portugal, had already published a poem in a magazine commemorating the anniversary of the country's first sports club, the Gymnasio Club Portuguez, where the dandy was pictured as someone frail, vain and frivolous. The style was ironic, although not very subtle: 'Look at him! What a grace! ... Complete! ... Irreprehensible! ... / Beautiful, carefree, tender, majestic' (Avellar 1888: 6). The poem reached its climax when all these questionable qualities were dismissed as effeminate: 'What a shame that this beautiful and excited ideal / This elegant and aromatic "girlie" / is made of such a different substance / from the well tempered substance of gymnasts' (Avellar 1888: 6). This kind of stereotype of romantic femininity was commonsensical, but it should not be read as a critique of women, who as such were not at issue here, at least no more than symbolically, or metaphorically. It just happened that their status in literature seemed fitting to contrast the real stuff gymnasts were made of to the frivolous image of the dandy.

In an article in the same issue of the magazine, Avellar even went so far as to defend exercise as a precondition for the regeneration of motherhood – contrasting the new wealthy mothers that Portugal needed to face the challenges of modernization with the, again very recognizable, images of nervous and anaemic female readers of romantic literature. It was not an unusual opinion. In fact, the 'magical effects' that so fascinated the reporter of *Tiro Civil* in the sporting life of Cascais were particularly appropriate to describe the gracefulness of sportswomen. As long as women practised sport properly, the benefits would be both physical and moral. The problem of sport's visibility was thus not in women themselves but in a lifestyle exclusively based on the exterior image of the body and generally associated, through literature, with effeminacy and figures such as the dandy.

As literary tropes, effeminacy and the dandy stood for the visibility that the champions of true sport found so disquieting. What was disquieting, then, was the regime of visibility itself, rather than the social figures represented by these tropes. In other words, the real social threat, to which the consensus around the definition of the sportsman as an aristocrat responded, was less concerned with questions of gender or sexuality than with new forms of visibility related to the popularization of sport. Whatever the threats looming over sport were, they would only become real problems if given social visibility by the press. That is why all issues related with the latter would inevitably become political, and that is also why we now have to move from the upper-class illustrated magazines and focus our attention on sports newspapers, targeted at popular audiences.

At first sight, an article published in 1910 in *Sport Nacional* – one of the first popular newspapers exclusively dedicated to sports – seemed to focus on exactly the same question as magazines, that of exhibitionism. From the newspaper's perspective, however, the question should be reversed: it was not so much that the lower classes wanted to become aristocratic by practising sports, but that the upper classes did not want to be seen practising the same sports as the people. Cycling, for instance, was by then becoming more accessible to those with lesser means, and the consequences, according to the journalist, were striking:

> So, the merchant often thinks that to be seen cycling side by side with a modest worker is a blow to his dignity and worth. The cyclist who owns a luxurious machine is almost embarrassed to ride with a colleague whose bicycle is a bit more rudimentary. In these circumstances, the merchant makes very little use of his machine, which he keeps like a relic and only uses at the crack of dawn, almost under disguise, when there are still not many people, to avoid being seen by a friend or colleague.[10]

The shift of perspective thus enables us to shift the problem. Sport was a site of class distinction and, as such, of class struggle proper. As an activity of growing visibility, it was also, if seen from below, an opening for social mobility. This is what made it so threatening to the status of the elites and why it was so decisive to keep it safe within the realm of the materially affluent. The magazines' insistence on the corrupting power of visibility did not refer to the proliferation of photographic images on display in those same magazines, but rather to the transformation of sport into a spectacle through the generalization of sporting competitions at all levels of society.

Duarte Rodrigues, the director of *Tiro e Sport* – the result of a merger between *Tiro Civil* and another elitist magazine, *Revista de Sport* – drew an explicit link between the problem of vanity as it was traditionally put – referring to the false sportsmen who considered 'their inalienable right to have their photo published in a magazine like ours' (Rodrigues 1910: 2) – and what seemed to be the growing threat to sport of its corruption by business: 'the best-selling newspapers give us plenty of information about major achievements, new clubs, gigantic initiatives ... while thousands of people are asked to drop a few coins for a spectacle we should be ashamed of in the twentieth century' (Rodrigues 1910: 2). What was worst, concluded Rodrigues, was that sport was becoming profitable not on behalf of sportsmen's merits, but simply because newspapers were transforming sporting competitions into modern versions of Homeric epics.[11]

He was surely right about the use of sensationalist journalism by business interests around sport. To say that spectacle had degraded a previously more authentic and respectable form of sport, however, was wrong. In his writings on gymnastics in 1888, Frederico Avellar tried to situate the emergence of new sporting practices historically. His account showed that the narrative of magazines – sport as an aristocratic activity being corrupted by popularization – concealed how sport, in the mid nineteenth century, had been no more than a circus attraction (Avellar 1888: 1–2). At this level, sport, as it became visible in the early twentieth century, was a direct successor of the acrobatic shows that had been amongst the most popular forms of entertainment for a long time, and only later had it been supplemented by modern concerns with health and physical well-being.

So the question was not that sport had recently become a spectacle. The problem, as a problem generated by the proliferation of images, was that these popular shows had entered a phase of much greater visibility. To keep sport as a prerogative of the upper classes was not primarily intended as a means of protecting privilege. The question of who practised sport was much less decisive than the determination of who should be seen doing it. Accordingly, the absent cause behind the strict definition of sport and sportsmen in sport magazines was the process through which the market had commoditized sport as spectacle.[12] If there was a threat to the status of the aristocracy, it was due less to any potential rise of the masses than the promise of social mobility brought about by the development of capitalism.

In his article, Duarte Rodrigues already numbered the audience of sporting competitions in the thousands. In newspapers, however, the word 'sport' did not refer to tennis, yachting and equestrianism, but rather to cycling, football and boxing. What the 'thousands of people' were being offered by these other sports, according to *Ilustração Portuguesa*, was nothing less than a spectacle of decadence:

> As in barbarian eras, the love of gladiators is back, hence the resemblance to Roman circuses when a handsome slave from Nubia with a strong chest, high-held head and a determined gaze sometimes appeared to fight the beasts … so now, in our progressive century, a gigantic black man will fight an equally strong white man.[13]

This excerpt refers to a North American competition where 'the black man Jack Johnson' beat a white boxer 'amidst the wild applause of the audience who enjoys watching these brutal sports'.[14] It is a powerfully evocative passage on many levels, but its meaning can be condensed into a familiar image, that of the crowd, or mob, since blackness and Americanization were just different aspects of the same threat to European – elitist, literate, intellectual – civilization. The spectacle of sport, like any other mass or indeed image-based phenomenon of the period, meant chaos. What was most worrying, however, was that those distant scenes had meanwhile become familiar to Portuguese audiences too:

> Lisboners applaud this every night … The ones who try to win at all cost, using excessive or forbidden blows, are insulted and jeered. The audience, nervous and aggrieved, intimidates the fighter in a general movement of protest, throwing canes, potatoes … and even boots into the ring! On those occasions, from the quiet spectator's point of view, the show given by the public is more interesting than the fighter's performances. Despite the emotional intensity of the matches, the house is full night after night. Wrestlers are discussed in the streets, people take sides, skills and tricks are commented [on] and criticized. And all this turmoil pleases the impresario, who sees in these professional championships one of the most profitable businesses.[15]

The tossing of potatoes and boots into the wrestling ring made apparent the differences between spectacle and the quiet afternoons of aristocratic sporting activities: sport, as an ethical model, turned into disruption; the sportsman lost their self-control and sense of fair play and became a ferocious animal; the elegant and orderly audience was transformed into a symbol of social degradation and chaos. Worst of all, though, and the ultimate proof of this general corruption, was that chaos seemed to be profitable, and true sport – amateur and disinterested – was obscured by business. Meanwhile, a new figure discreetly emerged guiding the whole process: the impresario who did not appear or take part, but organized and showed.

The above description of restless Lisboners watching wrestling was taken from *Ilustração Portuguesa*'s report on the Fourth Wrestling International Championship organized by the newspaper *Os Sports*, one of the titles that had appeared in the final years of the monarchy before 1910 as a cheaper alternative to the magazines of the elite. The championships were the most striking example of the collaboration between journalism and sport in the emergence of new forms of popular urban spectacle. The competitions started in 1906, and from then on were held every year for more than a month between May and June. In July 1906, right after the end of the first event, *Os Sports* felt the need to deal with the surprising impact of the championship and to evaluate what had just happened. In parallel with its self-congratulatory tone, the newspaper also had to respond to two accusations that had meanwhile been made about the initiative. The first was quite predictable: wrestling was not really a sport, just a form of entertainment. Ironically, the newspaper replied by evoking the use of foreign professionals – the kind of athlete that would not be considered a sportsman by the respondents of *Tiro Civil*'s questionnaire – which proved that the competition had prioritized the promotion of sport. This was reinforced by the private lessons given by the fighters, which transformed the championship into a unique opportunity to make 'useful and efficient publicity'.[16] According to the criteria used by the newspaper, then, publicity was not in itself a problem, as long as it helped draw the public into taking part in sport. The response also claimed that the audience – whose reaction initially caused some concern, as we can imagine after the account given in *Ilustração Portuguesa* – 'received the championship with open arms, following the different stages of the competition with delirious interest'.[17]

The second accusation was more serious, as it suggested that the results had been decided in advance. The newspaper vehemently rejected this as a despicable charge but nevertheless did not manage to entirely allay suspicion. The growth of audiences was thus ambivalent. If, on the one hand, the promoters of the championship could present it as a public service, the profits involved in the events made them particularly prone to fraud – a tendency that could only deepen as the competition became more spectacular. It is thus almost impossible to distinguish between a democratization of sport and sheer economic opportunism in the new event promoted by the newspaper in 1907. After the success of the Second Wrestling International Championship, the newspaper created the Championship of Newsboys, drawing them from the familiar swarm of peddlers – usually very young – that ran through the city streets every day selling newspapers. Considering their state of indigence and marginality, *Os Sports* thought that 'our modest and laborious collaborators' could simultaneously benefit from learning how to practice a sport and from making themselves visible to the public.[18]

The meaning of the event, or the intentions of the newspaper, here reached a peak of ambiguity. After the championship, *Os Sports* continually insisted on the idea that 'many [of those boys] benefited from what they had learnt', as the 'need to make the spectacle interesting and pleasant' had led the newspaper to organize, with the help of the professional wrestlers, private lessons exclusively for the young competitors. The conclusion was that, 'today these boys are more polite and have become fine examples of strength and will'.[19] Either because of 'the interesting and pleasant spectacle' or concern for the boys' education and improvement, the championship was another success. The event extended over several weeks and thousands of Lisboners had the opportunity to watch fights between little boys, weighing no more than 40kg, who bore cartoon *noms de guerre* like 'Sharp Nail', 'Knife Blade' and 'Truncheon'. It is of course impossible to assess if any of these neglected wrestlers gained anything, apart from some days of fame, from their participation in the competition. But it is easier to imagine that what attracted the audiences to these fights was less their strength or skills than the sheer spectacle of poverty.

Sport, in our narrative, here came full circle: these children, restless and suffering from malnutrition (the newspaper itself recognized this) stood for the exact opposite of the discreet and sophisticated image of the aristocratic sportsman. At this stage, we seem very far from quiet afternoons on Lisbon's hippodrome or summers in Cascais, but surprisingly close to the circuses where Frederico Avellar situated the origins of modern sport. Wrestling thus seemed to be part of an older urban culture. In fact, the evenings at the Lisbon's Coliseum – where the championships were held – had other attractions in addition to the fights. The event usually started at 8:30 P.M., but wrestlers only made their appearance two hours later. Meanwhile, the audience could see and listen to a series of attractions with musicians and dancers, but also, and most importantly, with the new machines of mechanical reproduction of images and sound. The fights were thus incorporated into a universe of expanding forms of entertainment, a true culture of attractions, rather than the other way around.[20] One evening's programme chosen at random from the Championship of Newsboys illustrates the structure of the event. Above all, it shows how everything was organized as a spectacle, and how at that moment it was already hard to distinguish sport from other phenomena of cultural massification:

First Part (8:30 P.M.)
– *D. Ramiro*, overture, by the Blancheteau Orchestra;
– The renowned and astonishing North American wonder Electrophone:
  – *Petit Tonkinoise*;
  – A new Fado from Coimbra;
  – *Tosca*, by the great tenor Caruso;
  – *Valsa de Apolo*, sung by actress Georgina Cardoso;
  – *O S. João Novo*, popular Northern song;
– The surprising and marvellous cinematograph:
  – *Çaid's nightmare*;
  – *Rome's military equestrian school*;
  – *The confession*;
  – *A husband's cleverness*;
  – *Slave's love* (in colour);
– Performance by the Graceful and Famous ballerina *La Flor da Andaluzia*;

Break
– *La Textulia, Zamanocca*, by the Chueca Orchestra;
– The renowned and astonishing North American wonder Electrophone:
  – *Pó, pó, pó*, song;
  – *Othello's death*, by the great tenor Tamagno;
  – *New year's eve*, by the bells of Milan's Cathedral;
  – *Cavalaria Rusticana*, by the great tenor Caruso;
  – *A cana verde*, popular Northern song;
– The surprising and marvellous cinematograph:
  – *Customs inspection*;
  – *Bathing in the sea*;
  – *Brothers Kremo*;
  – *A cyclist overcomes obstacles*;
  – *Modern robbers*;
– Second performance by the Graceful and Famous ballerina *La Flor da Andaluzia*;

Second Part (10:30 P.M.)
– *La Trempanica, jota*, by the Gimenez Orchestra;
– First session of the Championship of Colporteurs.[21]

Amongst other spectacles in a culture of attractions, sport emerged in the leisure habits of urban popular classes as a sign of modernity. The fights were exhibited side by side with the phonograph and the cinematograph, the most spectacular machines of the new culture. Fighters, either foreign professionals or the street kids of Lisbon, were there to be seen as one listens to music and watches a film: staged through new mechanisms of excitement.[22] However, all this visibility hid what was most decisive: the discreet emergence of the figure of the impresario. So, between the sportsman and his ethics and the urban public paying for enthusiasm, in other words, between aristocracy and the people, it was the bourgeois who, from now on, would decide what sport was.

A few years later, after the First World War, sport was already one of the most profitable businesses in the culture industries. In fact, if we resume our reading of sports publications right after 1918, it is impressive how much the war changed things. The whole question of social status disappeared, and when journalists talked about sportsmen, it sounded as if they were referring to virtually everyone. Exercise had become a habit, and readers could browse magazines and newspapers for information on the best hours to practise different sports, how to perform the movements correctly, recommendations about (not) smoking and drinking and so on. Cascais was still referred to as the best place for practising and watching, which means that class privilege did not disappear altogether, but even the way newspapers talked about motor cars – still a luxury good – gives us the measure of the change: the focus ceased to be on pleasure or the spirit of adventure, and shifted to the model's technical features. When journalists interviewed someone about cars, they spoke with the representatives of vehicle manufacturers rather than the drivers. The drastic decrease in concern for ethical issues and the apparent ease with which readers were supposed to know and engage with sport showed how the market had subsumed everything. Newspaper and magazine readers could well be potential sportsmen, but most of all they were treated as clients, and their relation to both sports equipment and the events of which they were spectators was that of the buyer to the commodity.

But despite the different types of change brought about by the war (democratization, commoditization), the conflict also meant an interruption, and a dramatic one at that. The participation of Portugal in the conflict can be seen as part of the social mobilization triggered by Portuguese republicanism after 1910, a political culture whose strong patriotic rhetoric presupposed, like sport, both an intellectual and a physical regeneration of the Portuguese (Catroga 2010). After several stagnant years, sporting activities slowly started to move in 1919 and 1920. It was not so much that attention had to remain focused on the war (although Lisbon's stadium, for instance, did close during the conflict). The question was more straightforward: the war transformed athletes into soldiers, and only after 1918 and their return from the trenches were the conditions for organizing championships again set in place. The return of men from the front, however, was more than an opportunity to give sport a second chance, for these men who had been transformed into soldiers came back as different athletes. War's unprecedented degree of violence and mobilization represented a unique challenge to the physical endurance of thousands who felt their lives completely changed (Bourke 1996). Moreover, conscription had set in motion a mass of young soldiers later seen, for better or worse, as a political force.

Sport entered the picture, therefore, as a solution to emerging social problems and a means to prevent potential political disruptions related to the mass discharge of soldiers – in this sense, it was not far from the spirit guiding *sidonismo*, a proto-fascist movement led by President Sidónio Pais in 1918. This was the context in which popular newspapers replaced the moralizing definitions of sport in prewar aristocratic magazines with a new type of ideological discourse: 'the European war … demonstrated the urgent need to take care of future generations both from the perspective of muscular energy and moral strength', one could read in *Os Sports*.[23] The replacement of aristocratic morals by 'patriotic ends' did not mean that class as the great divider had disappeared. On the contrary, the more class was concealed by the ideology of nationalism using sport as a stimulus for social bonds, the more we can read the anxiety of a moment when the threat of class struggle was all the more pressing – especially after the Russian Revolution of 1917.

In January 1920, *Os Sports* went so far as to publish an open letter to the minister of war, insisting that sport should be given priority in army exercises. The rationale still pointed to an individual malaise – 'when the struggle for personal gain seems to be society's only concern … it is absolutely necessary to put the people's will before anything else' – but the solution was clearly articulated in social terms, as sport stood for 'life, lucidity, energy and the will to create a future and build a single base through which society may be organized and learn how to dominate and dominate itself'.[24] On the one hand, then, sport still seemed to be an important way of articulating mind and body and thus enhancing individual existence. Contrary to the individual ethics of prewar sportsmen, however, the question was now put collectively, which meant that the stakes had become much higher: it was the entire nation that could be revitalized – or else lost by social fragmentation – through sport.

Be that as it may, the promotion of sport as an issue of national interest was not the only cause *Os Sports* engaged with in the passage from the 1910s to the 1920s; this was also the moment when the question of professionalism returned. In this sense, it is truly remarkable how the two major topics in postwar sport – capitalism and nationalism – not only did not collide, but seemed to combine harmoniously in journalistic discourse. The pragmatism with which newspapers championed professionalization indicates that, from the time when the aristocratic sportsman was publicly presented as an ideal model, the question had achieved enormous economic relevance. Paying athletes would simply regulate a situation familiar to all: producing a set of transparent practices and thus rationalizing economic relations that were impossible to ignore, let alone avoid, given the popularity of competitions. In this sense, it could be said – as Sacadura Cabral did, after all the 'noise' made by reporters concerning his attempt to fly from Portugal to Brazil – that there was no way back to the popularization of sports since the system of popularity, organized around the relation between press and its readers, was itself developing in tandem with the growth of newspapers' readership and impact.

The terms of the debate before and after the First World War can be directly linked to how the nature of available images changed between the two moments. From the beginning of the century to the 1920s, the cost of photographic reproduction dropped. In the 1920s, newspapers already published pictures on a daily basis, whereas the growth of audiences created the conditions for the publication of magazines exclusively dedicated to popular sports. Reading those newspapers and magazines allowed readers to fully enjoy the spectacular images of their favourite sporting events. The strict poses of sportsmen in *Tiro Civil* and the composure of ladies watching horse races in *Ilustração Portuguesa* already seemed to belong to a completely different era.

But the fall in the cost of photographic reproductions was not the only visible change in photojournalism. Film exposure times were now shorter, and with this came the ability to capture movement and make the resulting images sharper.[25] The relation between the popularity of sports in the 1920s and photography can in this sense be articulated in exactly the same terms as those between aviation and cinema in the previous chapter: photographers explored the camera's full potential to seize instants when, for instance, they captured a goal-keeper jumping and punching the ball while surrounded by other players (Figure 3.1).[26] In the third issue of *Sport Ilustrado*, a magazine dedicated to 'photography and football', a photographic reporter could even announce the exhibition of a 'sporting film' where he would show a succession of pictures from a match, thus inviting the reader to imagine the movement on the field between the different frames (Garcez 1924: 1).

Sport, in general, and football in particular, attained a position amidst cultural forms like cinema and music to the extent that they were all represented by the same forms of mechanical reproduction. So it was not only that audiences could see fights at the same events where they also watched films and listened to recorded music, as we saw in the case of wrestling championships; in addition, sportsmen themselves were increasingly shown as artists. The stronger defence of professionalism in the pages of *Os Sports* was given in the form of questions that challenged the reader to deny what should apparently be evident: sportsmen had become like movie stars.

Ano 1.°   SPORT   Número 3

ILUSTRADO

Publicação Quinzenal de fotografias de sport

Depois de um remate de João Francisco às redes do OLHANENSE e duma recarga de Jaime Gonçalves, o Keeper algarvio consegue desviar a bola

CLICHÉ DE NORBERTO DINIZ

Figure 3.1: *Sport Ilustrado* 3, 1924. Biblioteca Nacional de Portugal.

[I]f we step outside sport, aren't there thousands of creatures who make a living out of their exceptionally beautiful voice, musical talent, or histrionic abilities? You may argue: theatre, music, cinema, constitute basic needs of modern life. Well, couldn't we say the same about sport? Isn't it a fact that so many people already prefer a football match to a concert, or go to a rugby event rather than to the movies?[27]

Sportsmen, as modern heroes, had to be visible because visibility was value itself. An interesting example of this was published on the front page of *Diário de Lisboa* on 17 May 1925, where readers could see a photo of a man in a raincoat, lighting a cigarette and projecting the shadow of his silhouette against a wall (Figure 3.2). It looked as if he was being filmed in a studio. He could be a detective, or a reporter, or even an actor playing a detective or a reporter, something the public could see in so many contemporary films. He was, in any case, a very recognizable figure, standing for a lifestyle defined by a physical engagement with the world, a type of man who could see more than the others and participate in reality by being immersed in it. As we already know, reporters and detectives, or actors, were defined as the ones who saw – by being there – and, as such, had to be shown while observing. Accordingly, they had to be represented through images as their true meaning was invested in their bodies.

In this sense, it should come as no surprise that that mysterious picture of a man smoking against the wall was of Samitier, not a reporter nor a detective but a Spanish football player who was at that moment in Lisbon to play for his national team against Portugal. The image of him was both distant from that of Pinto Basto and close to Norberto Lopes's description of Sacadura Cabral. They were all modern and, as such, more than their particular occupation – reporting, investigating, playing football or flying – appearance was what defined them. 'Actors, sportsmen, are visual artists like no one else ... [S]ome lives are works of art' (Ferro 1987: 318); António Ferro's words outlined how he wanted to represent himself as a modernist reporter: the embodiment of a way of life in motion that could not but be represented through pictures.

The raincoat and the cigarette, the hat and the pose were in this sense a filmic image. Not that journalists needed to wear a raincoat or football players should smoke. But film, or the imaginary of cinema, was what unified all these figures as moving images. As modern heroes, the actors of modern experience, they embodied modernity through the senses.[28] Their impact was even bigger if what they did could also be attributed some nationalist symbolism, as in Sacadura Cabral producing new episodes for the epic of maritime expansion or football players re-enacting old battles against Spain, as we will see below. New narratives for old

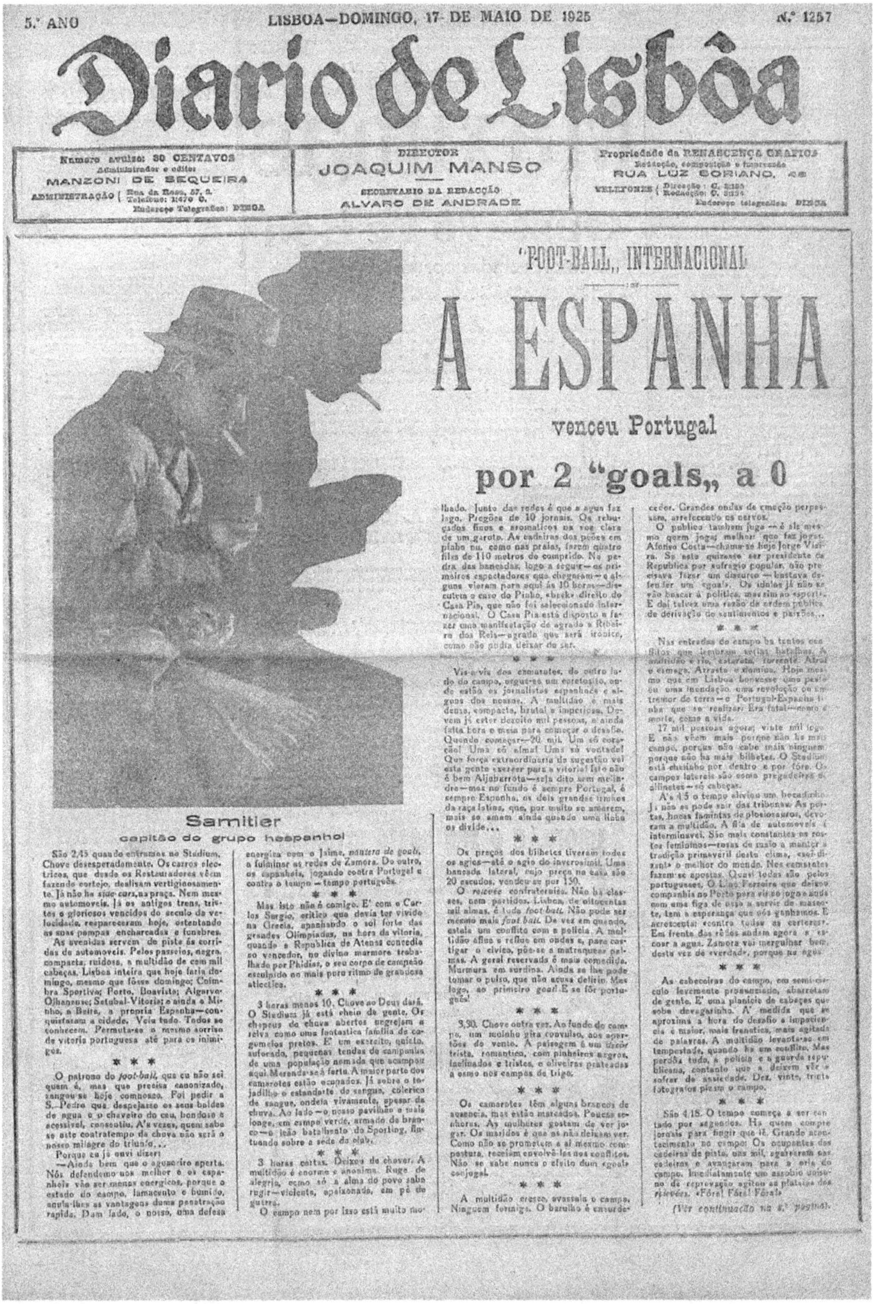

5.º ANO LISBOA—DOMINGO, 17 DE MAIO DE 1925 N.º 1257

Diario de Lisbôa

DIRECTOR JOAQUIM MANSO

SECRETARIO DA REDACÇÃO ALVARO DE ANDRADE

MANZONI DE SEQUEIRA

RUA LUZ SORIANO

"FOOT-BALL,, INTERNACIONAL

A ESPANHA

venceu Portugal

por 2 "goals,, a 0

Samitier

capitão do grupo hespanhol

Figure 3.2: Front page of *Diário de Lisboa*, 17 May 1925. Biblioteca Nacional de Portugal.

stories, one might say, with the proviso that the filmic dimension of these new narratives should not be underestimated. We have already seen a reporter trying to give an account of a flight as if he were a movie camera. Now we are going to read the report of a football match as if watching it in a motion picture.

The Fourth Portugal versus Spain Football Match

Only a few years after the First World War, a very interesting example of what, in relation to the social regulation of violence and instinct, Norbert Elias called the 'civilizing process' seemed to have taken place: the confrontation between nationalities moved from the trenches to football stadiums. Throughout the 1920s, most countries formed national teams in response to this trend. Among all the nations Portugal played, the one which sparked off most enthusiasm in the fans was of course that of neighbouring Spain. And of all the matches these two countries played against each other, the fourth, on 17 May 1925, had a special meaning: after three successive defeats, Portugal finally seemed to have a side that was well enough organized to overcome its opponent. Furthermore, the game took place in Lisbon, where a very supportive audience surrounded the players. Despite such high expectations, Spain finished up winning the match, but the public excitement around it showed how both football and nationalism were in the throes of a process of dramatic change (Melo 2004).

The day of the match was one of those when the main newspapers mobilized all their resources to cover an event. *O Século* organized its report by establishing a link from the stadium, where the reporter covered the game, to the telephone of the Countess of Alvalade, whose palace was nearby. Through this improvised connection, the reporter was able to transmit his commentary to colleagues downtown, where everyone who had been unable to get tickets to the game could follow the most important incidents as they were updated on the billboards. Meanwhile, these short telegraphic pieces of information were immediately composed by the paper's typesetters so that when the game was over and the last report had arrived, *O Século* could be printed without delay: 'before the spectators of this sensational spectacle have the opportunity to arrive at Rossio, a complete supplement of *O Século* will already be circulating in the streets of Lisbon' was the challenge for the day.[29] We are already acquainted with this image. On 18 May, the narrative of what had happened the day before strikingly resembles the exciting moments of the flight to Rio de Janeiro:

As we had announced, right after the match *O Século* had a two-page supplement in circulation in the streets of Lisbon, with a suggestive and complete report of yesterday's sporting journey from the early hours to the end of the game, as well as numerous photographs, some of them taken in the stadium, during the event. Lisboners eagerly read the supplement, and the large edition we printed sold out very quickly. In front of our billboard in Rossio, the news of what was happening was constantly updated, thus satisfying the curiosity of the crowd standing in front of it. Some of the spectators at the stadium had the opportunity to see some photographs from the game's most exciting moments when they arrived at Rossio. We also telephoned and telegraphed our branches in the provinces with news about the 4th Portugal–Spain [match].[30]

Once again, the event became the result of an intense negotiation between the narrative of what it was supposed to be (that is, a football match), its journalistic reports and the participation of the public with both the event and the different forms of circulating news. The participation of the public constituted an event of its own, which, in this case, allowed it to get even more closely involved than in the moment of the South Atlantic crossing, since the match was happening in the same place, Lisbon, where the news was being produced. The spectacle, in this wider sense, started the day before the match, 16 May, at the central railway station, where a crowd of football fans gathered to welcome the Spanish team. Newspapers agreed on how exciting the moment was, although they differed over the numbers of enthusiasts involved: while *Diário de Notícias*, usually more sober, mentioned the presence of two thousand people, *O Século* presented a more sensational figure of five thousand.

The day of the match started with heavy showers, but this was not enough to lower expectations. From the early morning, cars began to move towards the stadium as the gates were to be opened at 11:30 to let the most 'fanatic' in. Downtown, according to *O Século*, 'the agitation resembled that of revolutions'.[31] People assaulted trams despite where they were supposed to be going, and while the police felt powerless to intervene, the closer kick-off time came, the faster and more dangerously cars and motorcycles raced towards the stadium where everyone wanted to get first. After lunch, however, according to *Diário de Lisboa*, taxis were no longer available and other forms of public transport were stuck in a traffic jam. Strange scenes then occurred: old coaches that had been out of use for years reappeared in the streets, while in the opposite direction old-fashioned cars pulled by animals with flocks of people trying their best not to fall over brought in fans from the rural outskirts. As this chaotic swarm approached the stadium's surroundings, it became more compact. The image given by *Diário de Lisboa* described the moment when the disruptive crowd was transformed into a single mass, whose force was all the more disquieting:

The numerous conflicts at the entrance are reminiscent of real battles. The crowd is river, a waterfall, stream. It attracts and squashes. Drags and dominates. Even if there was a plague, a flood, a revolution or an earthquake in Lisbon today, the Portugal–Spain match has to go on regardless. 17,000 people now, twenty thousand later. And the only reason there aren't more is because there's no more room, there are no more tickets. The stadium is packed out. People in the surrounding fields look like pinhead dots – just heads.[32]

The image inside the stadium did not seem very different. The reporter, however, tried to get closer to specific individuals and hear details of their conversations. The crowd was still anonymous, but voices could be isolated from the overall roar, expressing opinions about the players, the teams' strategies and the probable score. As the hour of the game approached, the roar itself seemed to have a different meaning. It was still 'violent' and 'passionate', but the journalist was able to identify the 'soul of the people' in it. When the game finally started, the crowd had somehow transfigured into an embodiment of the whole nation, and the event – again like the flight to Brazil – into something bigger than itself, a historic moment synthesizing national past and national present:

It's still one and a half hours before the beginning of the game and there are already 18,000 people in the stadium. 20,000, when it really starts. A single heart! A single soul! A single will! This is not exactly Aljubarrota[33] – let's say it bluntly – but ultimately it is Portugal and Spain we are talking about, the two big brothers of the Latin race, who, precisely because they love each other so much, love each other still more when a line divides them … The audience fraternizes. There are no classes nor parties, Lisbon, with its 800,000 souls, is all football … The people play as well – it can even be said that it is the main player; or better still: what triggers the game. Afonso Costa[34] today is called Jorge Vieira. If he wanted to be elected President by popular suffrage, he wouldn't have to make a speech – just defend a goal. Idols are no longer found in politics but in sport.[35]

The nation, the historical past, current politics: when the referee's whistle started the game before a completely paralysed crowd of hypnotized eyes showing 'mortal anxiety', the twenty-two players seemed to have a lot on their shoulders indeed.[36] However, it was only a football match, and all the excitement of the next hour and a half was entirely diverted to kicks and tackles, defensive moves and goals, rather than medieval battles and mass political rallies.

The various pieces of report published in *Diário de Notícias*, *O Século* and *Diário de Lisboa* on 18 May all looked practically the same. Their narratives, composed of brief notes in succession – rather like the telegraphic information on the night of the second transatlantic flight – suggest that they also matched the pieces of information displayed on newspaper billboards while the game was going on. Reading it may then give us, as before, the chance to reconstitute both the immediate experience of those standing in front of billboards during the game (as something as close as possible to the experience in the stadium) and the simulated simultaneity performed by the morning reader. At first sight, however, a post facto reading of these close descriptions, where the game's duration was broken down into a series of details unfolding almost minute by minute, seems rather dull. And yet, if we read the narratives of the three newspapers closely against each other, not only can the most exciting moments be highlighted against the monotony of irrelevant information, but it may also become possible to recognize some signs of a plot properly speaking. In fact, even in accounts as hurried as these, reporters had the chance to insert brief comments, discreet clues between the lines. Especially towards the end, then, we will have the opportunity to discern the drama of how reporters struggled to come up with an anticipated explanation for the defeat.

The Portuguese kicked off at 4:30 P.M. Surprisingly, in its first attack (*Diário de Lisboa* was very specific about this: exactly fifteen seconds into the game), João Francisco, the Portuguese striker, hit the post. 'Bad luck', sighed *O Século*.[37] 'The Spanish hadn't even touched the ball', pointed out *Diário de Lisboa*.[38] It was a promising start, which made it even more difficult to endure Spain's first goal, only five minutes later: a strong finish by Carmelo that threw cold water on the stadium's initial enthusiasm. The Portuguese seemed a bit bewildered with this hectic start, and Spain's intense pressure did not help. Things would get even worse just before twenty minutes had gone, when the visitors scored their second goal. This time, the reporters were less surprised than annoyed: according to the consensual opinion among Portuguese journalists, Piera, the scorer, was offside when he received the pass. From this moment on, the narrative became more involved, and the journalist of *Diário de Lisboa* started inserting criticisms – 'our midfielders are playing too much on the rear of the field' – and accusations – 'the Spaniards are playing rough' – into the report.[39] *O Século*'s reporter also started to intervene more explicitly, although in a different way: during the rest of the first half, he would talk about the Portuguese, almost ignoring Spain's attacks and thus giving the wrong impression that Portugal was reacting well and getting close to scoring a goal. As a result, his final remark at the end of the first half was rather surprising: 'So far, the Portuguese have only managed to hit Spain's goal once, right in the first minute'.[40] Apparently, the visitors had been in fact playing much better, but what the reports stressed was the perspective of Portuguese fans. Portugal's attacks were highlighted, while its failures were either ignored or transformed into complaints. The second half would merely reinforce this tendency.

The weather seemed more favourable for the locals when the teams changed ends. The wind was now behind the Portuguese team and, according to *O Século*, the latter started with some good attacks that frightened the Spanish defence. Ten minutes after the break, the reporters were becoming rather optimistic. Portugal was playing much better and their first goal seemed imminent. This makes what came next even more intriguing. Only a short while into the second half, the initial enthusiasm gave way to concern: 'The Portuguese are now playing really well. Zamora's net is constantly in danger. A very strong kick by A. Silva hits a defender's back. We're definitely out of luck'.[41] *Diário de Lisboa's* reporter was clearly excited with what seemed like a promising performance, but the delay in Portugal scoring their first goal while time ticked away introduced a hint of fatalism: 'we're definitely out of luck'.[42] It was just a small note ending an otherwise frankly confident remark. But the Portuguese were playing against the clock, and despite the team's superiority at that stage – 'we were installed in the Spanish area for long periods' – no one could avoid the 'waning of enthusiasm' as, according to *O Século*, the end approached.[43]

Hence, after the first fifteen minutes of the second half, all narratives seemed progressively sure that things were already decided. It was as if, despite all the efforts and the good performance, the game was bound to finish as a 2–0 defeat by Spain. Somehow, reporters started preparing themselves, and readers, for this. The concrete facts of the game no longer stood for themselves. If Portugal, despite its better game, was indeed going to lose, some sort of explanation had to be inserted into the reports.[44] In the last half hour, all three newspapers would give readers the single picture of a game that should be remembered not by the excellence of the winners or the bad luck of the losers, but for it being ruined by a lack of fair play. The similarity of the three accounts, at this moment, reached its peak. *O Século*: 'Zamora takes ages to put the ball back into the game. The other players kick the ball out on purpose'; *Diário de Notícias*: 'The Spaniards, especially the forwards, play hard and violent …'; *Diário de Lisboa*: 'The Spaniards, especially in attack, are playing "*muy sucio*" [very dirty] (in Spanish in the original). Ferreira was brutally hit again by an opponent and falls'.[45] Near the end, *O Século* finally became explicit about the relation between the score and the adversary's behaviour:

15 minutes to go and still 0–2. The Spanish intensify their manhunt! … There are tackles (*rasteiras*), kicks (*caneladas*), and several tricks. Mr Vallat [the referee] is not strict enough. We might even say that he's too benevolent. The public won't have it and protests, asking for the toughest, most violent and incorrect players to be sent off … At 18h10, Ferreira is violently hurt. He leaves the field in pain, and the public protests, calling for the exclusion of the Spanish player. But the game starts once again. Peña, with a kick, throws Mário de Carvalho to the ground, in pain. At 18h13, the Spanish start doing something better with their time, wasting time. The last hopes are gone. Portugal will be defeated.[46]

According to *Diário de Lisboa*, when the referee blew the final whistle, only 'a breathtaking silence' was left.[47] The report ended with this silence as if it had been, from the start, the voice of the audience. Back at the offices, when the reporters finally had time to digest the game and give their instantaneous narrative a closure, they confirmed what had already been pointed to in their brief notes and tried to wrap the whole narrative up. According to *O Século*, Spain's behaviour had been deplorable, 'marked by tricks and violence',[48] while for *Diário de Notícias* this could be used to assuage the defeat: after all, only brute force could have defeated the elegant game of the Portuguese. The same reporter, however, spotted a danger: 'In simple numbers yesterday crossing the frontier by telegraphic wire or through the waves of Marconi's invention, surely it may seem that our neighbours achieved a brilliant triumph'.[49] That was why the mere telegraphic enumeration of what went on was not enough and further remarks had to be inserted in order to explain the final score.

The editions of 18 May, however, added an extra element that must be considered: the interviews with Spanish players showed another point of view. To *O Século*, Samitier complained about the public's behaviour in the stadium, and even suggested that he would refuse to play in Lisbon again under such conditions: 'the crowd was too passionate'.[50] This countered the version given by Portuguese fans and reporters. Apparently, then, the home-team supporters had played rough as well, but that was completely invisible in the reports of Portuguese newspapers. As such, the coincidence between the reporter's complaints about the Spanish and the referee with the protests of the crowd in the stadium suggests that, in the heat of the game, those journalists were writing in very similar conditions to the ones experienced by *O Século*'s anxious editorialist describing the country's anxiety during the most decisive night of Coutinho and Cabral's transatlantic flight: close to the public in the stadium, cheering for the Portuguese team just like any other fan, they were completely immersed in the event.

In this sense, we are once again in one of those situations in which it is hard – or indeed impossible, not to say irrelevant – to say whose narrative this was. For reporters were to a large extent sharing the event with the audience while simultaneously assuming that the audience corresponded to the readership of their newspapers. Within this closed community, morning readers who had been at the stadium or spent the match in front of billboards could reactivate the intense relationship with events we have already seen in the Ultimatum in 1890 and the transatlantic flight in 1922. From this perspective, the involvement of readers with events like the flight and, to a greater extent, the football match, may help us understand more clearly how 'glancing over' stood in for conventional reading. If 'glance' is still a good word for describing this relationship at all, it is of course not only because front pages were by now more illustrated or readers busier people. For the glance was the form of perception inherent to that physical involvement, which allowed the reader to overcome the mere simulation of events that had happened on the previous day through the succession of telegraphic frames and add their own perceptions to what the reporter wrote and thus compose a montage of different perspectives on what had happened.

Frame and montage are, of course, elements of film technique. Contrary to Norberto Lopes, however, I am not using them as metaphors. It just so happens that, as in my initial questioning of Jonathan Crary's work (Crary 2000), concepts dealing with images, and all the more so with images in movement, somehow seem more effective in giving an account of this form of perception.[51] In a way, the status of these reports, between the short – telegraphic – information, and a whole narrative enclosing the event, brings to mind Hayden White's definition of the chronicle as a narrative of a sequence of events distinct in its causal artic-ulation from the mere enumeration of the annals, but still too dependent on a strict obedience to chronological succession to become a narrative proper (White 1987). We might suggest, then, that the reporter's attempt to anticipate – and thus justify – the outcome of the match, during the second half, arranged the chosen episodes in a way that was already close to a plot: 'we lost because our opponent played violently'.

This is what allows us to extend the parallel between journalistic readership and filmic spectatorship to the level of filmic and journalistic narratives as well. For the distinction between chronicle and narrative in Hayden White presents a remarkable similarity with the distinction between continuity and discontinuity, the third and fourth genres in the 'theory of genres in early film' proposed by Tom Gunning (1990b). Initially, the reports cut the game's flow by breaking it down into suc-cessive episodes, but continuity was restored by linear chronology. The stage of discontinuity had to wait for the final comments written at the newspaper office, because only then did reporters edit their stories and all the disparate plots that constituted the event (what happened outside the stadium, the description of the match, the audience's behaviour in the stands and in front of billboards, and so on) came together within the newspaper layout.[52] At this stage, the newspaper – in its printed form – became the final synthesis waiting for the reader to assemble the loose pieces and give a unified meaning to the whole thing. What readers did, then, was to re-enact the constellation of visibilities circulating through the newspaper I mentioned earlier. In this sense, if reportage as the film of events and reporters as movie cameras are to be understood more than metaphorically, this is because readers themselves overcame the simple enumeration of different moments and were able to transform simple continuity into a complex story resulting from the montage of many different things.

And yet, one might think that by 1925 this was no longer a very interesting question. Newspapers were not made to render images in movement, and anyway, cinema was already in place to capture the movement of a football match. In fact, there was a camera filming the fourth Portugal–Spain match at the stadium on 17 May. Unfortunately, those images were lost and we can no longer check whether Portugal really deserved to win or if the Spanish players were indeed that violent. But we can try to imagine how that film showed the game by briefly looking at the still existing footage of another Portugal–Spain match, from 1928. Here, during the first half of the game, the camera was positioned among the spectators in the stands, far from the players. We are given a picture of the entire field, but it is hard to distinguish who was doing what: this becomes an even bigger issue with the permanent obstruction of the camera by the spectators' heads and hats. The cameraman seemed to be aware of the problem, and at half time decided to get closer to the pitch. The action become much clearer, but the camera's new position only captured a small area close to the Portuguese goal. All we see, then, are Spain's attacks in a very small fragment of the field. Surprisingly, then, the written report of the 1925 Portugal–Spain game seemed much more exciting than the film from 1928.

The same difficulties felt by the cameraman, or indeed the limitations of the artefact, were also visible in the footage of Coutinho and Cabral's *Fairey 16* flying over Fernando Noronha, where similar problems are apparent: when the camera that followed the flyers vertically aligned the shot with the plane's route, it was impossible to have a sense of its speed; when the plane crossed the frame horizontally, it disappeared too quickly, as the camera moved very slowly and was unable to track a travelling object. Here too, the report by Norberto Lopes was in a sense much more 'cinematographic' than the existing footage of the flight. So even if filming events remained a mere metaphor, an impossible task for journalism, it must be added that, in the 1920s, cameras were still struggling with speed and movement. In this sense, it only seemed possible to capture the true movement of modernity through montage – as in the synthesis of several different events on the same page. Interestingly, then, the intensity of the written page, the ubiquitous power of reportage as an event shared by reporters and readers at different times and in different places, was still barely matched by 1920s newsreel based on continuity. Things looked different, however, whenever the fast-paced montage used by modernist film-makers was used to respond to the challenge of modern life. In this sense, it is a happy coincidence that in 1928 a film was made fictionalizing a day in Lisbon from the perspective of one of the city's most typical experiences: the making of a newspaper.

Notes

1. As part of events, reporters became, according to Gumbrecht, the writers of lived experience: 'whereas the traditional truth-claims depend on a distance between the observer and the world … the fact that reporters are concerned with lived experience means that there is an emphasis on physicality in their public image' (Gumbrecht 1997: 186). This physicality, one might argue, becomes even more crucial in the journalistic coverage of sporting events.
2. 'A que vimos', *O Auto* 1, 1 April 1923, p.1.
3. *Tiro Civil*, 15 October 1903, p.9.
4. *Tiro Civil*, 15 October 1904, p.2.
5. Norbert Elias analyses sport as one of the main features of the 'civilizing process', with its establishment of rational rules of behaviour: '"Sportization", in short, had the character of a civilizing spurt comparable in its overall direction to the "courtization" of the warriors where the tightening rules of etiquette played a significant part' (Elias and Dunning 1986: 151).
6. This socio-professional distinction was probably what Stefan Zweig had in mind when he confessed that sports had been completely absent from his youth in late nineteenth-century Vienna: 'The newspapers did not yet send reporters to fill columns with Homeric rapture about a hockey game. Fights, athletic clubs and heavy-weight records were still regarded in our time as things from the outer city, and butchers and porters really made up their audience' (Zweig 1964: 58).
7. 'Jogos sportivos – Cascais', *Tiro Civil*, 1 November 1903, p.1.
8. 'Concurso hípico em Palhavã', *Ilustração Portuguesa*, 13 June 1910, p.757.
9. According to Laura Mulvey, these figures who are shown while seeing enact 'the possibility in the cinema of shifting the emphasis of the look'. Their importance to my argument is directly related to their origin in, or at least kinship with, film: 'It is the place of the look that defines cinema, the possibility of varying it and exposing it. This is what makes cinema quite different in its voyeuristic potential from, say, strip-tease, theatre, shows, etc. Going far beyond highlighting a woman's to-be-looked-at-ness, cinema builds the way she is to be looked at into the spectacle itself' (Mulvey 1975: 16).
10. *Sport Nacional*, 13 April 1910, p.1.
11. It was a two-way relation, though, as Alan J. Lee shows: newspapers may have contributed to turn competitions into 'Homeric epics', but the excitement inherent to sports also led to a new sensationalist tone that would soon become the norm in the journalistic narratives of other social phenomena, such as 'police news' and 'divorce cases' (Lee 1976: 128).
12. Such narrative is very close to the critique of modern civilization as a society of the spectacle put forward by Guy Debord: 'In the essential movement of the spectacle …

we recognize our old enemy, the *commodity*, who knows so well how to seem at first glance something trivial and obvious, while on the contrary it is so complex and so full of metaphysical subtleties' (Debord 1994: 26).

13. 'Os desportos brutais – o campeonato do mundo de boxe', *Ilustração Portuguesa*, 4 July 1910, p.1.
14. 'Os desportos brutais', *Ilustração Portuguesa*, 4 July 1910, p.1.
15. 'Campeonato Internacional de Luta', *Ilustração Portuguesa*, 18 July 1910, p.73.
16. *Os Sports*, 29 September 1906, p.1.
17. *Os Sports*, 29 September 1906, p.1.
18. Quotation from *Os Sports*, 28 September 1907, p.1.
19. *Os Sports*, 28 September 1907, p.1.
20. Drawing on Sergei Eisenstein, Tom Gunning uses 'attraction' to speak of early cinema in a way that seems close to our description of these sporting events: 'the cinema of attractions directly solicits spectator attention, inciting visual curiosity, and supplying visual pleasure through an exciting spectacle' (Gunning 1990a: 58).
21. *Os Sports*, 28 September 1907, p. 1.
22. Adorno's use of the word 'sportification' relates sport to mass culture in a context from which both become impoverished: sport and culture mutually reduce themselves to the status of spectacle: 'The sporting events from which the schema of mass culture borrows so many of its features and which represent one of its favourite themes have divested themselves of all meaning. So it is that "sportification" has played its part in the dissolution of aesthetic semblance' (Adorno 2001: 89).
23. *Os Sports*, 6 April 1919, p.1.
24. *Os Sports*, 11 January 1920, p.1.
25. André Gunthert's history of photography in nineteenth-century France is shown as a constant search for simultaneity. Sports worked, in this context, as a particularly challenging field of experience in 'the exercise of surprise, the arrest of the accidental, the interrogation of the visible, the invention of topics and, above anything else, the search for photographic performance, the struggle with the limits of the apparatus' (Gunthert 1999: 298).
26. Siegfried Kracauer, a contemporary of the phenomenon, immediately perceived the impact shorter exposure would produce in the public perception of sport: 'Sometimes it is the fraction of a second required for the exposure of an object that determines whether or not a sportsman will become famous to the point where illustrated magazines commission photographers to give him exposure' (Kracauer 1995: 59).
27. *Os Sports*, 9 March 1922, p.1.
28. In his description of the reporter as a figure of lived experience (*erleben*), Gumbrecht notices how 'reporters are constantly stimulating their senses with cigarettes' (Gumbrecht 1997: 186).
29. *O Século*, 17 May 1925, p.2.
30. *O Século*, 18 May 1925, p.5.
31. *O Século*, 18 May 1925, p.1.
32. *Diário de Lisboa*, 17 May 1925, p.1.
33. The Battle of Aljubarrota was fought between the kingdoms of Portugal and Castile in 1385. The Portuguese forces won, thus guaranteeing the country's independence from the Castilian crown.
34. Leader of the Portuguese Republican Party, Afonso Costa was probably the most renowned politician during the First Republic.
35. *Diário de Lisboa*, 17 May 1925, p.1.

36. The relation between football and national consensus – or indeed depoliticization – is discussed by Modris Eksteins: '"Athleticism is no unimportant bulwark of the constitution", mused Charles Box, a cricket writer, in 1888. It "has no sympathy with Nihilism, Communism, nor any other 'ism' that points to national disorder". On the contrary, sport developed pluck, determination, and public spirit; sport, as the *Times* put it on the Monday after the English football final in 1899, was of great value in the battles of life' (Eksteins 1989: 121).
37. *O Século*, 18 May 1925, p.1.
38. *Diário de Lisboa*, 17 May 1925, p.8.
39. *Diário de Lisboa*, 17 May 1925, p.8.
40. *O Século*, 18 May 1925, p.5.
41. *Diário de Lisboa*, 17 May 1925, p.8.
42. *Diário de Lisboa*, 17 May 1925, p.8.
43. *Diário de Lisboa*, 17 May 1925, p.8.
44. This is why the usual distinction in histories of the press between story and information, or (sequential) narrative and (immediate) photographic coverage, is insufficient to render this journalistic experience, as both things (the display and the narrative – and analysis – of the event) seem to happen simultaneously: 'Journalism driven by narrative carried along in its wake the reader, who anticipated sequence, emplotment, and resolution. Realist press photography trades away temporal narrative in exchange for other things, such as immediacy and emotional impact. Photojournalism is exciting and startling, but by doing it more it may, in fact, do less to bring readers into the storytelling of news' (Barnhurst and Nerone 2001: 138). On the contrary, my account seems to show that the 'filmic' reading of text and photography allowed the reader to insert some sense of progression into different moments of the narrative.
45. *O Século*, 18 May 1925, p.5; *Diário de Notícias*, 18 May 1925, p.5; *Diário de Lisboa*, 18 May 1925, p.8.
46. *O Século*, 18 May 1925, p.5.
47. *Diário de Lisboa*, 18 May 1925, p.8.
48. *O Século*, 18 May 1925, p.5.
49. *Diário de Notícias*, 18 May 1925, p.5.
50. *O Século*, 18 May 1925, p.5.
51. In fact, all the most familiar images of early twentieth-century film phenomenology can already be seen at work in the journalistic experience when seen from the perspective of readers. Vanessa Schwartz is very close to this point: 'Early actuality films were embedded in narratives that occurred off-screen in illustrated newspapers and at wax museums. Films often served as visual corollaries to the printed world, in a reversal of the way that the printed word in the newspaper offered a written digest of the flâneur's mobile gaze' (Schwartz 1998: 193).
52. 'The third genre, which I refer to as the genre of continuity, consists of multi-shot narratives in which the discontinuity caused by the cuts is de-emphasized by being bridged through continuity of action on the story level. The fourth genre I call the genre of discontinuity, in which a multi-shot narrative conveys action which is continuous on the story level through a disruption caused by editing on the plot level' (Gunning 1990b: 89).

Chapter 4

The Film of Events

This chapter starts with an interesting and promising paradox. I have been trying to argue that we can use filmic categories to render the modern experience of newspapers. However, as I suggested at the end of the previous chapter, film as such, at least until the 1920s (although things were rapidly changing), was still struggling with that same experience of simultaneity journalism already seemed able to express. Paradoxically, then, it can in some circumstances be suggested that journalism was more filmic than film. The visibility and circulation of newspapers reached such a level of technological sophistication that it enabled the press to become a symbol of modern life better than any other medium, while at the same time making it harder to represent the press with its own narrative resources. The paradox is thus the following: while newspapers were still the most powerful mechanisms for producing narratives in movement, the circulation of journalism could only be fully represented through filmic montage.

This is what *Como se Faz um Número do Diário de Notícias* [The Making of an Edition of *Diário de Notícias*], a film commissioned by the newspaper in 1928, demonstrates. The film seems to be a typical example of a 1920s city symphony, a key genre in modernist cinema. Its narrative structure is organized around twenty-four hours of city life, drawing on the coincidence between this time unit and the temporality of the daily newspaper. Journalism was thus transformed into a narrative while the stories published in the newspaper were relegated to a secondary role so that the newspaper itself – its production – emerged as an event unfolding throughout the entire day.[1] So, what did the narrative of a newspaper look like, or, what was there to narrate about a newspaper? The short answer was the paper's ubiquitous presence in the world (which, in this case, largely coincided with Portugal's national territory). Only montage could have made this possible. Here, the already familiar metaphors used by reporters that related journalism to film can be read as something much more than stylistic convention: for they now refer to a metonymical relation to the material existence of newspapers as narratives in motion.

The intersection between cinema and journalism enhances the horizon of a narrative of modernity. For in this filmic narrativization of journalistic narratives we may have reached the ultimate synthesis created by newspaper readership: a moment when not only the simultaneous readings of the same news stood for the quintessential form of Benedict Anderson's 'imagined community' (Anderson 1991), but one that managed to represent the imagined community on the move, that is, in the process of being imagined.[2] In other words, the mental concept of the community becomes visible as newspaper production and circulation are shown, and we are able to see what filled the imaginary on that particular day and what such a community organized around the press looked like. In this sense, such an intersection becomes something like the overlap between different spaces and temporalities Fredric Jameson (2009) pointed to as the prerequisite for any representation of modernity as capitalism.[3] A synthesis between the gazes of both reporter and reader glancing over the ensemble of reports on the page – a spatial experience of ubiquity (all events in the same space) – enhanced in the film by the representation of simultaneous readership – a temporal experience of simultaneity (all readers sharing the same events).[4]

The Making of an Edition of *Diário de Notícias*

What I will now do is a rather conventional breakdown of the film.[5] As we already know, the plot takes place across the twenty-four hours it took to make a daily newspaper. The film relies on a succession of familiar urban motifs interposed with the different activities involved in the organization of journalistic narratives. As such, city life can be seen through the perspective of the making of the newspaper's edition. However, the specific representation of journalism in the film is exclusively established through cutting and editing, which makes any written narrative almost useless (in fact, the only intertitles now visible in the film were inserted at a later date). More than through the stories narrated on that specific edition of the paper, city life is disclosed as a specific rhythm whose pace is set by the newspaper.

This allows us to begin our own description of the film's narrative by slightly changing the posed questions, in order to ask when (that is, at what time) did this production start. According to the present cut of the film, not at dawn, when the rotary printing presses began to roll (this is relegated to the end) and the newspaper was physically coming into existence. This seems obvious enough: the production of the newspaper should start with the production of the news. The question is, as we will see, that in order for the newspaper to be finalized, that is, in order for the news to be produced, not only a lot of work was involved, but quite a few things would already have to be set in place before any events occurred.

The newspaper edition was only the final outcome of a process without which the finalized product would remain incomprehensible. In other words, the meaning of this particular material artefact depends on the complex assemblage of the three moments of the synthesis described in Chapter 1: the contingencies of a particular day, a systematized line of production of printed narratives, and the final production of meaning by readers. As a production of news, then, the production of the object itself – a composition of folios with folded sheets – was almost a secondary event between the initial events – contingent or not – of that particular day, and the final reading when the meaning of those events was established. The temporality of the newspaper is thus very complex, composed as it is by three different layers, and this was what film montage had to come to terms with in order to render the whole experience.

Therefore, it is very suggestive that the film seems to begin with what in one sense represents the end of the whole process of producing the news, by showing different forms in which newspapers are handled by readers: men reading while chatting, a peasant eating and reading after putting his tools aside. What is interesting here is that this image adds yet another layer of complexity to journalistic temporality: one is entitled to assume that this edition is not the one whose making of the film is supposed to be narrating, but one produced on the eve and now being concluded – by being read, with readers finally giving sense to the events reported – in the morning of the day the film is supposed to follow. Mornings are, in this sense, a moment when two simultaneous things happen in the realm of newspapers: the making of the next day's edition and the reading of the edition made the day before.

Such a structure not only gives viewers a sense of continuity – newspapers are produced every day – but it also reinforces the idea that more than reflecting the everyday life of the city through the news, the newspaper actively participates in it. This is a key idea of the film, in the sense that it blurs the distinction between making the news and producing the everyday. The choice of those particular moments and protagonists – men chatting, a worker eating lunch – is also very meaningful, as it suggests that while reading newspapers may well be something for breaks in the production system, this is precisely what inserts it in the world of labour at large. The first sequence finishes with images of a factory and a car approaching, which completes an image of this world as one of capitalist production based on movement, that is, relations. Its representation thus necessarily has to render the multiple connections produced by human activities, and in particular those of workers around a single and continuous community of newspaper readership.

This focus on production, if not indeed industry, is immediately confirmed through subsequent shots of the newspaper offices, the centre organizing everything else. The first of these shots is of the entrance of *Diário de Notícias*'s headquarters with people hurrying about and waiting in a queue to place advertisements in the following day's edition. The displacement between events and news we have already seen during the transatlantic flight to Rio de Janeiro (the city reacting to events that had happened the day before as if they were occurring simultaneously) is here confirmed. Not only does the edition only finish its work the day after being produced (in the hands of readers), the newspaper begins to gain shape even before the arrival of any news – the film is now in the early hours of the edition's eve. Before any events happened that day, there was already a lot taking place: people acting in a world of exchange unfolding through daily tasks based on communication, and the newspaper at the centre of it all. In other words, tomorrow's edition might appear as a paper filled with the news happening the day before, but the newspaper, in order to guarantee a continuous flow of news, relies in advance on ongoing forms of sociability and exchange in the public sphere.

It should be stressed how counter-intuitive this introduction to the production of a newspaper seems to be: the point of departure is not the accidental event but morning routines, not the extraordinary but everyday business.[6] The following cut to inside the offices reinforces this, by allowing us to see procedures in more detail. With newspapers, and thus in narratives about the way they functioned, all the work involved in the making of the next edition started by a structure set in place to capture an already existing circulation of information: busy men writing, reading and talking at the same time; women lined up making repetitive gestures in front of their typewriters as if in a production line – all these workers are acting out their everyday control of that flow. So far, then, everything is shown as if newspapers were machines producing daily information independent of the unexpected event, the sensational accident that made the press so recognizable, as if the communicational routines I was just talking about could, if nothing else happened, replace the news.

The rest of the sequence completes the description. The network of telegraph and telephones allows the cameraman to draw an impressive geometrical picture of crossing wires before cutting to men mediating the flow of information by simultaneously receiving a telegram from a machine while talking on the phone and pressing a bell that triggers a number on a small board.[7] The scene is of course very sophisticated, but the ease with which these men do everything at the same time shows that what could be almost seen as a futurist embodiment of machines of mass communication is, once again, just daily routine. Likewise, the unloading of casks containing huge rolls of paper in a scenario of intense traffic of rushing people and cars suggests not so much how lively cities are or the industrial dimension of newspaper production, but rather the opposite: production is naturalized as just another familiar motif of the urban landscape.

As soon as the structure is set up – the standard process of receiving, transmitting and reproducing messages by both people and machines, and the arrival of the paper's raw materials – the narrative immediately moves to the production of news proper. Journalists can finally step into the picture. And yet, in their first sequence, these seeming heroes of the film are shown as just another element in the bureaucratic structure we have just seen: a group of young reporters lining up, waiting for tasks that a clerk sitting on a desk is about to give them. Gradually, however, the film opens to exterior sequences and the engagement of reporters with the world can finally begin outside the newspaper office.

Almost instantaneously, we are shown frames of reporters juxtaposed with typical scenes of modern life – youngsters dancing to a jazz band – or trying to capture events – peeping inside train carriages, interviewing politicians – and the film suddenly becomes a hectic succession of visibilities, with events unfolding rapidly interspersed with eager reporters looking and struggling to write what they see in their notebooks. The reporter thus becomes the central figure, or mediator, of associative montage. Time and space are synthesized around him, as the figure whose ubiquitous presence in the film embodies the ability of the press to see, almost like the panopticon, the whole of society. The sequence reaches its climax when the images of events, in fact any signs of social life, simply disappear and all there is left to see are the reporters themselves watching, in an extraordinary shot that recalls Norberto Lopes's moving gaze on the ship deck. Now, two reporters – one with a notebook in hand, the other with a camera – are shown through a medium long shot standing on the top of a hill restlessly glancing over the landscape (that remains invisible to us). Somehow, the world is reduced to an abstraction whose representation entirely depends on what reporters are able to observe – and later show.

When reporters are finally given centre stage, it is reportage itself (the narrative genre used by the press to appropriate reality) that becomes the true object of the film's narrative. It can then be said that at the point when a famous reporter – António Ferro, the most famous of all – is shown boarding a ship just before setting off on a mission, *Como se Faz um Número do Diário de Notícias* becomes a narrative of narratives. Or better still, the narrative of making a newspaper was to be seen as a master narrative subsuming other types of event, if anything because the latter would never have become visible if it were not for the action of the press in the first place. From the perspective we have explored in the previous chapters – from the reporters' close involvement in public suicides, heroic flights and football matches – this becomes the key point of newspaper production. Newspapers were structures that were not only meant to capture the ongoing flow of information that organized modern life, but also a true informational machine prepared to seize virtually everything that happened and transform it into journalistic events.

And yet, by now we have seen only half the film. The most decisive production at stake in the film is still to come. At this stage, the narrative has reached an impasse and has to be interrupted at precisely the moment

Figure 4.1: Still from *Como se Faz um Número do Diário de Notícias*. ANIM/Cinemateca Portuguesa.

when reporters were apparently getting hold of reality. The director, or whoever edited the copy and tried to give the narrative some plausible sense afterwards, faced two options: either to continue, presumably with the return of reporters to the offices, the writing up of the news and the final arrangements of the following day's edition before it was printed, or to go back to where it had started, the other decisive aspect of *Diário de Notícias*'s presence in the city: the circulation of the edition of that day. In other words, more than following one single edition from when it started to be produced to when it was given full meaning by readers (for which the narrative on the making of one edition of *Diário de Notícias* would have to last at least two days) the film seems to choose to focus on something slightly different from what is promised by the title: the making of an edition of *Diário de Notícias*. As we have already seen, by opting for an account of the various forms of presence of *Diário de Notícias* in the city during a single day, the film had to narrate two different editions simultaneously: the next day's, being prepared by the office structure and the reporters; and the one that had been published that morning and had begun to circulate while the offices received advertisements and messages, and while the reporters went out into the city. More than the making of an edition, then, the film shows the coexistence of two newspaper editions (one being made, the other being read) on the same day. In this sense, the first part of the film is about the production of the following day's edition. The second, starting now, would be about the edition already circulating.

As the narratives shift, the protagonists also change: inside the office, the images of men and women writing and receiving messages are replaced by hands counting money and putting it in tills; outside in the streets, the same places observed by reporters are now invaded by an army of newsvendors shouting out the headlines.[8] More importantly, the immaterial, that is, communication and the gaze of reporters, has now materialized into money and papers. From now on, from the entry of the material artefact into circulation, the film becomes a narrative about a commodity and its value. This will introduce poverty and conflict as interior elements of journalistic production, rather than simply external phenomena potentially convertible into news. The film here returns to dawn so that we can see a long sequence with the early morning negotiations between vendors and the distribution services of *Diário de Notícias*. This is production at its lowest level: newsboys were the *lumpen* of this industry, and the images we are given of them – frames of very close shots making their physical misery all the more evident – are, as such, very impressive. The first faces appear right after a scene where great amounts of money are being handled, exchanged and kept in a deposit box, which dramatizes the contrast with the following shot of very young boys leaning against a door and carrying sacks. As the camera moves closer, we can see they are shivering. It is still dark and the kids wait for the door to open and the paper to be delivered. Meanwhile, they pass the time by chatting, playing cards or sleeping. When a door opens, they enter a room with a bar where two adults give them something hot to drink. The camera zooms while they slurp eagerly. Some look only six or seven years old.

What happens next is even more impressive. Another door opens, giving access to a counter. The same men we have seen counting and handling papers now stand behind a little window. The boys, who only a few minutes earlier were still asleep, suddenly start fighting each other furiously for a position in front of the counter's narrow window. When this finally opens, the camera is inside, giving us a reverse-shot of the kids' excited faces while they frantically try to put their arms and heads inside the small aperture. We can see them screaming while close-up shots stress the pathetic expressions of despair in their faces. What is this all about? Inside the counter, the men are now receiving money in exchange for batches of newspapers. The fury of vendors suggests they were fighting for something decisive to their share of the business: either protesting against the meagreness of their cut from the deal or competing

Figure 4.2: Still from *Como se Faz um Número do Diário de Notícias*. ANIM/Cinemateca Portuguesa.

with each other for more newspapers (which would mean more sales and bigger earnings).

Very suddenly, however, the film changes to another sequence in completely new surroundings. The boys' scrapes, as dramatically charged as they looked, played in the film the role of just another picturesque motif in the city landscape. The viewer, in 1928, was not supposed to be distracted by the newsboys' misery and vagrancy (at least, not in a fundamentally different way from the distraction spectators paid for in the wrestling championship organized by *Os Sports* in 1907): boy vendors were just a restless crowd whose lack of discipline went along with the unstable rhythm of the urban life they helped to animate. That is why they were able to change so suddenly from sleepy boys into fierce negotiators. Now, with their sacks filled with papers, they lead the narrative when it becomes truly epic.

From this moment on, the film focuses on how the specific product – the newspaper as a weighty folio of ads, information and reports – was distributed. Even more than in the montage that interposed scenes of observed events and reporters observing, the film's ability to render circulation is here at its peak. Whereas reporters are the centre of the first part, when we are given the power of journalism to observe and capture events, now, when the question is the paper's circulation, newsboys become the protagonists. From now on, the film unveils what the newspapers ultimately produced, the constitution of a community of readers sharing narratives and images, simultaneously producing meanings in distant places. For, despite the efficiency of the office structure, the sophistication of the network of telecommunications and even the exuberant participation of reporters in events, everything journalism set in place was motivated by pursuit of a readership. This was why newspapers, with their tendency to become protagonists of their own stories, always emphasized the public's participation in events. What the film thus shows is this decisive but usually invisible moment – the absent cause – when the finished product was consumed throughout the national territory and, as such, structured its imagined community. In other words (and as I have already suggested), with the film's second part we no longer need to imagine the community as it is being shown to us in the closest possible representation of what a public sphere looks like.

After leaving the building of *Diário de Notícias*, the camera shows the vendors running down the street, spreading out from Bairro Alto – the bohemian quarter where most of Lisbon's newspapers were based – to the rest of the city. They here become a spectacle in their own right, filling the streets with animation and joy while passers-by stopped to look at them; earlier images of suffering and bargaining seem now long gone in the long shots where, rather than the details of misery, we see the vendors as part of the landscape. To give a true sense of their movement, the camera filmed from a car while one of the vendors ran down an avenue. Meanwhile, some of his colleagues jump into a tram and start selling papers to commuters. Seeing them shout titles and headlines, it is impossible not to remember that the limits of silent film prevent us from hearing how they also filled the streets with sound. But what is most decisive here is the way in which the rhythm imposed by the quick editing of scenes showing the vendors selling newspapers in different circumstances extended their presence throughout the city. The rhythm of editing, once again, creates a perception of simultaneity. The speed with which newspapers are sold assembles the community of readers, and we are led to imagine that if all those different copies are being sold at the same time – to a middle class woman in a car, to a housewife leaning on a windowsill, or thrown at someone's house or taken up the staircase of a building, thus ensuring the news arrives everywhere for everyone to read – then we can also suppose that they will all be read simultaneously.

We have never been so close to a full picture of newspaper circulation and simultaneous readership: newsboys, and thus the newspaper, seem to reach every corner of the city, becoming something that virtually everyone can find and no one ignore; their ubiquity, as we have just seen,

Figure 4.3: Still from *Como se Faz um Número do Diário de Notícias*. ANIM/Cinemateca Portuguesa.

necessarily entailing a sense of simultaneous readership. In these circumstances, if the newspaper was everywhere this was not so much because
anything could become news and become part of its content, but literally,
because everyone had easy access to it. The next sequence comes as the
necessary corollary of this, by showing successively a worker sitting on
the pavement while his wife brings him lunch with the newspaper, a
man reading while sitting at the docks, a doorman, a fishwife and even a
middle-class couple in bed waking up with their breakfast and *Diário de
Notícias*: a whole social portrait organized around readership.

The paper, however, did not stop at the city limits, and thus neither does the film. In fact, the paper's journey towards the public has
barely started, but in order to go further, newsboys have to give way
to other means of transportation. Now the copies of *Diário de Notícias*
are loaded onto a railway carriage. As the train leaves the station, the
camera goes with it, thus enabling us to see the landscape passing by,
first the plains of Ribatejo, right after Lisbon, then the northern moun-
tains and coast all the way up to Porto, as if it was drawing a map
of the country by crossing its several regions and stopping at all the
main cities. At every station, a batch of newspapers is thrown onto the
platform, but the sequence's most expressive moments happen whilst
the train is in motion. The camera is then able to perform all kinds

Figure 4.4: Still from *Como se Faz um Número do Diário de Notícias*. ANIM/Cinemateca
Portuguesa.

of effects – filming the rails from above, capturing the moment when another train passed by in the opposite direction – enhancing the sense of speed of distribution.[9] As in the scenes with the newsboys, what is left here after the train has moved on is readers enjoying their newspaper. In fact, the paper's readership is first seen inside the train, with a carriage full of passengers each reading their own copy. The most remarkable scene, however, is in an idyllic setting with an old man sitting on the porch of a rural house reading *Diário de Notícias* while his daughters are sewing around him.

The episode could have taken place in any remote village of the Portuguese countryside, but when the camera zooms in for a close-up of the front page we can see that the peasant is reading about events in Italy. The geographical range of the news was apparently unlimited. The simple picture of a peasant reading about a foreign country in a paper just printed and transported from the capital gives us a glimpse of how newspapers had condensed and shrunk the world.[10] What the film showed, however, was how this centripetal movement towards the page had a centrifugal counterpart in the multiplication of copies distributed throughout the city by newsboys, to the rest of the country by train, and also, as the sequence finally shows, to even more distant or remote places by mail, to the colonies by ship and to other countries by plane.

The paper has now been produced and distributed. But not, as we know, the same paper. More precisely, the next day's edition is being produced while today's is distributed. The third part of the film follows the day to its end,[11] not to accompany the readers' reaction to the news or the paper's arrival in distant places, but rather to resume the first narrative at the moment when the next edition is about to go to press. For the first time, the need was felt to give some kind of further meaning to what was being shown and intertitles finally make their appearance: 'And while Bairro Alto is asleep, the big rotary machines, perfect and prodigious, capable of printing 100,000 copies of *Diário de Notícias* in forty-five minutes, start singing their clear song of progress'. The making of the newspaper is here clearly presented as industrial production. And yet, after showing the circulation of the daily edition, this narrative of production is no longer the same. The image of the city asleep while a hundred-thousand copies were being printed assumes that it was the day itself what had been transformed into a narrative, and thus that the following day's narrative – people communicating, taking decisions through information, or simply spending time reading about yesterday –was already on its way as the outcome of an industrial form of mass production.

Bodies and Screens

'The song of progress', the film said, about industrial journalism: What did it sound like? What made journalism this narrative machine, with film the only thing to match it within the horizon of expectations of the era? Film was able to represent the production of a newspaper in at least two ways. I have already analysed the first at several points in this book: montage was the language of journalistic ubiquity and simultaneity. The struggle with temporality in *Como se Faz um Número do Diário de Notícias*, on the other hand, suggests that having to produce an edition every day opened journalistic narratives to a form of contingency akin to film's opening to continuity.

The sheer fact that days always follow each other forces newspaper production to keep going, one daily edition after another. Both journalism and cinema thus proved such convenient narratives for modern times insofar as continuity was the ultimate expression of flow, here understood as the temporal structure of progress as modernity's (that is, capitalism's) key ideological feature. The borderline between a mere metaphorical figure of speech and a more palpable analogy legitimizing the relation between cinema and journalism is of course thin, and I would like to put it now by focusing on fictional feuilletons published in the 1910s and the 1920s. A close reading of some of the period's most famous writers – whose popularity was largely won through the press – will allow us to see how the female body, insistently used as a literary trope, worked as a mediator between literature's written word and the new culture of images emerging through journalism. More specifically, we will follow the transition from neo-romantic to modernist feuilleton as a process in which the idealized figures of romantic femininity will become increasingly material and determinant in the definition of the twenties as a period in which historical change was perceived, above all, as a break in the forms of perception. This was done, I will argue, because the proximity to journalism and the pervading presence of a filmic imaginary in the literary unconscious allowed writers to come closer to the representation of (female) bodies and senses. The narrative that follows will in this sense try to show how journalists used their increasing ability to materialize women's bodies through images in order to present the press itself as a materialization of the world.

The contemporary suspicion that newspaper readers and film viewers – surely often the same people – had a common perception of time and narrative in both filmic and journalistic representation was behind an initiative promoted by *Diário de Notícias* and film producer Invicta Films in 1919, almost ten years before *Como se Faz um Número do Diário de*

Notícias. The idea was very simple: Invicta Films would produce a series of films based on feuilletons initially published in *Diário de Notícias*, 'thus allowing the reader', said the newspaper, 'to complement his reading by accompanying some of our most brilliant actors and actresses on screen cinematographically reproducing the literary creations of our land's most distinguished writers'.[12]

To have the making of a newspaper represented on film was not the only contact between the press and other non-journalistic narratives for, as we already know, feuilletons were an important part of the contents readers expected to find in their paper. Despite the clear separation between fiction and reportage within the paper's layout, the combination of the two was complex and ambiguous, as we have seen in Júlio César Machado's literary games. Feuilletons, together with the other contents of the newspaper, composed a narrative ensemble that helped define a period's literary style. Therefore, if it was possible to draw a connection between reportage in the second half of the nineteenth century and realism (with the emergence of mass produced photography in the background) in the 1920s, we should be able to establish the necessary relation between reportage in a world progressively becoming cinematographic and whatever literary movement was simultaneously responding to the same challenge. I will thus try to argue that modernism was, here too, as with aviation, the solution found by modern reporters to the challenge of coming up with a kind of journalism that would be able to perform the film of events, as they often said.

Before starting to read our modernist journalists, however, we have to come to terms with the hegemonic genre they reacted against. It was no coincidence that the initial plan for the collaboration between *Diário de Notícias* and Invicta Films – which never went ahead, and is here used merely for the sake of the argument – was to start by adapting stories of the two most popular authors of 1919, the 'land's most distinguished writers': Júlio Dantas, who we met contemplating birds in a church when Gago Coutinho and Sacadura Cabral arrived in Rio de Janeiro; and Antero de Figueiredo. Both writers had evolved from late nineteenth-century realism to neo-romanticism, which, in the case of Dantas, took his fiction close to a light-hearted imaginary populated by young and frivolous women, whereas Figueiredo went from there to a progressively moralistic and religious stance. They also shared a close friendship with Augusto de Castro, a journalist and writer who became the director of *Diário de Notícias* only a few months before the proposed project with Invicta Films – and who we also met, comparing the flight to a Shakespearean drama in the editorial of his paper. This is the nucleus of neo-romanticists dominating the literary and journalistic system against whom young modernists will have to compete in the 1920s.

On 30 March 1924, Augusto de Castro's friends came together in the pages of *Diário de Notícias* as a tribute to his five years as the newspaper editor. Interestingly, the conservative Antero de Figueiredo wrote to emphasize his friend's role in bringing *Diário de Notícias* up to modern standards. These coincided with our own insistence on the newspaper's autonomy as a social actor in its own right: as 'a modern journalist', Castro was able to 'give life to the newspaper', by transforming what was 'heavy and circumspect' into something – and these are all Figueiredo's words – 'happy', 'lively', 'restless', 'sagacious' or, in what summarized it all, 'modern'.[13] This modern journalism, according to the writer, responded to the emergence of a new reader, those men and women immersed in the speed of modern life and eager for knowledge, however little, about virtually everything so as to be able to 'pretend to have their own ideas'. More than a moral judgment on modern mass media and its consumers, Figueiredo tried to emphasize the analogy between newspapers with what, for him, were the most up to date forms of representation:

> The art of making a 'daily' shares a lot with the art of making a play, in the movement of the plot; in the quick cut between scenes; in the dramatic endings; in the thick paint of stage sets; in the mystifying lights, converting cheap garments into gold; and even in the ephemeral voice on the stage, ostentatiously declaiming but quickly vanishing.[14]

By choosing the theatre rather than cinema as the genre to be associated with the journalistic 'song of progress', Antero de Figueiredo seems to fail to live up to the standards of modern journalism as seen in the 1920s. And yet, one would hardly fail to notice how all the elements he uses to describe the technical achievements of modern drama – the cut, lights, illusion and transience – could already be said to belong to the rhetoric of film. In any case, his description seems closer to the point when it came to the director's literary talents. According to Figueiredo, if Castro could be considered a modern writer, capable of giving life to a newspaper, that was because he had the ability to use his 'agile hand … to grab all opportunities' and, just like a reporter, 'brilliantly improvise' articles that were 'written without batting an eyelid'.[15] In short, his writing should be seen as a form of action rather than a thought, the deployment of an agility that seemed more physical than intellectual. In his own writings, however, the director of *Diário de Notícias* was more prone to criticize than praise this modern imaginary and its physicality.

In 1933, Castro published a book symptomatically titled *Sexo 33 ou a revolução da mulher* ('Sex 33, or women's revolution'), where he tried to establish a relation between the era's tendency to disaster – at a moment when it was becoming progressively clear that a second world war was to follow the first – to the frivolity of women. The book encapsulated the crisis in a formula, the 'triumph of number', originating in 1914 and defined as 'the emergence of disorganized social forces coming up against a now defeated orderly individualism from before the war' (Castro 1933: 159). Women, or a certain public image of femininity, appeared in this context as the most visible of all 'numeric forces precipitated by the conflict' (Castro 1933: 160). The choice of women as the epitome of a world corrupted by images and the period's revolutionary chaos is truly remarkable, and shows how ambivalent the central role of femininity in the fiction of writers like Augusto de Castro, Antero de Figueiredo or Júlio Dantas was. For women were simultaneously shown as the most idealized images and the more palpable embodiment of contemporary historic change. The comparison used by Castro to illustrate this suggested how someone who was old enough to have started a literary career before the war could not help feeling that his object of representation moved much faster than his ability to represent it: 'by then, she had lit a cigarette, got a monocle, bought a cane, and by 1917 – good gracious me, so much time had passed since 1914! – an eighteen-year-old girl resembled an eighteen-year-old girl from 1907 as much as I, a man of my time, resemble a man from the Crusades' (Castro 1933: 160). Obvious as it may seem, this excerpt reminds us that the existence of these women was simultaneously historic and literary. And what made them so ambiguous for these authors was, on the one hand, the latter's own ambivalence towards historic change and, on the other, the circulation of what they wrote through both fiction and journalism.

This may help us situate the role of women in our analysis: women were used as a literary trope that helped mediate historical perception, thus entitling writers to experience the crisis as a literary problem. According to Castro, the fact that his 'generation was intoxicated with literature to the bones' (Castro 1933: 163) had been one of the main causes for the disaster. The responsibility of women for this, however, seemed difficult to establish, for if for Castro himself they were a mere object of a 'romantic and materialist civilization that transformed [them] into the beings of passion, luxury and sensuality with which we adorn our salons and decorate our existence' (Castro 1916: 63), Júlio Dantas, on the other hand, seemed to support the opposite view: 'modern literature is everywhere an excited, nervous and sick kind of literature. It weakened, became tired and collapsed on voluptuous contact with women' (Dantas 1916: 269).[16]

The hesitation between the place of women in history (or society; that is, the mundane world narrated by journalism) and fiction was in fact a negotiation. If women epitomized the historical period and if they could be represented as both literary tropes (with which 'we adorn our salons') and readers (whose 'voluptuous contact' weakened literature), then the ambivalence of their status in the genre can be read as a way to deal with readership at a moment when 'number', that is, massification, seemed unstoppable. In other words, between women's voluptuous power and literature's corruption, Augusto de Castro and Júlio Dantas were attempting a new balance between the now defeated orderly individualism prior to the war (here represented by the writers themselves) and the disorganized social forces emerging after 1914 and that women stood for.[17]

The new social landscape may have looked threatening, but simple mathematics would also suggest that the emergence of number could also represent an opportunity for popular writers such as these. It is thus not enough to say that fictional women were simply a literary representation standing for materialist society or the spectacularization of culture, since these female representations were already figurations standing for concrete social relations of power. In other words, newspaper feuilletons became intensely political because the power display of forces between men and women was experienced as a relation between (male) writers and their (female) readers. The reason why women – rather than, say, the urban lower middle classes (never mind the proletariat) who probably constituted the biggest segment of newspaper readership – seemed such an appropriate figuration for feuilletons should be approached as a literary question to be analysed through the conditions by which the genre's popularity was used – despite their rhetoric of crisis – as an instrument of power.[18]

Sometimes this authority was very explicit. The war was one such moment when writers like Augusto de Castro used their ambiguous status within journalism – between fiction and opinion making – to exert it. It is difficult to imagine any other circumstance when a public intellectual could address his readers with the censorious 'Is this a time to think? Is this a time to discuss?'(Castro 1917: 120) with which Castro demanded unconditional faith in military victory over the Germans. Castro's command, however, would become even more efficient when he used an imaginary female interlocutor to reinforce his patriotic statement and thus transformed plain authoritarianism into paternalism: 'Oh! No, my charming and annoying friend, whose delicious mouth has no idea of what it is talking about!'(Castro 1916: 99). His female 'friend' had shown some sympathies towards Germany, the reason why he reacted so aggressively. And yet, more than the aggression itself (she was 'annoying' and her 'mouth had no idea' of what it said), what was really violent here was the way the female's sexualization (the reference to her charm and 'delicious mouth') undermined her opinion and submitted her to a mere corporeal, non-intellectual, form of existence.

More often, however, such an authority was put in fictional, and thus more insidious, terms. In the second half of the 1910s, both Júlio Dantas and Augusto de Castro achieved huge success by assembling their feuilletons in books that became bestsellers. The titles established an unpretentious, rather frivolous atmosphere from the start: *Ao ouvido de Madame X* ('Whispering to Madame X') by Dantas and *Fumo do meu cigarro* ('The smoke of my cigarette') by Castro suggested a genre close to the senses and thus able to apprehend and express the era's fleeting – or feminine, as they would say – nature. In *Fumo do meu cigarro*, Castro described Dantas's *Ao ouvido de Madame X* as an example of that 'infinitely difficult and … delicate art of talking to women' (Castro 1916: 176). In his next volume, simply titled *Mulheres* ('Women'), Dantas would in his turn show his gratitude by referring to Castro as 'insinuating' and 'sparkling', a writer whose relation with readers was as modern as one, in that context, could imagine: 'to read him is to see him, is to listen to him' (Dantas 1916: 242). In his own following volume, *Fantoches e manequins* ('Dummies and mannequins'), Castro would again praise 'my dear friend's new book' – *Mulheres* – for 'its series of feminine kodaks [snapshots] taking … a soul, a profile, an ankle, a tear, or a woman's neckline by surprise' (Castro 1917: 197). This intense exercise of self-indulgence had already started when, in *Ao ouvido de Madame X*, Dantas wrote a review of *Doida de amor* ('Crazy for love'), a similar kind of work previously published by Antero de Figueiredo, where the ambition of this literature to be more than just an external manipulation of women's image was first established:

> You are now going to meet, through reading *Doida de amor*, a subtle, sharp, rigorous, accurate, psychologist, who circles endlessly around a rose petal, explains the brief reflex of a woman's whim in twenty volumes of analysis, puts in third degree equations complex episodes of sentiment, and knows, much better than you do yourself, my lady friend, what you are thinking as we speak. (Dantas 1915: 123)

'Much better than yourself': the key talent of these writers was not intellectual (those 'twenty volumes of analysis' were based on observation rather than meditation) but sensorial, located in their supposed capacity to be read as one sees and hears. It thus seems that, as portraitists of modern life, their ambition was to collapse the world into a single image of femininity and further invert hierarchies so completely that representation came to prevail over, not to say colonize, its own referent. Women readers were thus invited to search for their true selves in a literary land-scape. And yet, the exercise came with a price. The absolute submission of a particular social and historical actor to a literary trope could not but fall into formalism. Instead of images of women proper, then, all the reader could see and hear in those feuilletons were strawberries with 'opulent bosoms' whose 'flesh trembles close to us', or cats as 'evanescent as a woman' (Castro 1916: 9). In short, a long portfolio of stereotypes where women were objectified through catachresis and objects feminized through personification.

These female characters, a series of stereotypical madams, misses and ladies, were usually very shallow. Lady Futility, one of Dantas's fictional interlocutors, told him how she had just broken up with her lover in the most frivolous manner: 'Was it his fault? Was it mine? No. Neither his nor mine. It was life's fault, where everything is vague, fleeting and ephemeral'. Such moral relativism seemed simply a pretext to explain the character's name: 'I've got a golf match today. My husband woke up in a terrible mood. Don't forget my Loti. You know I would be heart-broken if António killed himself? And my hats, what's taking so long for them to arrive from Paris?' (Dantas 1916: 54).

And yet, superficiality here was twofold, since this behaviour was supposed to take place in a world made of surfaces. It can thus be said that these plots' own repetitiveness – everything was decided accord-ing to the whims of rich ladies and spoilt girls – was already superfi-cial in itself. The formal inflexibility of the stereotype would eventually turn against the genre. Miss Kate, another of Júlio Dantas's imaginary friends, proved that if women were really just these evanescent impres-sions, ultimately they could flow away from literature: 'what's variable, instantaneous, fugitive, delicate, almost divine in women – is completely overlooked by men's observation and intelligence' (Dantas 1916: 208), she told her creator. The circularity of the narratives – the effort made by literature to remain superficial in order to represent superficial women – signals the limits of the genre: to show women as mere images will take any material anchorage away from female characters, which would made it impossible to represent those same women beyond the bodiless veneer of literary form. This was exactly where modernists found a win-dow of opportunity, and where António Ferro (the reporter travelling in *Como se Faz um Número do Diário de Notícias*), as the new leading figure of feuilletonism, established the break in direct dialogue with his predecessor, Júlio Dantas:

I know her as Mademoiselle Y, because I don't know of any other letter in the alphabet that can draw her better. She is a perfect Y, with her small head, her body in the shape of I, her feet thrown like commas ... I could have called her X, which is an old-fashioned letter, used to designate mysterious women, but the letter X is an unfriendly letter, round and fat, a letter that manages to photograph only short and voluminous women with precision. Mr Dantas must forgive me, but his Madame X, in addition to being deaf (as we have to whisper close to her ear), surely has the mumps as well. (Ferro 1923a: 24)

The genre's most recognizable motifs did not seem to change in Ferro's modernist turn. Women were still young, aimless and their 'natural' shallowness submitted them to exactly the same stereotypes. The status of Ferro's images of women, however, was completely different, for they now seemed to have bodies and, as such, a material presence anchored in the scenario. Where X was just symbol, standing for what remained invisible, the name Y radicalized verbal representation beyond literalness by actually drawing the referent. To assume the full consequences of this transformation and allow his characters to emerge in their materiality, Ferro had to resort explicitly to the filmic apparatus: 'at a table next to mine, Madame Film – with a filmic body in permanent movement – had fallen a long time ago under the lens of my eyes. Immensely cinematographic, immensely photogenic, Madame Film, unfolded, through smiles and facial expressions, a whole film in less than fifteen minutes in the hotel lobby' (Ferro 1923a: 80).

As a body of image and movement, Madame Film could only be seized with a lens.[19] But because António Ferro himself was not a film-maker, he had to somehow demonstrate that what he wrote – like Norberto Lopes on the deck of the ship on which he was crossing the Atlantic – was the result of direct observation. This entailed something similar to reportage, where the narrative's credibility depended on the reporter's ability to enact his own involvement with the referent. In this sense, modernism, defined by these writers as any artistic form stemming from an engagement with modern life, seemed the stylistic answer to a new situation where it was impossible to tell a reality suddenly transformed into moving images without the modern mechanisms of representation.[20] In this sense, the fact that Ferro was still writing frivolous feuilletons about shallow women is not the decisive point. My point is that the real difference between Mademoiselle Y and Madame X was that between Dantas, a traditional writer (whose fiction remained detached from reality), and Ferro, a modernist reporter whose literature rendered movement because he himself was a writer in motion. We must now try to detail this profile of modern writer further.

One of António Ferro's most significant texts of the period, *A idade do jazz-band* ('The jazz-band age'), was initially read out at a conference in Rio de Janeiro in 1922, when Gago Coutinho and Sacadura Cabral were arriving in Brazil from their flight. What makes it so important to the author's work is less the fact that it was presented as a performance

– whose impact was necessarily circumscribed – but mostly for its insistent effort to produce a definition of the period (the jazz-band age)
while simultaneously trying to stretch the limits of its representation. I
suggest we follow the text closely for a while, for it may indicate how
far this modernist journalism could go in the representation of modernity
through the use of women as a literary trope.

While in front of his audience, Ferro's reading was occasionally interrupted by a dancer whose movement was supposed to illustrate what
the text tried to express in words and sentences. And what the text struggled to say was what by 1922 probably already looked like a familiar
– if not indeed banal – modernist landscape made of 'big cities' bar-
baric streets, crazy streets with moving eyes gazing at the luminous and
fleeting placards, streets already taken by automobiles and buses, streets
where cinemas wear posters as make-up and behave like feline worldly
women inviting us to get in, ferocious streets, panther streets, streets
decorated with signs, dresses and screams' (Ferro 1923b: 56). *A idade
do jazz-band* gives a comprehensive account of the modern world by
encompassing its most recognizable tropes (or indeed stereotypes), especially those related to communication and transportation. More than
an enumeration, however, these mechanisms related to each other as the
objects and subjects of the same representation: the urban streets – with
their 'moving eyes gazing' – should be seen as both the space and the
content of cinema, with their posters resembling women with make-up.
In other words, more than a succession of busy cities and sophisticated
mechanisms of representation, this modern age should be seen as a relation between a space and the visual forms that made it visible.

Interestingly, however, cinema did not epitomize the era. Instead, this
was identified with the 'jazz-band', which, for Ferro, should be firstly
recognized as a dance rather than a musical form. Somehow, dance,
as 'one's multiplication, like having a different body in each gesture',
seemed able to fill narrative with motion by generating 'images from
image itself, [and] to unfold like a film' (Ferro 1923b: 42). Like the
busy streets to whose movement the presence of cinemas contributed
so decisively, so too dance was able to generate images through its own
movement. Conversely, all these busy streets and moving bodies needed
cinema to appear as such: 'all the images of modern life fit into a jazz-
band as in a screen' (Ferro 1923b: 55). Like sport, then, the ability of
dance to represent modern life directly depended on whether it could be
expressed by film. The same happened with journalism in *Como se Faz
um Número do Diário de Notícias*: beyond the identification of cinema
and modernity, modern reality was defined as what had a filmic quality
by being made of those same images and movement that only cinema

could render. Dancing as a multiplication of gestures seems to take us back to Ferro's definition of moving bodies as the ultimate art form, which, for him, not only brought actors and sportsmen together under the same bodily ontology, but raised it up to the status of lifestyle: 'Actors, sportsmen, are visual artists like no one else ... some lives are works of art' (Ferro 1987: 318), and this was the reason why a reporter like himself could join the club of those whose lives resembled a work of art.

But for this to be possible, the representation of modern existence would have to provide a technological update to the images of femininity exhausted by Júlio Dantas and Augusto de Castro. This was the task of filmic tropes in modernist feuilletons. So, the question in *A idade do jazz-band* was not simply to establish a symbolic difference between X and Y, because if Y was a body and thus could be filmed, Ferro's narrative necessarily had to enhance its filmic quality beyond metaphor and manage to somehow put it in motion. In formal narrative terms, playing with letters in feuilletons was the only solution the author managed to come up with to make bodies move, while using the plot to reinforce women's transience through their lack of goals. The inability of female characters to stabilize in any depth in Ferro's novels, was the author's solution to duplicate the unfolding of film in his narratives for it made 'them different at every hour and every minute'; after all, he added ironically, 'women get very tired of themselves' (Ferro 1923b: 49).

The call of *A idade do jazz-band* stretched the challenge of modern literature when it asked its own writings to come to terms with the ability of dance to 'disarticulate' women's 'flesh, bone and blood'. Ferro's own literary ambition – to make and unmake female bodies as if his words were film frames being projected onto a screen – was explicitly defined as a process where the personality of his female characters 'would be ripped apart' (Ferro 1923b: 39). When one gets to this point of ripping apart women's personality by 'disarticulating flesh, bone and blood', what before was a mere abstraction, a figure of evanescence, suddenly becomes a gesture to be inscribed on their own bodies. In other words, what in the hands of Dantas and Castro was a rhetoric of authority seems to become, in Ferro, an instrument of torture. And yet, if we take a look at one of the most insistent images used by Ferro in his efforts to define the boundaries of the modern representation of women, we will find out how close he still was to the rhetoric of older literary tropes. Images like 'Woman is the cover. Man is the book' (Ferro 1923b: 53) – or 'Books are men's dolls; dolls are women's books' (Ferro 1923a: 112) – showed, by equating female dismissal with the intellectual values of male-centred literature, how female objectification through stereotype aimed at maintaining their role as passive readers. As such, the violent narrative of women's bodies can also be read as a sign of powerlessness. As Ferro himself had to recognize, despite the Promethean promise that 'each sentence is a woman' and everything is 'born from words', his own words were not enough to sing 'the spontaneity of the hour' (Ferro 1923b: 43).

All this frantic drive towards metaphor thus seems to represent an anxious response to the limits of the written word in a moment of 'cinematographic uneasiness'. When Ferro declared that women could be seen as the 'models of the century's restlessness' just because they were 'influenced by modern art' (Ferro 1923b: 63), all he did was to add the expressiveness of movement to that same literary authority already set in place in Augusto de Castro and Júlio Dantas. Symptomatic as Ferro's treatment of women may have been, then, modernism's major break with traditional feuilletons should be grasped at another level. To put it schematically: if new times needed a new literature, that literature would in turn need a new type of writer. Accordingly, we may now be in a better position to confirm the idea that has been guiding this analysis of journalistic literature in the 'jazz-band age': what changed from Madame X to Mademoiselle Y – just two metaphors, although the Y is almost a metonym – was less significant than the difference between Júlio Dantas and António Ferro, that is, between the sitting writer and the moving reporter. Or, if Ferro is at all capable of stretching the limits of representation in the jazz-band age, that is not because of something particularly groundbreaking he wrote, but because he embodied the new literary figure of modernist journalism.

When Afonso de Bragança, the editor of *Contemporânea* and fellow reporter from *Diário de Lisboa*, protested against how badly women wrote, Ferro was magnanimous, asking in return 'What does it matter if they write without punctuation?' After all, 'all those commas and full stops are our inferiority' and to some extent lack of grammar could be seen as the solution to overcoming their own literary impasses: 'My dear Afonso de Bragança, you, a modern journalist, so modern you only write in print characters, ... wouldn't you say that the most beautiful literature is that of shouts, exclamation marks and loose words?!' (Ferro 1923a: 42). For once, let us not focus on yet another repetition of this by now already too familiar trope of femininity – women's loose writing as a reflex of their physical evanescence – and get hold of why, according to Ferro, Bragança should be able to identify the era's true literary novelty: 'you, a modern journalist, so modern you only write in print characters'. If journalism was the literary form of modernity, then reporters should be seen as the epitome of modernism. But Bragança knew this only too well. In fact, when he tried to situate Ferro's position in the literary field of the 1920s, he ended up with the first description ever made of a modernist journalist:

> Our literature is becoming more and more journalistic – which doesn't mean our journalism is becoming more literary. There are two different categories of literary journalists. Those who, through talent and effort, get there after a busy professional life, and those who, originally coming from literature, don't know how to write journalism in any other way. The journalist-literate [i.e., journalists who also wrote fictional works] started writing for an audience. And never forgets he is writing to an audience. His prose, even when it's not vulgar, is at least clear. The literate-journalist [writers who also wrote in newspapers] ignores the public and artistic etiquette. Today, Mr Ferro is one of these journalists.[21]

Bragança's main point – a hierarchy of 'journalist-literates' and 'literate-journalists' based on literary talent – is hardly acceptable. In fact, the distinction is blurred as journalist-literates – those reporters who sometimes wrote fiction but whose main activity was reportage – often came up with much better solutions to the challenges of modern representation than literate-journalists – writers, like Ferro, who also wrote reportage. We have seen as much in the efforts of Artur Portela (a modernist reporter much better known for his work as a journalist than as a writer) and António Ferro to narrate the flight of aeroplanes, where the former was able to escape from literary conventions and get much closer to the narration of speed.

Moreover, Ferro's growing public visibility showed how even the most autonomous writers, that is, the most modernist journalists, were still in tune with the audience's traditional expectations. But Bragança was right in locating the new forms of literary legitimacy within newspapers. In the era of modernism, literary reputation seemed to have become directly dependent on the writer's ability to engage with the dynamism proper to reporters. This was particularly visible in the images they used to talk about themselves. Whereas Júlio Dantas and Augusto de Castro liked to present each other as writers who could feel reality through the senses, now, with the new impulse brought by António Ferro, Afonso de Bragança and João Ameal (the author of *A religião do espaço*), literature imposed itself over the mundane precisely as if it was just one of those new machines of visibility and circulation.

We here reach a new level of this whole constellation of metaphors. In order to represent women as the objects of filmic representation, men would have to incorporate the mechanical features of its reproduction. This is why it was so important for Ferro to say of Ameal that he was 'the cameraman of today's Portugal', or that his book *A semana de Lisboa* ('Lisbon's week') read as a 'newsreel' (Ferro 1921a), or Luiz de Oliveira Guimarães – yet another member of this generation – to compare Ameal to 'a vertiginous limousine, running, flying and jumping nervously'

(Ameal 1922: xxviii). António Ferro also used a motorized metaphor to describe the group's leading figure, himself: 'António Ferro's soul is a poster astonishing the crowd. His prose is a red car blowing his horn while running everything over' (Ferro 1987: 20). His soul as a poster was impossible to ignore, but Ferro's impact went beyond the astonishment usually produced by images as his prose should be seen as a car violently invading the tranquillity of readers. As cameras, posters and cars, these writers were now like those machines that not only captured and screened images, but that also had made urban daily life in the restless, busy, modernity that required machines to capture and screen it in the first place.

Once again, it is hard to see how Ameal could be a 'vertiginous limousine' and Ferro a 'poster astonishing the crowd' if not through the same literary procedure that transformed women into film and screen, and made it possible for writers to be heard. But these young modernists were in a situation that somehow allowed them to move beyond mere metaphor and behave as if to reproduce reality as machines was not an unreasonable undertaking. As reporters, they could argue that their presence in the city resembled motorized traffic since publishing in newspapers transformed what they wrote into narratives in motion. This became explicit when both Ameal and Ferro had the opportunity, in the early 1920s, to create and edit their own magazines. When, in 1924, João Ameal proposed to Luiz de Oliveira Guimarães that they create *O Chiado*, their dialogue acted out in the magazine's presentation suggested they were already equipped with the technical features of the camera:

> OLIVEIRA GUIMARÃES: About Chiado? A magazine about Chiado? But that is a *tour de force*! You will cease to be a writer and become an athlete. Allow me to congratulate you … And when does *O Chiado* start?
> JOÃO AMEAL: What do you mean? Now. Immediately. Today.
> OLIVEIRA GUIMARÃES: Today? But then it's not a magazine: it's a photograph.
> JOÃO AMEAL: A photograph, of course. All we have to do is to stroll down Chiado together, for the magazine to be done. (Ameal and Guimarães 1924: 3)

As for António Ferro, when he was made responsible for the modernist revamping of *Ilustração Portuguesa* in 1921, it already seemed clear that, in order to thrive, the magazine had to fulfil the function of a movie theatre: 'more than the book, more than theatre, magazines have to live their era, to document it, to fix its memories. Magazines have great affinities with cinema. Paper is the screen used by magazines' (Ferro 1921b: 232). Beyond the metaphorical power, or banality, of these images, what is key here, I would like to argue, is the extent to which the circulation of periodicals, whose visibility was enhanced in the case of magazines by prolific illustrations, somehow made these assertions seem feasible.

To a certain extent, then, Ameal and Guimarães did give life to their magazine just by walking down the street, whereas Ferro, even if he was still being merely figurative when comparing *Ilustração Portuguesa* to a screen, may be said to have a point when he added the promise of 'turning Lisbon weekly', and, 'if necessary, inventing Lisbon' (Ferro 1921b: 232). It is hard to imagine how the material presence of literature through journalism could go any further.

To conclude, contrary to what I suggested at the end of the previous chapter, sometimes the journalistic film of events did go beyond simple metaphor. Newspapers, as the narratives in motion we are trying to come to terms with, could be seen as metonyms for the textual dimension of reality, the structure over which the everydayness of modern society was made by people communicating, deciding about and acting on information, or simply spending time reading. In this sense, reporters were more than just the narrators of reality: when António Ferro stated that he would 'turn Lisbon weekly' – and, if necessary, 'invent' it – he was assuming the authorship of nothing less than time itself and imposing its passage through the writing of daily newspapers and weekly magazines. Journalism, in these circumstances, literally became a production of the everyday.

Notes

1. Obviously, it is not film that imposes the time unit on newspapers. In fact, one could go as far as saying that if many modernist films matched their urban narratives with twenty-four hours in the life of a city – *Lisboa, Crónica Anedóctica* (1930), Lisbon's own symphony, is the closest example to *Como se Faz um Número do Diário de Notícias* – this was because the temporality of urban life was already organized by the rhythm of newspaper editions and the imaginary of journalism. Peter Fritzsche seems to suggest as much in relation to Berlin and Walter Ruttman's *Berlin: Symphony of a Great City*: 'emphasizing the movement, contrast, and transitoriness of urban inventory, the newspaper moved away from a textual or narrative organization of reality and constructed a visual or tactile encounter with it. Without photographs and making only slight use of line drawings, lithographs, or half-tones, the boulevard press generated image after image whose selection had been made according to formal properties rather than thematic substance. In this way, the printed media anticipated the nonmimetic, purely visual effects of cinema. The 'urban spectacle' that is so manifest in Walter Ruttman's acclaimed 1927 documentary, *Berlin: Symphony of a Great City*, for example, embellished a visual field already prepared at the turn of the century by the publishers Ullstein and Mosse. As readers and thus as consumers, the prewar public approached the city more and more completely in terms of visual pleasure and spectatorship' (Fritzsche 1996: 130).
2. My insistent parallel between journalism and film reaches here a purely formal point, where the elements of the filmic image – the frame, the shot – and of filmic narratives

– the work of editing, montage – could be interchangeably used to describe the articulation of different reports within the circulation of newspaper copy. Francesco Casetti's definition of cinema as the 'eye of the century', combining the particular shot with sequencing – a combination between fragmentation and transience – could be used to describe both *Como se Faz um Número do Diário de Notícias* and *Diário de Notícias* itself: 'Film effectively seized this emergent duality of modern vision, assuring a dialogue between the two. With the shot, film puts a limited perimeter of vision on screen; but every film-take seeks to restore a striking, "epiphanic" vision of the world. Through editing, each shot proposes one and one vision only, but the sequencing of shots permits multiple – even ubiquitous – perspectives' (Casetti 2008: 32).

3. In a discussion of Benedict Anderson's *Imagined Communities* (1991) and simultaneity (to which newspapers decisively contribute), Fredric Jameson argues for simultaneity as an 'intersection of several different temporalities', which allows for the contradiction to be seen, that is, 'the thing itself only becomes visible at moments of temporal coexistence, of simultaneity, of the contemporaneity without coalescence of several distinct subjectivities at once' (Jameson 2009: 531–32).

4. What allows this to happen is, once again, the correspondence between the basic element of film's discontinuity – editing – and the circulation of newspapers, where the successiveness of the making of the news gives way to a moment of simultaneity in reading: many different readers doing exactly the same thing far away from each other: 'A selection of two shots had to be read not only as signifying temporal successiveness and relative spatial proximity, but as potentially also signifying an inverse relation: that of temporal simultaneity and spatial distance' (Elsaesser 1990: 23).

5. Even this linear description of the original film has its risks, as the only copy left, deposited in Portugal's national film archive, the Arquivo Nacional de Imagens em Movimento, contains only less than half of the original feature. My analysis will in this sense be limited to an extract of the original film. Moreover, the current order of the negative was established at the archive, and although it follows what is presumably the most coherent sequence, we cannot be absolutely certain that it matches the original. Despite these limitations, there are two things the remaining footage allows us to assume: the film follows the temporality and some formal elements of other contemporary 'urban symphonies'; and its structure oscillates between the narratives of the making of two different editions: the edition produced the previous day, and circulating 'today' (so to speak), and that being produced 'today' to be circulated 'tomorrow'. On the other hand, the film, premiered in 1928, was originally called *Diário de Notícias*. I will keep the working title given to it at the archive to distinguish the titles of film and newspaper in my own text.

6. This can be traced back to the origins of modern newspapers in the nineteenth century, before the emergence of information as it would be later defined, when daily newspapers were basically vehicles for classified advertising.

7. In her analysis of *Berlin: Symphony of a Great City*, Sarah Jilani shows a similar moment where modern communication sets the tempo of urban production: 'When the clock strikes eight, the film focuses on the beginnings of the business day. As telephones, typewriters, account books and filing cabinets are readied, the large modern bureaucracies are set in motion. Two secretaries begin tapping away, and with that intra-framic prompt, an inter-framic visual rhythm similar to the factory sequence begins. This time, it is driven by the hyper-efficiency of modern communication. As the sheer simultaneity of this communication is matched by rhythmic montage, the kino-eye and our own is finally overwhelmed by a spiral' (Jilani 2013).

8. Alan J. Lee shows the importance these figures had in the development of the popular press in England: 'Street news-selling was an old tradition. Every public place had its newsboy, even before 1855, but it expanded enormously after the appearance of the cheap daily, and especially of the cheap evening paper' (Lee 1976: 65).

9. The development of railways and train transportation allowed distant places to feel they were sharing the same news (that is, the same sense of novelty) as the centre where the news was produced: 'there was a time when the tiny London News-letter was very patiently expected in the provinces, reaching its destination in days or weeks … Now each of the quick morning-trains drops its bundles of damp letterpress at every station … Travel where you will on the iron network, you can never lag many hours behind the times' (Rubery 2009: 3).

10. 'The nation's contraction into a metropolis … conversely appeared as an expansion of the metropolis; by establishing transport lines to ever more outlying areas, the metropolis tended to incorporate the entire nation' (Schivelbusch 1986: 35).

11. Given my initial disclaimer about the remaining reel of the film, we have good reasons to think that the night sequences were indeed at the end of the film's first version, as this would match the narrative structure of most urban symphonies.

12. *Diário de Notícias*, 19 November 1919, p.1.

13. *Diário de Notícias*, 30 March 1924, p.2.

14. *Diário de Notícias*, 30 March 1924, p.2.

15. *Diário de Notícias*, 30 March 1924, p.2.

16. Patrick Collier found in the English magazine *Nation and Atheneaum* a similar type of discourse on journalism and its feuilletons. The quotation, from the early 1920s, is anonymous: 'so, about thirty years ago, the "New Journalism" was born. Headlines, scareheads, "snappy pars", and "stunts" took the place of literature, serious news, and discussion. The note of papers rose from modulated reason to the yowl of an American baseball match, calculated not to convince but to paralyze the opponent. Pictures appeared, with adjectival commendations: "A Delightful Photo of a Charming Little Hostess"… The change has been so complete that one no longer notices anything about it'. Collier's following remark reinforces this anonymous proximity to Castro's and Dantas's own critiques: 'As we shall see, several terms of this critique are paradigmatic, among them the equation of the deplored newspaper and the feminization of its content (note the Charming Little Hostess caption) and the sense of degraded political discourse' (Collier 2006: 12).

17. The First World War was seen by many contemporaries as an active participant – as both cause and consequence – in a generalized process of language corruption; see esp. Sherry's discussion of 'the journalistic turn' (Sherry 2003: 32–47).

18. It is interesting – but hopefully not surprising at this stage of my analysis – that one of the best accounts of this power relation should be found in film analysis. Laura Mulvey also identifies the 'split between active/male and passive/female' as the representational outcome of 'a world ordered by sexual imbalance': 'the determining male gaze projects its fantasy on to the female form which is styled accordingly. In their traditional exhibitionist role women are simultaneously looked at and displayed, with their appearance coded for strong visual and erotic impact so that they can be said to connote to-be-looked-at-ness' (Mulvey 1975: 11).

19. Ferro's move is an interesting example of what W.J.T. Mitchell calls 'ekphrastic hope', 'the claim that [written signifiers] *do* take on iconic characteristics, achieving verbal artifacts that "resemble" at some level the visual form they address' (Mitchell 1994: 158). Ekphrasis, 'the verbal representation of visual representation', deals with

the same questions at stake in these feuilletons, as narratives struggling to become images while reducing reality – and women in particular – to an image: 'If a woman is "pretty as a picture" (namely, silent and available to the gaze), it is not surprising that pictures will be treated as feminine objects in their own right' (Mitchell 1994: 163).

20. Interestingly, as we have seen, this drive towards images by the written word was felt by journalism before the popularization of cinema. Kate Campbell identified some early twentieth-century discourses that are very close to my argument: '"the journalistic eye is now of far greater importance than the journalistic pen" ... – not so much in respect of illustrations as such as the way in which the visual and other senses were permeating daily journalistic prose' (Campbell 2000: 42, quoting a source from the early twentieth century).

21. *Diário de Lisboa*, 28 March 1922, p.2.

Chapter 5

The Body of Literature

The classic codes of journalism are very strict in the distinction between news and fiction. Journalism should remain close to what can be verified without interfering much in it. When journalists like João Ameal and António Ferro promised to write Chiado or to organize Lisbon's temporality, we know that to a certain extent they were just putting on a literary pose. In this sense, the most modernist thing about their magazines, or the journalistic work of modernist reporters in general, was a certain acceleration of an already old realist trope according to which – as we have seen with Júlio César Machado's characters in *A vida em Lisboa* – there were no differences between discourses of fiction and the narrative of reality newspapers were supposed to produce. Traditionally, writers rather than journalists explored this blurred area between fiction and reality. Fiction often tried to use the mundane to its advantage, by incorporating the authority of real things. When António Ferro, facing the scandal unleashed by one of his plays, *Mar alto* ('High sea'), guaranteed that '*Mar alto* was written by life' and that 'it often wandered through Chiado' (Ferro 1924: 11), he was precisely trying to use that authority to protect himself as an author writing about sensitive matters. However, the suspicion that what newspapers published was not far from fiction could be very damaging to the credibility of journalism.

To a certain extent, the temptation felt by reporters to be creative was still a question of literary status. When Afonso de Bragança sketched his distinction between 'journalist-literates' and 'literate-journalists' inside newspapers,[1] many journalists were starting to react against the rule of anonymity that prevailed in the press. The profession was growing, with more people contributing to each edition, which made it hard to identify even the most stylistically autonomous and those with literary ambitions. In these circumstances, the tendency to stress personal style was reinforced, and sensationalism, as the most immediately recognizable literary technique of journalists, became a token of authorship. The moment when the narratives of reportage seemed to prevail over the events narrated should thus be read in the context of a struggle between reporters and between newspapers.

The birth of *Diário de Lisboa* in 1921 was seen by many as the modernist version, or moment, of that tumultuous style of journalism already familiar to readers in *O Século*'s recklessness regarding events and in the impulse given by Augusto de Castro to *Diário de Notícias* after 1919. The most distinctive characteristic in the work of the young modernist journalists emerging in public with *Diário de Lisboa* was a new genre of interviews where the reporter's permanent interference in the dialogue often made them more visible than the person interviewed.[2] This was where the trouble started. On 26 September 1921, one young reporter, Artur Portela (the author of 'Asas trágicas', where he cleverly narrates a plane crash), arranged an interview with the famous actor Nascimento Fernandes. Through 'The Life of Nascimento Fernandes On and Off the Stage', readers gained access to Fernandes's intimate secrets, such as the ways he spent the large amounts of money he earned, all the women he had had affairs with and his very harsh views on impresarios. Next day, *Diário de Lisboa* published a letter where the actor complained that everything the reporter had written had been said in confidence. Two months later, on 30 November, Portela wrote an article, 'Newspapers and Newspapermen – How to Do a Modern Interview', where he implicitly justified his indiscretion with Nascimento Fernandes and explicitly used literary categories to define the interview as a genre based on dramatization, and where careful depictions of setting and gesture would allow journalists to unmask the depths of an interviewee's personality and the secrets of their life: 'details are everything; not what the excellent guest said, but what he didn't want to say' (Portela 1921: 5). In consequence, he proudly concluded, journalism becomes 'indiscretion' and 'imagination'.

This was a provocation, of course, and, as such, still part of an attitude that reporters like Portela presented as modernist.[3] But what should interest us here is the way in which this kind of interference could jeopardize the trust of readers, for if reporters claimed the right to imagine things, then readers might as well wonder if anything at all had in fact happened the way reporters narrated it. This was even more dramatic when the muddle between real events and the imagination of reporters was not as explicit as in the episode involving Artur Portela and Nascimento Fernandes. For even in reports that did not raise questions of credibility, newspaper readers often had to deal with literary challenges that were very close to those presented by fiction: interviews created characters and reports developed plots in narratives whose structure was similar to novels.

This is the perspective through which I would like to introduce the journalistic coverage of the murder of the actress Maria Alves. The truth about her death in 1926 depended to a large extent on the way reporters handled the event. Conversely, by reading reports closely, we can try to reconstitute what was required of the reader to give meaning to the mystery. This case becomes particularly useful to my analysis because it allows us to take a step further from the indiscreet take on an actor's life to the violent death of an actress, and thus we can revisit several of the questions raised in previous chapters in relation to a single episode. In fact, issues like the frontier between private and public and the objectification of the female body were, as we have seen, particularly significant topics in the drive of reporters towards using reportage as fiction. Time, on the other hand, was key to the structure of journalistic narrative. In the case of the press coverage of the murder of Maria Alves, the unfolding of reports over several weeks – as in the narrative of Coutinho and Cabral's transatlantic flight – rigorously demonstrates how periodization was journalism's specific way of inventing reality by making it daily or, like António Ferro with his magazine, weekly.

The Murder of Maria Alves

On the night of 30 March 1926, a woman's dead body was found in the middle of a dark street in one of Lisbon's most infamous quarters. While the morning edition of *O Século* was still wondering if it had been a crime, in a short note with a discreet reference to the girl's youth and beauty, and her hair cut 'à la garçonne',[4] *Diário de Lisboa* not only identified the body in the afternoon as being that of the famous Maria Alves, but immediately offered an explanation: that this had been a job of 'apaches', underground slang for robbers who strangled their victims.[5] Anyone who read more than one of Lisbon's daily newspapers the next day would nevertheless have been puzzled by the many questions and few and contradictory answers in circulation: was there money involved? Some people had heard that the victim had been carrying a large sum of money with her. Was it a robbery? *O Século* said no, as there were no traces of violence, whereas *Diário de Notícias* and *Diário de Lisboa* maintained it was, and mentioned marks on the body attributed to the violent removal of jewellery. Was it a crime of passion? Was she killed in a car? Could it have been a heart attack? After all, she did seem to have a cardiac condition.

On 2 April, *Diário de Lisboa*'s report dramatically introduced readers to the crime scene with a vivid picture of its 'reprehensible aspects':

'by night, electricity wires are frequently cut – and our readers can imagine what follows'.[6] That day *O Século* also came up with a sexual angle: 'it had to be' a lover – three days was enough for the murder thesis to be unconsciously taken for granted – but as Maria Alves apparently had two of them, the reporter added with a hint of malice, the question was whether it was the actress's public companion, Augusto Gomes, a famous impresario in Lisbon's theatre, or a mysterious gentleman friend from Porto.[7] Meanwhile, *Diário de Notícias* insisted that robbery had been the murderer's motivation. It is not clear if the day of the funeral, 3 April, signalled a truce in the intense speculation triggered by the press reports, which had been promised as a sign of respect for the victim. In general, for once, newspapers did focus on the grief of the family, and in particular that of Augusto Gomes. But this also meant that the impresario somehow came to occupy centre stage in the case. For the time being, although no one was being explicit about it, the ongoing controversy around robbery or passion as the motives for the crime was gradually becoming a discussion about Gomes's guilt or innocence. This is what transpires from a close reading of details between the lines of daily reports for an entire week (rather than something I can explicitly quote): some hypotheses, expressions and names disappeared, while others became insistently reiterated. Without a clear idea of what happened – and especially of the strategy guiding police investigation – readers too had to navigate their way through loose details and subtle repetitions.

In any case, something already familiar to us had become very clear only a week after the crime: the details of the investigation and the public's response to the crime had taken the place of Maria Alves's death in the priorities of journalists and in the content of the news. Newspapers insistently criticized the obsession with the murder, to which they were obviously contributing themselves, and the general atmosphere of suspicion that was poisoning everyday life in Lisbon. But what most annoyed journalists was the eagerness shown by people to get involved and to act as detectives, or reporters. The police had meanwhile made some arrests, which enhanced the circulation of rumours and further reinforced the competition between *Diário de Notícias* and *O Século*. While *Diário de Notícias* asked for patience and called on the public to trust the detectives, *O Século* was clearly contributing to public tension by suggesting as soon as 3 April that the police were 'asleep', and expressed regret for the 'Five Lost Days' (the number of days that had passed since the crime) in a front page headline two days later.[8]

Just as with the flight to Brazil in 1922, *O Século* tried to make its own theories coincide with its idea of how public opinion saw the case, while

Diário de Notícias remained closer to the perspective of the authorities. So, it was as if *Diário de Notícias* wanted to represent the nation by reproducing the discourse of power, whereas *O Século* engaged in a less mediated relation with readers, here treated as the people itself. In the latter's demand (in its 'Five Lost Days' editorial) that the police should interpret 'the feeling of the whole country's population … arrest who should be arrested, and follow every clue instead of stubbornly sticking with just one',[9] readers would not find hard to infer an accusation against Augusto Gomes. Either way, the joint action of the press had made the murder of Maria Alves a national case (with contributions, often quoted by Lisbon's newspapers, from the press in Porto).

Less than one week after the crime, *O Século* seemed to argue, everything that needed to be investigated had been, and the time had come to deliver justice. Conversely, when *Diário de Notícias* dismissed the case by dropping its coverage to page two on 5 April and reiterated its support for the police ('We are still confident that the police will do their job and won't be influenced by the impatience of the sceptics'), its action was in fact a critique of *O Século*, which had become, in the pages of its rival, the symptom of an attitude one could find throughout the entire city before the crime was committed: 'Factions have been formed, detectives appear at every corner, everyone makes accusations and points to criminals, everyone knows details that explain the crime, there is no one in Lisbon, smart or dumb, who doesn't think he can shed the light on this case'.[10]

By the beginning of the second week, only *Diário de Notícias* and the police seemed unconvinced by the argument that Augusto Gomes was guilty. Implicitly, all the other newspapers did everything they could to reinforce a silent agreement with the public about the case. 'The police are convinced that Augusto Gomes has nothing to do with the death of Maria Alves' was *Diário de Lisboa*'s way of suggesting that what the police were trying to deny, a hypothesis nowhere legible in written words, had already been established in the familiar vox populi formed between newspapers and readers.[11] *O Século*, whose daily publication of evidence and testimony against Augusto Gomes went as far back as Maria Alves's own written declaration before she died that 'this bum will kill me',[12] seemed more straightforward. And yet, the accusation that 'the police keep embarrassing Mr Augusto Gomes' published on 6 April suggests that gossip had taken over: in order to rid Gomes of all suspicion, the police should call him in for questioning. The request was presented on his behalf, for if 'it is possible, … even probable, that he might be innocent',[13] the police had no alternative but to dispel an accusation that had already become a verdict on the streets.

On 8 April, *O Século* made its boldest step yet in its attempt to influence the course of events. At a moment when investigations seemed to have reached an impasse, and while *Diário de Lisboa* kept the coverage going with 'empty' information – 'another day lost in useless investigations'[14] – and *Diário de Notícias*'s own investigations were now limited to deconstructing *O Século*'s thesis, the latter tried to mobilize the whole country – assuming the presumptive role of the people's tribune – by launching a public subscription for a reward for those with information that would lead to the killer of Maria Alves. It is easy to imagine how this initiative could have triggered a manhunt by the public, intensifying its obsession with the case even further. The police reacted quickly, but ambiguously. On the same day, Augusto Gomes was arrested, which seemed to contradict the official line taken up to that moment. *O Século* immediately boasted about this supposed confirmation of what had been its suspicion from the start, whereas *Diário de Notícias* tried to embark on what seemed to be a new phase in the case by arguing that Gomes's arrest only proved how right they had been in trusting the police in the first place. *Diário de Lisboa*, which had meanwhile been wavering between both theses, complicated things further by insinuating that the police were merely bluffing, and their strategy would leave the real criminals unsuspecting, thus making it easier to catch them.

Be as it may, Gomes's arrest – and he was immediately released after interrogation – seemed to have worked. Those who protested his innocence assumed that his name had been cleared, while the accusers were forced to diminish their attacks on the police. More importantly, tension waned for a few days. Not that the newspapers dropped the case, of course, but the display of power seemed to have convinced the press that the authorities were on top of things and that it would be just a matter of time – and hence patience – until the mystery was solved. During this pause, *O Século* bided its time exploring other aspects of the case, in particular the family life of Maria Alves, her abandonment of her daughter and the poverty of her parents. In another sensational move, the newspaper publicly assumed, on behalf of the family, all legal expenses related to the case.

On 11 April, while everyone was still waiting for the police to come up with a solution, *Diário de Notícias* published a report of what seemed to be just a casual incident, but one which would nonetheless eventually lead to the murderer.[15] The newspaper knew that a taxi driver had consulted a lawyer for advice on how to handle a serious incident that had occurred in his taxi on the night of 30 March. When the reporter investigated this rather vague piece of information, he managed to uncover the man's secret: one of his clients had killed a woman in his taxi that night and made him get rid of the body. That client was Augusto Gomes. The police took the information seriously and arrested the taxi driver. Next day, 12 April, while *O Século*'s asked in a headline 'Is the Mystery Solved?',[16] *Diário de Notícias* celebrated its own story of the previous day as an example of what the 'the true mission of the press' should look like, in an implicit critique to *O Século*'s hasty behaviour throughout the whole affair.[17]

If proof were still needed as to the extent to which journalistic investigation had taken over the coverage of the event, what came next surely provided it. According to the newspapers, the outcome of the case had nothing to do with justice and the arrest of the putative murderer. As the affair had turned into a journalistic story, the verdict should also legitimize the most persuasive narrative of the events. On 13 April, *O Século* claimed a 'great victory' for its investigation, as 'the police seem definitively interested in the hypothesis presented from day one' by the newspaper.[18] As evidence for this claim, the reporter quoted the reaction of a police lieutenant to the closing of the case: 'congratulations to *O Século*, which has just won an important press battle and rendered a great service to the country'.[19] In a similar move, *Diário de Notícias* claimed victory for itself, citing the testimony of the man who had initially yielded the information about the taxi driver's visit to a lawyer (though not what that visit was about). When the reporter interviewed him, he was puzzled:

– Isn't what our newspaper has published the truth?

– It is, indeed! But I am amazed because I don't understand how you discovered the information. I am perplexed. I'm sure I didn't commit any indiscretion! How did you 'dream' about this?

– It's a professional secret … Would you like to put our information right in any way?

– No, sir. It's precisely because it is absolutely correct that I am as astonished as I am. You are unbelievable! Who would imagine anything like it?![20]

At this point, all the attention of the press focused on journalistic procedures, its investigation techniques and the structure of reportage. The movements of the police or indeed the events of the crime itself were by now a distant concern in a battle between reporters.[21] *O Século* responded to the boast made by *Diário de Notícias* about its professional methods by assuring its readers that 'it was not because of a hint but as the result of reasoned thought and self-conscious reportage that *O Século* held the only logical version of the crime'.[22] Whereas its rival had had a simple stroke of luck, *O Século*, whose reporters were the 'most famous and experienced', had consistently worked with the thesis that would ultimately 'enlighten both the public and the confused spirit of the police'. The justification for overriding police authority and claiming the role of public guide was a combination of expertise (the experience of reporters) and cognitive skills (the logical interpretation of what had happened). The question of whether Augusto Gomes was guilty or innocent became the object of a dispute between journalistic styles. What really mattered were not so much the details of and motivation for the crime but the ways in which the press managed to establish a convincing relation between the production of reliable information and the publication of persuasive narratives. In other words, more than the truth as such, what seemed to matter was the means of producing it.

This focus on the procedure by which the narrator disclosed the structure of the narrative process should not be seen as a sign of the power journalists had to manipulate facts but, on the contrary, the guarantee that their competence was based on reflexivity. The violent attacks launched by *Diário de Notícias* against *O Século* after the case stressed the direct link between the 'shameful methods of falsity and lies' used by its rival and 'its incompetence and bravado'.[23] Dishonesty, in other words, or the lack of transparency in relation to methods of investigation, was directly equated with lack of competence. *Diário de Notícias* was especially aggrieved by the 'insulting collection in the community' organized by *O Século* to reward whoever found the murderer. This had been an illegitimate interference, the accusation went on, and, as such, an active contribution to the atmosphere of suspicion that surrounded the event. And yet it was not just the attack itself that was exceptionally violent (*O Século* was treated as an 'excrescence' and 'pathological abortion'). The terms used by *Diário de Notícias* to explain its technical superiority over other newspapers also seemed to take its own reporting techniques to a much higher level of interference: 'our information services are designed and organized in a way that makes it almost impossible to let anything, even what seems unimportant, pass unnoticed'.[24] The mechanisms of interference boasted by *Diário de Notícias* and *O Século* thus seem the exact opposite of one another. For, whereas *O Século* interfered by trying to mobilize its readers around the event via its pages, *Diário de Notícias* was much more insidious as the design and organization of its informative structure seems to suggest that the whole of society was under its control. The newspaper presented itself as a panopticon.[25]

We have already had an opportunity to verify what this apparatus looked like in *Como se Faz um Número do Diário de Notícias*, where the mechanisms used to capture the flow of information were shown.

And yet, we should remain sceptical about this power to control every urban move and consider how this image of efficiency was still part of the press's permanent effort of self-promotion. If newspapers were able to be this vigilant, this was surely due less to their ability to stretch their tentacles across the whole of urban space than their capacity to organize the temporality of everyday narratives. The rhetoric of control, in this sense, worked as a complement to Ferro's ambition to invent reality. Newspaper periodization not only set the rhythm through which narratives unfolded, but also encompassed everything as it happened. In this sense, although the daily rhythm of publication was what established the dramatic quality through which readers experienced the event, this was just the threshold of journalistic temporality. The press, in order to truly control the events, could not just follow them. This would leave it too vulnerable to temporal contingency. Somehow, then, after having shown the events, journalism had to find temporal mechanisms to stop, step outside and gain the necessary distance from events to be able to explain them.

As the absence of any description of what exactly had happened inside the taxi on the night of 30 March may suggest, after the race for truth was over and scores between the competitors were settled, there was a need for something or some agency to explain, that is, to show, how things had really happened. This was the role played by weekly publications, and it gave the opportunity for yet another modernist reporter, Reinaldo Ferreira, the mythical Reporter X, to display his investigative skills and journalistic technique in the pages of a popular illustrated magazine, *ABC*. Ferreira had also championed the 'automobile thesis' from the start. Like his colleagues at *O Século*, he believed that Maria Alves had been killed in a car and dumped in the street where she was found, rather than robbed and killed locally. However, the weekly rhythm of the magazine – *ABC* published its first edition after the crime on 8 April – gave Ferreira two advantages over those journalists who proposed the same theory in daily newspapers: time and images.

Throughout that initial week, as he would explain in his first piece on the case, 'Two Hypotheses on Maria Alves's Murder', he had the opportunity (that is, the time) to spend 'two nights in a row at the crime scene, at the hour of the crime (no agent has had this experience yet)' and to verify 'that it was impossible to kill someone, let alone to drag a corpse in that direction' (Ferreira 1926a: 4). The report was illustrated with three images: a map of the neighbourhood with the street where Maria Alves was found; and two photos, one with the body being carried by two men (the robbery thesis) and the other with that same body being thrown from a car into the street (see Figure 5.1). The images were there to confirm what the reporter had written as if their indexical value – a real body photographed while being dragged and dumped – could prevail over the fact that they were just simulations.[26] However, images like these were more than mere illustrations of the written text, for they were part of a report that was less the narrative of an event than of the reporter's own speculations about how things were supposed to have happened. In this sense, the pictures were evidence of Reporter X's engagement with the event: 'when I knew about the event, as a good sniper-reporter, I immediately got going with some of my colleagues. A car took me to the crime scene'; Reporter X could then become a participant in his own right, and pretend to be 'replacing our detectives when these can't or don't want to do their job' (Ferreira 1926a: 4). Here too, his report was strictly about the investigation of the crime, rather than the crime as such.

When, a week later, and following the taxi driver's testimony, the case was closed with Augusto Gomes confessing everything to the police, Reinaldo Ferreira also celebrated his journalistic triumph, but over the police rather than other journalists: 'Augusto Gomes killed Maria Alves in a car ... Whose antenna received this revelation? The Police? No. The press. Who acted? Reporters' (Ferreira 1926b: 4). As before, newspapers had been the true scene of the event and journalists the main protagonists of the narrative. In this case, the control assumed by reporters was so forceful that a complete reversal of the journalistic order of discourse can be said to have taken place: almost one month after his confession, Augusto Gomes, already in prison, asked for an interview in an urge to explain to Reinaldo Ferreira – and thus the public – how he himself had experienced those dramatic days in early April:

'The biggest emotion, the one that seemed to strangle me, was caused by you. Yes – by you! It occurred when I opened *ABC* and read your story and the photographic reconstruction of the crime. Bowled over, I cried: "This man knows everything! This man has been spying on me!"' And then, putting his heavy hand on my shoulders, he concluded: 'You saw me killing Maria, didn't you?' (Ferreira 1926c: 5)[27]

As we can imagine, Reinaldo Ferreira had not been in that alley on the night of 30 March. He had not really seen Augusto Gomes opening the car door and, with the engine still running, dumping the body of his lover after having strangled her in a fit of jealous rage. But that was beside the point, especially if we consider how reporters were shown to embody those powers of observation that, according to *Diário de Notícias*, made it almost impossible to let anything go without notice. Maybe they were absent when things happened, but they could always come back and revive those events in some other edition. In this sense, the observing power of reporters, especially those who were compared to cameras and

AS DUAS HIPOTESES DO CRIME DE
MARIA ALVES
Pelo REPORTER X

O crime de Maria Alves é um dêsses folhetins que ficariam bem em qualquer roda-pé civilisado. No nosso meio pacato, provinciano e amortecido, toma ele proporções de acontecimento nacional. Seria um crime dos muitos que os nossos detectives, sem bigodeira, porque a raparam, e sem bengalão, porque o reservam de alicate, de *tira-dentes* nos seus gabinetes do Govêrno Civil, — que os nossos detectives, repito, deixariam armazenado nos arquivos, num cemiterio de poeira (como o do capitão Vaquinhas, como o do chinês, como tantos outros) — se a opinião publica, sobressaltada, enervada, não exigisse a descoberta dos assassinos, como o publico do Principe Real exigia, noutros tempos, a morte do cinico e do traidor e a reabilitação dos inocentes.

A noticia encheu, a transbordar, as colunas das gazetas: numas, com ancias de luz; noutras, com demasiada boa fé e demasiada confiança no faro dos nossos *Sherloches*, que lazem da *Chic*, de mistura com as coristas do Eden, laboratorio policial. Os senhores sabem como o crime foi relatado. Numa madrugada alguem chamou uma policia de guarda para acudir a uma mulher caída de borco na Rua Francisco Foreiro, à esquina do Regueirão. E a mulher golfava sangue ainda. E o coração ainda palpitava. Não era ainda um cadaver. Um automovel. O hospital. A mesa de marmore da Morgue.

Quem era? Quem não era? Ás onze horas da manhã dava-se um nome à morta. Maria Alves, corista feita actriz pela amisade dum emprezario, que triunfara sobre a ribalta, que conhecera o estralejar das palmas, os coloridos berrantes dos cartazes — e que, dotada dum genio herdado da padeira de Aljubarrota, se degladiava, frequentemente, com o protector de um dia. Dizia-se até que, por ciumes, ela larçara às aguas do Atlantico, numa noite de viagem para o Brasil, uma corista rival do seu amor. Sobre este enigma lançaram-se todas as areias do Nilo, até o abafarem por completo.

Quando a noticia chegou ao meu conhecimento, eu, reporter-franco-atirador, pus-me em campo com varios companheiros meus. Um automovel me conduziu ao local do crime. Havia ainda, sombreando as pedras da rua, o sangue

O grafico do local do crime, paragem do electrico e residencia da victima que vem tornar um pouco inverosimil a hipotese policial

da actriz. Por essas manchas vi, nitidamente, que o corpo fôra lançado do meio da rua para a valeta.

Depois fui a casa de Maria Alves. As visinhas choramingavam. Só sabiam que, de manhã, uma pequena que estava à janela, tinha visto aproximar-se Augusto Gomes — o emprezario, outrora prctector da vitima, — que vinha em direcção do falso-lar. Eram dez horas da manhã. As dez e meia o emprezario batia à porta cêsses visinhos, mostrando o assombro por vêr a cama intacta. Saíu. E, cinco minutos depois, voltava, gritando que tinham morto a *sua* Maria. Como o soubera? Lera nos jornais. Os jornais diziam, de facto, que fôra encontrada uma mulher estendida, proximo duma valeta, cujo nome se ignorava.

Fui à Morgue. Na Morgue havia o cuidado de não deixar entrar os jornalistas. Que sinais apresentava a morta? Feridas na testa, devido a uma queda de chofre, uma mancha negra no braço e a rcupa esfarrapada. E na garganta? Nem uma revelação de estrangulamento. E o misterio dessa morte, mereceu, poucas horas depois, da boca dum chefe de investigação, a fantasia que and.u propagando pelos cafés que ela fôra vitima duma navalhada no ventre . . .

Entretanto o emprezario Augusto Gomes (os senhores lembram-se, não é verdade? Esse homem de teatro que o Destino fez testemunho involuntario de tantas tragedias, como, por exemplo, a morte de Machado Santos e o incendio do barracão onde tinha uns scenarios pertencentes ao emprezario José Loureiro? —) foi chamado à policia. E contou que, na vespera, fô·a cear com Maria Alves, a acompanhara ao Maria Vitoria, e ali se encontraram com Oscar Ribeiro, emprezario tambem, da *tournée* ao Porto, donde ela regressara pouco antes. Oscar Ribeiro, que estava cm atrezo de alguns *cachés*, declarou que não podia entregar-lhe imediatamente a soma em debito.

— Não te apoquentes ! — diz Augusto Gomes. — Eu adianto-te os mil e quinhentos escudos — e Oscar Rbeiro liquidá-los-ha depois comigo.

Este gesto é tanto mais notavel, quanto é certo que, publicamente, as finanças do ilustre emprezario estavam abaladas. Ainda ha pouco, na empreza do Teatro Nacional, Augusto Gomes tivera de fazer um emprestimo de quatro contos.

Desceram os dois a Avenida. Noite de verão. Noite de optimismo. Noite excitante de optimismos cu pessimismos para o temperamento dos dois namorados. Augusto Gomes acompanhou a actriz até à Rua da Betesga. Para quê? Para que ela tomasse o penultimo carro do Arco do Cego. Imprudencia! A actriz chamava a atenção. No seu saco havia um conto e novecentos escudos!

E ela lá foi pelo labirinto penumbroso das ruas que irradiam da Rua da Betesga até Santa Barbara.

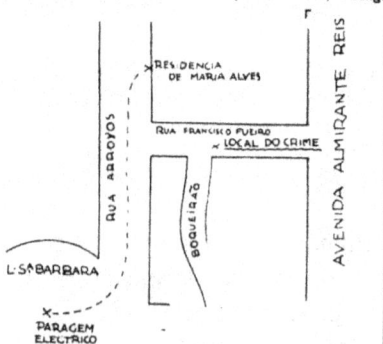

Figure 5.1: *ABC*, 8 April 1926. Biblioteca Nacional de Portugal.

Depois . . . depois . . . Um cadaver — um cadaver ser.i joias, sem saco . . . e sem casaco. Onde ?

Apeou-se — e era logico que o fizesse — no Largo de Santa Barbara. Os ultimos carros vão sempre apinhados — e, como a essa hora, — 1,50 da manhã, pouco mais ou menos, — já não passam os electricos de Almirante Reis — muita gente se apeou, provavelmente, nesse largo. Pelo grafico que acompanha este artigo vêr-se-ha que o caminho era recto até à residencia da actriz na Rua de Arroios. A essa hora e à saida do *ultimo carro* (e eu já vivi para esses lados) a rua tem certo movimento. Contudo o cadaver aparece fóra da recta logica, num desvio, na Rua Francisco Foreiro. Ora, para ter sido assassinada na Rua de Arroios e para que os assassinos a levassem para o local onde foi encontrada — era necessario que ela tivesse ido a pé, fóra das horas de paragem do carro, quando a rua está deserta . . .

Em que ficamos ?

Admitindo a hipotese de um assalto de gravateiros — a opinião dos peritos não o prova e a nossa tambem não —, veem os detalhes do pseudo-movel a desmenti-la. Os gravateiros são os mais profissionais dos criminosos. A vitima aparece sem aneis, sem saco de dinheiro — e sem brincos que *foram tirados cuidadosamente e sem o casaco de peles.*

Estes dois pormenores, que teem todo o ar de uma *despista* — são inverosimeis. Estive, duas noites seguidas, no local do crime, *à hora do crime* (nenhum agente fez ainda esta experiencia) e vi que era impossivel, não só matar, como arrastar para ali o cadaver. Porquê ? Porque, áquela hora, o movimento é grande ; razoavel é a iluminação e existe todas as noite — e até na noite do crime (a policia ignora-o ; e eu sei o) idilios amorosos em redor.

Se não ha possibilidade do crime ter sido cometido naquele local ; se não ha possibilidade do ca 'aver ter sido arrastado — muito menos teria o criminoso vagares para desaparafusar os brincos e para levar o casaco. Sobre os brincos existe uma explicação policial: que foi a propria *granata* que os arrancou das orelhas. *Laissez passer . . .* E o casaco? Qual é o criminoso profissional, que, depois de encher os bolcos com joias e dinheiro, facilmente escondiveis, leva um casaco de peles, casaco de senhora, dependurado no braço, chamando sobre si a atenção de todos?

Não e não! O crime deve ter sido cometido ou numa casa ou num auto. E esta ultima hipotese deve ser verdadeira. E admitindo-a — deve admitir-se que, quem a atraiu a

A HIPOTESE POLICIAL: Maria Alves, assaltada pelos «gravateiros», segundo os processos habitualmente empregados por estes criminosos. Foto de simulacro «A B C» feita no local (Rua Francisco Foreiro) e à hora (duas da manhã) a que o crime devia ter sido cometido

uma casa ou a um auto, devia merecer à victima toda a confiança.

Alem disso, o tempo que vae da saida de Maria Alves da rua da Betesga até ao encontro do seu cadaver é de quarenta minutos — que adensa mais ainda o misterio. O sr. Augusto Gomes viu-a meter no carro? Bem. Nesse caso ela apeou-se pouco depois para tomar um auto . . .

Mas ha mais. Ha a minha duvida sobre a verdade do estrangulamento — e para ela rogo a atenção dos peritos. O electricista que a encontrou afirma que o coração da actriz batia ainda. Se batia — vivia. Ora os senhores lembram-se decerto do caso de Shackspear no *Otelo*. Otelo asfixia Desdemona, abafando-a com almofadões. Depois de a libertar — ela discursa, fala do seu amor — e morre. E' um erro. Se ela discursou — é porque poude falar. Se falou, respirou. Se respira vive — e se vive está salva — porque não chegou a dar-se a asfixia. E' o mesmo que sucede com Maria Alves. Se o coração da actriz palpitava ainda, é porque vivia; se vivia, é porque o estrangulamento não a asfixiara. Se não a asfixiara — ela não podia morrer depois em consequencia dele.

F. agora vem o reporter passar a interrogar a policia. Porque não selou imediatamente a casa da victima . . . e das pessoas suspeitas? Não me desmentem porque eu . . . e quatro colegas meus estivemos lá, dentro de casa, quinze horas depois de se saber quem era o cadaver da rua Francisco Foreiro. Porque razão a policia, tão severa e tão prompta a pôr sob incomunicabilidade qualquer operario ou ladrão vulgar — não guardou — sob a sua alçada, os suspeitosos do crime? Porque motivo a investigação não foi entregue a alguem que estivesse fóra dos boatos de *fraternidade* politica que correram por ahi ?

Estou quasi a dar um conselho : e de pedir á policia do Porto para tomar parte na investigação. Ela tem-se mostrado, neste caso, tão habil e tão imparcial . . .

REPORTER X

A HIPOTESE DOS REPORTERS: Maria Alves assassinada dentro dum auto e projectada dum auto para rua. Foto «A B C», feita no local (Rua Francisco Foreiro) e à hora (duas da manhã) a que devia ter sido cometido o crime

automobiles, went beyond the panopticon: the power to show everything did not depend on the ability to have one's presence felt everywhere at all times, but to reduce the scope of what could happen – of what could become an event – to what could be framed in words and images within a journalistic narrative.

We have, of course, many reasons to doubt the content of Reinaldo Ferreira's interview with Augusto Gomes – although the latter never contested it. After all, Reporter X was famous for writing about his visits to places, like the Soviet Union, which he had never been to, and his acquaintance with people, such as Mata-Hari, whom he had never met (Ferreira 1926d). Again, what is important was that the story accompanied by a picture of Augusto Gomes side by side with Reinaldo Ferreira – and the caption 'You Saw Me Killing Maria, Didn't You?' – was in fact printed and circulated inside *ABC*'s edition of 13 May. True or false, it became an important part of the narrative of an event kept alive by the press, not only during the days and weeks immediately after it, but also over the following months. The case had a strong impact in the public sphere both because it proved a good opportunity for reporters to show the resources of journalism, as we have seen, and because it involved people from the theatre, with its display of all the related tropes of violence, passion, betrayal and sleaziness. Gradually, reports abandoned the perspective of the journalists – and the urgent rhythm of daily newspapers' temporality – and focused instead on the moral issues raised by the case. When the murderer was exposed and the investigation concluded, attention shifted towards the two figures who comprised the tragic couple and started exploring both Augusto Gomes's criminal past and the intimate life of Maria Alves, the other major figure who had up to that point been almost completely absent from the narrative.[28] In fact, neither the aggression between newspapers nor the anxious turmoil of the investigation contributed as much to the dramatic atmosphere of the case as did the disappearance of the initial act of brutality perpetrated by Augusto Gomes on the body of Maria Alves. When the obsessive engagement with clues and theories finally ceased, the real protagonists in the murder could finally emerge.

The lives of Augusto Gomes and Maria Alves, and in particular the last tragic episode of their love affair, were explored in all its aspects – their unorthodox behaviour and unconventional lifestyle, the sordid details of their sexual relation – and disseminated through dime novels, pamphlets with rough drawings and fado songs with very simple lyrics. The characters' relationship was given a gloomily dramatic quality, and Maria Alves eventually became the victim, the 'trembling little girl' who succumbed to the hands of an 'evil criminal' (Maria n.d.: 6). The biography of Augusto Gomes was meanwhile dissected in many different places – Reinaldo Ferreira wrote a series of articles about him in *ABC* – and his terrible past, comprising fraud, robbery and violence, revealed. Gomes was made responsible for all sorts of accidents and tragedies: burning down a warehouse to collect the insurance money, and the killings of the infamous 'Bloody Night' of 1921, where three renowned republican politicians were killed, were attributed to him. Even more seriously, suspicions were cast about the mysterious deaths of other women he had been romantically involved with.

By the end of the year, and after the trial that sentenced him to deportation to the African colonies, the two reporters in charge of *Diário de Lisboa*'s coverage, Artur Portela and Norberto de Araújo, laid down the case for posterity with the publication of *O crime de Augusto Gomes* ('The crime of Augusto Gomes'). To a certain extent, the book was an attempt to regenerate the image that the public had become familiar with of a man who until that moment was just a lustful and violent person capable of all sorts of crimes. Maria Alves's portrait as the helpless victim, on the other hand, would also suffer a dramatic transformation. The reporters took the trial as an opportunity to humanize Gomes and to point out how excessive his trial by journalism and the public had been: 'every crime committed in Lisbon in the last ten years is now attributed to him. The public hungrily demands more drama, more scandal' (Portela and Araújo 1927: 126). Apparently, however, it also demanded compassion, and the reporters describe a defendant looking older and consumed by remorse. With this new image, all sins of the past seemed not only distant but also somewhat unreal. How could the same man who appeared in court as the loving father of the child he begged, with 'tears in his eyes', 'to pray for him' and 'search in God for the mercy men refused' (Portela and Araújo 1927: 130), how could this man be the monster everyone thought he was? The answer was Maria Alves. Or, better still, the reckless lifestyle and perverted sexuality that their relationship was notorious for. In that relationship, violence was the name of the game, something that Augusto Gomes not only dished out, but to a large extent something that Maria Alves consented to, if not actively desired: 'it was a sordid, ferocious, primitive love, dominated by low instincts. After these epileptic crises, they kissed and made up. The fury multiplied desire – renovated it, satiated it' (Portela and Araújo 1927: 111).

The book concluded with the authors' own moral interpretation, not so much of the murder, but of the reprovable relationship and behaviour of both Augusto Gomes and Maria Alves. The question thus became whether Gomes had sufficient motivation for such violent jealousy or not. After all, Maria Alves was unfaithful, living on the edge of

NO PATEO DO LIMOEIRO
Augusto Gomes (á direita); Reporter X (á esquerda)
— ... O unico remorso da minha vida consiste em te-la abandonado na Via Publica. Cem vidas que ela tivesse, cem vidas que eu lhe tirava...

Reporter X e Augusto Gomes

(Cinco horas no Limoeiro com o assassino de Maria Alves)

Na carta que recebera de Augusto Gomes, que, ao assina-la se adjectivava de «desgraçado»—dizia-me o assassino da Maria Alves.
«Até mesmo aos condenados à morte lhe é dada assistência; e por isso lhe peço o lavor de vir a esta cadeia, ouvir-me»...
E fui. Não era uma entrevista. A situação e o crime de Augusto Gomes não me permitiam entrevista-lo; a minha propria atitude jornalistica, tomada logo a seguir ó tragedia não m'o consentia. Mas se Augusto Gomes queria falar-me—para paz da minha consciencia devia escuta-lo.
Se dissesse que foi sem nervosismo que puchei a sineta macabra do Limoeiro, nessa tarde de sol — mentia! Não conhecia pessoalmente essa figura extranha de criminoso que conseguira, durante quinze dias, sujestionar uma multidão, num lekirismo sobrenatural. Não o conhecia, mas acusara-o de frente, da primeira hora — da hora em que êle, numa estrategia de defesa, ameaçava de morte «quem lhe insultasse a honra, supondo-o autor da morte de Maria Alves.»
Continuara a acusa-lo, para alem da confissão, vasculhando-lhe o passado, procurando uma nepita de luz para as trevas que lhe marginam a vida, como bastidores de crepe. Ele tambem não me conhecia. E neste periodo quantas vezes êle não me vira, em pesadelo, como fantasma a persegui-lo? Quantas vezes não me teria amaldiçoado? Por isso aquele encontro de dois pugilistas que se bateram na negrura — havia, por fôrça, sacudir-nos os nervos, pôr-nos na garganta uma secura de febre.
... Augusto Gomes aparece. No seu rosto não há nem basofias, nem alegrias, nem compungimento. Ha uma serenidade burguesa, uma serenidade que era egual á que exibia quando empresario, quando jogava no teatro como quem joga na roleta. Traja um fato de campo «kaki» amarelo e vem sem colarinho:
— Quem me procura?
Avancei:
— Sou eu.
— ?
— O «Reporter X».
Esperei uma contração, um gesto, uma atitude. Mas não. Augusto Gomes, sereno, tão sereno como se eu fosse um actor ou um baritono à procura de contracto, levanta um pouco a gola para o pescoço nú e pede-me:

— Mil perdões... É a hora da visita... Suplico-lhe que me deixe falar com a minha familia. As duas horas estou à sua disposição...
...... As duas horas volto a chamá-lo; e ele torna a aparecer-me. É outro. Não que a serenidade tivesse sido substituida por qualquer pose. Mas mudou de fato. Vem cuidado; camisa llamante; gravata impecavel. E repetiu:
— Estou à sua disposição.
Não estava. Era eu que estava à disposição dele. Foi ele quem falou sempre. Fechei-me num silencio impressionavel como de celuloide, como um disco de gramofone; como um cliché fotografico.
— Antes de mais nada devo dizer-lhe o seguinte: Não lhe peço misericordia. Sou um criminoso e tenho a noção nitida do meu crime. Apelo só para a sua imparcialidade.
E começou:
— Acusam-me o senhor de ser o assassino de duas mulheres: da minha primeira mulher legitima — Virginia de Jesus ~ e de Piedade Vamos primeiro ao caso de Virginia de Jesus...
Fala sem me desfitar. Nos seus olhos claros, insinuantes, não ha uma esquivança, uma miradela de esguelha; as palpebras fazem prodigios de imobilidade. Se os olhos fossem espelho da alma — a alma de Augusto Gomes seria de arminho ou de cristal puro. Ha só um detalhe que perturba a sua sugestão de simpatia: as mãos — as mãos sapudas, com os dedos polegares curtos, largos na cabeça — mãos de estrangulador. Se ele tivesse morto Maria Alves numa cegueira de ciumes e se Maria Alves tivesse sido o seu unico crime — ele teria obedecido a um estigma imperioso.
E prossegue:
— Minha mulher morreu... porque não queria ser mãe segunda vez. Evoco o testemunho do medico — Dr. Mota — que já morreu. Viviamos então em Aldeia Galega. Era eu director da fabrica Abecassis — logar que é hoje ocupado pelo meu irmão. Tinha raptado uma pequena, Ana Baptista, e que estava tambem para ter um filho. Deviam nascer ambos ao mesmo tempo: o de Virginia e o de Ana. E a minha mulher soube. E não quiz. Quem me trouxe as hervas que a mataram — foi o Eusebio, que fazia ainda recados entre Aldeia Galega e Lisboa. Eusebio, coitado, não sabia... Eu ignorava essa

Figure 5.2: *ABC*, 13 May 1926. Biblioteca Nacional de Portugal.

A B C   Pag. 5

conspiração da minha mulher. Começou a sentir-se mal, muito mal.
Veiu um medico, um medico que já morreu...
— O Dr. Mota?
— Não. Esse ainda vive. Era outro cujo nome ignoro. E ela morreu, coitada. De Virginia tinha eu um filho de dois anos — o Augusto. Ana Baptista tivera, simultaneamente à morte de minha mulher, um petiz. Mandei os dois petizes para a companhia de meu pai. Depois gastei um dinheirão para trazer o cadaver de Virginia para Lisboa — onde está, num coval florido, no Alto de S. João. E fiz-lhe um enterro como ela merecia. Um dinheirão!
E descreveu-me um enterro — um enterro a que ele assistira; acompanhando a morta, atravez do rio, atravez da cidade, chorando saudoso e inconsolavel.
— Mas dizem que a morte da Virginia foi devida a um pontapé brutal que a atirou da escada abaixo, estando ela grávida...
Augusto Gomes é sempre espontaneo nas respostas.
— Calunias. Realmente o juiz recebeu uma carta anonima, denunciando-me. É possivel que essa denuncia se baseasse nas frases que a minha mulher pronunciou no delirio da febre. O medico quis saber os antecedentes da doença — e ela, para ocultar o assunto das tais hervas que o Eusebio lhe trouxera, contou-lhe uma historia de escadas...
— E o medico quem era?...
— O Dr. Mota... o que morreu...
Havia ali uma evidente confusão entre medicos vivos e medicos falecidos. Indaguei:
— E o filho de Ana Batista?
— Ah! Esse morreu...
— Em casa de seu pai?
— Em casa do pai de Ana. Foi uma congestão pulmonar.
Toquei então, directamente, o caso de Piedade. Ele narra:
— Conheci Piedade, quando ainda corista, no Avenida. Era então amante dum camareiro. O meu caracter não suportava uma situação equivoca. E disse-lhe: — Ou eu ou ele! — E ela veiu para a minha companhia. Era a mais antiga de todas — mais antiga do que a Miquelina e do que a Maria Alves.
«Era doente. E eu — não nego — dava-lhe desgostos, muitos desgostos — tudo por causa da Maria. Levou pontas de fogo. Foram seus medicos o Dr. Lopes e Dr. Fradique. Um dia chego a casa, e ela queixou-se-me de tonturas. Caiu, redonda, no meio do chão. Assustei-me. Investiguei.
Ergue os sobrolhos, aproxima mais a cadeira de mim e informa, grave e solene:
— Era cocaina! Era éter! A desgraçada tinha o vicio dos paraisos artificiais. Queria esquecer-se dos desgostos que eu lhe dava — coitada... Até me zanguei!
E vem a seguir a noite da morte:
— Cheguei a casa. Foi ela —como V. Ex.ª diz muito bem— quem me abriu a porta. Depois começou a sentir-se mal... muito mal...
— Como Virginia de Jesus?
— Exactamente. Como Virginia. Suores, febre, o corpo a gelar-se. Procurei um medico. Foram as pequenas do telefone, coitadas, quem me indicaram o Dr. Tudela...
— E a morte foi devida a essa uremia?
— Parece que sim.
— E não admite a hipotese de uma entoxicação que...
— Talvez... quem sabe? A cocaina? O éter?
Corta, rapido a conversa, e refere-se ao filho de Piedade, com exaltação:
— Afirme o senhor que eu abandonei o filho de Piedade — o Armando. É falso! A hora da morte Piedade pediu-me: — Tem dó de meu filho, Augusto. Tem dó dele! — Eu morro... tinha que

ser! Mas do nosso filho... tem dó dele... Não o leves para a Maria Alves...»
«Fiz-lhe a vontade. O Armandinho está com o meu pai.
«E ainda, sobre a Piedade preciso esclarecer um caso: o dos Seguros.
Tosse; recosta-se, e manosinhando muito as palavras, continua:
— Fiz sempre o seguro de todas as minhas amantes. Era para fazer a vontade aos agentes da companhia. O da Piedade foi feito na Garantia. E se esse seguro não foi para diante foi porque me zanguei com os seguradores... E de todas as fermas, era insignificante: oito ou nove contos... Compreende o senhor que eu não ia matar a Piedade por oito ou nove contos!
Foi a altura de eu intervir. Indaguei:
— Nunca lidou com a familia de Piedade?
— Sim. Fui uma vez a Cezimbra, visitar uns parentes.
— Nunca impediu que qualquer parente de Piede te exigisse a autopsia?
— Nunca...
Teatralmente abro a carteira e exibo lhe uma carta que recebera dum primo de Piedade, de Cezimbra, uma carta comprometedora em que me era prometido um documento sensacional.
Inerva-se um pouco Augusto Gomes. Depois retoma a serenidade.
— Esses parentes sao deveras engraçados. Eu nunca os vi... É certo que lhe mandei participar a morte de Piedade. Talvez se retiram a essa paticipação...
E como quem compõe o ultimo capitulo dum romance, declama:
— Faz agora, a 29, um ano que morreu... Fiz-lhe um enterro, coitada, como merecia... Lá está, no Alto de S. João, numa cova coberta de flores... numa cova que eu trato como quem trata um jardim...
— Como a de Virgina de Jesus?
— Igual!
E a seguir, noutro tom:
— E a Miquelina —esta Miquelina é uma santa!— teve a delicadeza de lhe mandar uma coroa. É que ela sabia o valor, a resignação da Piedade. Eram ambas irmãs do martirio — do martirio a que eu as obrigava por causa de Maria. Essa Maria é a minha desgraça. E olhe, quere saber? Maria Alves nem sequer teve a delicadeza de enviar umas rosas a pobre Piedade!

NA ESCADA A' DESPEDIDA
Augusto Gomes (em cima); Reporter X (em baixo)
...« — O senhor viu cometer o crime, não é verdade?...

Eu considerava-me satisfeito. Ele não. Ele quis descrever-me a sua vida com Maria Alves, os misterios da sua morte. E, ora lúgubro, com as veias a incharem-se-lhe—ora comovido, com os olhos a merejarem-se de lagrimas—ora epileptico de violencia, contou-me como a conhecera, corista anonima, na pensão dum Sr. Leal da rua do Carmo; descreve-me as sovas historicas que lhe pregara; os sacrificios que lhe fizera.
— Uma vez, estavamos no Porto e aparece no hotel uma pequena andrajosa, suja, descalça... — «Quem é esta criança? perguntei eu. E Maria explicou: — «E minha filha!» Fui eu quem abriga a mãe a traze-la comnosco para Lisboa. Fui eu quem a educou, quem a brindou, quem fez dela uma «senhora». E, apezar disso, a filha da Maria, que tudo me deve, vae dizer que eu deixei em casa da mãe não sei que documento na vespera da morte de Piedade. E' uma mentira! Não fui lá essa noite...
E o desfile dos pormenores prosegue: o dinheiro que lhe deu durante o tempo que esteve no Porto; as razões porque lhe aconselhou a entregar-se a um homem rico — tudo por dedicação por ela, desde que ela tivesse a lealdade de o prevenir a tempo! — e por fim a morte tragica; o auto do José Fernandes que fora seu chauffeur; a busca de José Fernandes durante o dia: a razão porque ele estava

(Continúa na pag. 7)

prostitution. On the opposite side of the reporters' moral balance sheet, the trial had seen the appearance of Miquelina, the mother of Gomes's two sons, who had decided to stay with him, no matter what. Her attitude could not be more different to the lack of family values shown by Maria Alves. The end of the book almost sounds an unspoken condemnation of the victim: 'Maria Alves! … Why don't you lean over this man, whose regret doesn't sleep, and forgive him? You know he is not the only one responsible for this crime. Wake up! Speak! Maybe your conscience can give a last verdict' (Portela and Araújo 1927: 131). The same press that had discovered the murderer now seemed to transform the victim of this violent crime into the one who was truly responsible for what had happened. Despite the fact that these words were published by reporters in a book subtitled 'Notes of reportage', *O crime de Augusto Gomes* was obviously very far from the standard criteria of journalism. After all, Artur Portela and Norberto de Araújo were interpellating a death woman on a matter of consciousness. Nothing could be more distant from a narrative of the everyday. But this did not seem to matter. Some creative licence only enhanced the appeal of the narrative by making it more vivid while the authority of real events kept it grounded in journalistic legitimacy. It is hard to imagine a situation where fiction and reality could be more completely blurred.

Proletarian Fiction

Not long after Maria Alves's death, *O Século*'s reporter Belo Redondo published yet another book titled *O crime de Augusto Gomes* in the cheap collection of short stories 'Grandes criminosos' ('Great criminals'). Some reporters used this very popular format to publish their fiction and thus become authors. Contrary to his colleagues on the 'modernist' *Diário de Lisboa*, Artur Portela and Norberto de Araújo, Redondo did not have the option of signing his pieces of reportage in the more 'popular' *O Século*. Under the label of fiction, however, he was able to upgrade his cultural status, even if the narrative itself was just copied from the pages of *O Século* into those of a volume in the 'Grandes criminosos' series with almost no changes. One of the few notes inserted by Redondo in the book version of his story plays a role similar to the appeal launched by Artur Portela and Norberto de Araújo to Maria Alves, that of supplementing the narrative with a moral note. In this case, however, the critique of the victim's lifestyle shifted from sexual to political mores, with explicit references to post-First World War speculation, exploitation and class differences:

And yet this crime, with all its ferocity, brutality and cynicism is an appropriate product of a selfish society, a corrupt milieu, a wicked era ... We are the victims of counterfeiters, those getting rich at the expense of essential goods, leaving our children and women on the verge of misery, slowly decomposing and dying. But, as all these tragedies happen in miserable invisible places, the majority don't realize they take place, and even think these things don't happen at all. (Redondo n.d.: 14)

According to Redondo, then, the intense visibility given to a crime among the privileged had ultimately contributed to hiding – or at least was a lost opportunity to show – a whole world of misery and deprivation. Visibility, here, and especially the effect of the journalistic agenda on social perception, was for once given a political content. In fact, his fellow reporters rarely matched Redondo's social consciousness. On the contrary, one of the reasons why the crime kept the attention of the public for so long can be found in the appeal exerted by the bohemian, sophisticated lifestyle of Maria Alves and Augusto Gomes. They were, in many ways, representatives of the 'jazz-band age' described by António Ferro (1923b). Reinaldo Ferreira's Reporter X, who was familiar with various aspects of the bohemian scene, from the clubs of the upper classes to the sleaziest dives, was probably one of the best observers, in his fictionalized report, of the ambivalent nature of this world: 'newspaper work is inevitably determined by the thundering routines of journalism: more or less focused kodaks [snapshots] of a cosmopolitan existence in hotel lobbies, wagon-lits [sleeping cars] and jazz-bands; the vertigo with which the "today" mixes with the "tomorrow" where we all live, or think we live' (Ferreira 1923: 2).

Whereas Ferro became famous for the evanescence of his narratives of women named after films or letters, Reporter X was much more concrete in his descriptions of smoky atmospheres in cabaret clubs with prostitutes and drugs, where jazz ceased to be the basis of a fleeting movement and became instead a material sound 'penetrating ... like a hammer' (Ferreira 1923: 2). Afonso de Bragança's distinction between 'literate-journalists' and the 'journalist-literates' who laboured to become known at the bottom of the journalistic profession with bold reports from the lower depths of society seemed to find in people like Reinaldo Ferreira and Belo Redondo the counterparts to António Ferro.[29] Whereas the latter saw fiction as a device to create abstract representations of images and time, journalist-literates published short stories using the raw material of the already dramatic journalistic narratives of their profession, as the demands of newspaper work always seemed to lead them in the direction of crime and marginality.

When a headless body of a woman was found in *O crime da carne branca* ('The crime of white flesh'), one of the stories written by Norberto de Araújo, the immediate reaction of a policeman is to say that reporters will inevitably make a 'novel out of it' (Araújo 1923: 2). The regular presence of newspapers in the narratives of popular fiction was surely a consequence of the familiarity reporters had with the crimes, accidents and other tragedies that populated its landscape. Such a presence, however, was felt well beyond the themes, spaces and protagonists of the stories. For the press itself could influence the narrative, whether because reportage organized the plot – the crimes, in most cases – and gave it an atmosphere of mystery and excitement, or because of the way in which the mundane presence of newspapers interfered in story plots. This interference could be either indirect, through the vague idea that the press increased the propensity to violence, or absolutely direct, when reporters participated in the development of fictional events. 'Arrest them … [T]hey're the ones who create the environment for crime' (Araújo 1923: 3), someone says to a police officer when a pack of reporters harasses the staff of the morgue where the decapitated body in Araújo's story is being kept. Araújo was surely familiar with this type of situation. As in the murder of Maria Alves, the event he covered for *Diário de Lisboa*, so too in *O crime da carne branca*, reporters exercised huge pressure on police investigations.

Their interference was thus felt in both real and fictional events. The most intriguing forms of this fictional representation were those moments when the actions of characters were determined by the reading of newspapers.[30] These fictional episodes with newspaper readership are very useful, as they give us rare (and particularly dramatic) glimpses of what the real impact of the press looked like. It is in this sense interesting, but not surprising, that the best example of reading newspapers in fiction from my universe of reporters was written by the reporter who was probably the most important representative of this lower level of journalist modernists: Ferreira de Castro. Castro, somewhere in between the modernist imaginary of António Ferro and Belo Redondo's proletarian condition and political consciousness (Castro was famous for both his journalism and anarchist activism), based the whole plot of one of his short stories, 'Os paramos do desejo' ('The height of desire'), on the characters' reactions to particularly dramatic news they read in newspapers. The narrative fictionalized two pieces of news published in *O Século* on 6 and 10 February 1922. The first was an account of the double suicide of a mother and her adolescent daughter due to a crime committed by her son with his own sister. The second was the tragic closure of the first: after reading the news of the suicide in *O Século*, the son who had been imprisoned for his crime decided to commit suicide himself. The story's outcome is the consequence of a distant interaction: the man only commits suicide because his mother and sister also took their lives, but he does not see the tragedy with his own eyes, isolated as he is in a prison cell; what triggers the tragedy, then, is the circulation of the news - that which creates the imagined bond that allows distant people to somehow – in this case quite literally – participate in the same event.

It can be argued that 'Os paramos do desejo' gives us the clearest representation of the material presence of newspapers in the world – probably clearer than *Como se Faz um Número do Diário de Notícias*. This is mainly due to the specific situation of Ferreira de Castro as a proletarian journalist, someone close to the material production of newspapers. The professional situation was thus what distinguished the worldview, and the journalistic narratives, of these proletarian reporters from those of more privileged modernist journalists. More specifically, what distinguished these narratives from the superficiality of the modernist journalism analysed in the previous chapter should be seen as a material question: the proximity to production and bodies. We have already come across four female corpses in this chapter (most of them killed in crimes of passion). The literary representation of women's bodies, and not only of the female as image and literary trope, thus seems a key element in situating these writers and their narratives.

'Os paramos do desejo' was published in the 'Ten Minute Short Story' section of *A Hora*, a short-lived magazine with which the author (who was also the magazine's editor) tried to come up with a popular alternative to the more sophisticated and expensive magazines of João Ameal and António Ferro. What made these other publications more popular (in both senses: more widespread and presumably read by the popular classes) can be seen at the level of narrative and, more specifically, in the tropes used to represent women. For what was most noticeably different in the transient Madame Film of António Ferro was the constant deployment of erotic themes and sexually suggestive episodes to spice up crime narratives and its wounded bodies.[31] The crime in 'Os paramos do desejo', which had been left unsaid in the news story drawn on by Ferreira de Castro, was an incestuous relationship between the two siblings, for which only the adult brother was convicted. From news to fiction, that is, from the pages of *O Século* in February 1922 to the short story in *A Hora*, the case became surrounded by an intense atmosphere of lust with the girl transformed by Ferreira de Castro into a 'bottle of desire' with 'virgin breasts' (Castro 1922) and the protagonists inevitably succumbing to a proliferation of erotic adjectives.

What the author did, then, was to add a fictional supplement of vivid sexuality to the family tragedy initially published in *O Século*, thus attracting even those readers who already knew the story from the newspaper. It should be stressed that these bodies – decapitated, being thrown out of cars or committing suicide after sex – always belonged to women. What made them appear so distant from Madame Film (just an image, a screen), let alone Lady Futility (composed of words in an imaginary dialogue), was not only their physical materiality, but also the fact that they had invariably been engaged in more or less illicit sexual intercourse. This was decisive in the case of Maria Alves. Her embodied self could be seen as pursuing the same lifestyle of immaterial superficiality as the women depicted in the fictions of Ferro and Dantas, but she also had a concrete body whose life was violently curtailed.[32]

The distinction between titles like *O crime da carne branca* and 'Os paramos do desejo' and the feuilletons of Júlio Dantas and António Ferro can be further explored by highlighting the nuanced difference between the literary genres circulating in the wider community organized around the press. For, unlike the 'literate-journalists', what 'journalist-literates' wrote were not exactly feuilletons. Their contribution to newspapers was made exclusively through reports on all sorts of daily violence and accidents. In this sense, their quotidian lives were also ones that were more familiar with women's material presence in the world, whether this took place by engaging in sexual intercourse, suffering bodily assaults or being eventually killed. But the press was usually reluctant to use their fictional section for the stuff of the news, both because it could make feuilletons redundant and because the latter were an opportunity to invite prestigious writers to grace the pages of newspapers. Cheap pulp novels with sensational stories were, in these circumstances, the only outlet reporters found for their fictional creations. The most interesting of the genre were published between February and August 1923, with the suggestive title 'Novela sucesso' ('Success novels'), of which *O crime da carne branca* was the third of twenty-three issues. The affinities with journalism were visible at different levels, from the intense rhythm of publication (forcing writers to create under the pressure of deadlines, just as in newspapers) to the sensational plots of violence, sex and scandal that were similar to those in news stories. Not surprisingly, almost every 'journalist-literate' already mentioned contributed his own story. In fact, Norberto de Araújo, Ferreira de Castro, Artur Portela, Reinaldo Ferreira and Norberto Lopes all published in the 'Novela sucesso' series and came from the lower ranks of journalism.

This did not stop the collection from presenting itself as 'absolutely in love with the wonderful and modern conceptions of art', as a press advert put it. On the contrary, the link between modernism, with plots written like reportage, and authors who were also professional reporters was very straightforward, although it could mean different things. On the one hand, these stories could also be read as those expressions of modern life we have already analysed through feuilletons describing the jazz-band age. The difference, or, what was specific to this second genre, was the degradation of the referent, which had an immediate impact on the narrative through the complete submerging of modernity by the sensationalist discourse of journalism. But modernity for these writers also meant the subversion, or at least provocation, of conservative mores, especially those concerned with sexuality. In *Delicioso pecado* ('Sweet sin'), Mário Domingues described the passionate love story between a father and his daughter as a form of liberating repressed impulses (Domingues 1923). As in 'Os paramos do desejo' (despite social condemnation, Ferreira de Castro described the whole affair as the 'tyranny of prejudice'), here too incest appeared as a natural inclination. However, there was nothing naturalistic about the heavily carnal hyperboles to which the lovers succumbed. Women in particular were represented using a luxuriant vocabulary that sexualized all things and events. The combination between moral transgression and literary voyeurism thus created an ambiguity. For, despite the militancy with which most of these reporters remained attached to moral libertarianism and political anarchism, the erotic charge of their fictional narratives gave way to yet another moment in the intense reification of women's bodies, or women as bodies, we are already so familiar with.

Any potential subversion at work in these narratives was in this sense undermined by a very schematic rhetoric of lust. The sexual atmospheres this fiction reproduced were invariably built around the repetition of metaphors with erotic implications further dramatized by a proliferation of adjectives: objects were lascivious, and everyone was dominated by the flesh. But the key word seemed to be voluptuousness. Everything was voluptuous, but if this insistence helped create the sensual mood of the novels, the word itself seemed to play different narrative roles: in *Delicioso pecado* it helped to define the daughter's 'agile body' that 'trembled in happy voluptuousness' (Domingues 1923: 15); in *Divina* ('Divine'), by Artur Portela, and *A metamorfose* ('The metamorphosis'), by Ferreira de Castro, two stories we will read in more detail, voluptuousness was associated with opposed feelings of pain and pleasure. The cover of *Divina*, Artur Portela's contribution to the series 'Novela sucesso', was drawn by Stuart de Carvalhais, a very popular exponent of modernist illustration and caricature, whose style was very familiar to newspaper readers. His stylized female model still evoked those fleeting bodies in movement that defined the age of the jazz band (see Figure 5.3). However, the sexual tension at work in the closed eyes and half-opened mouth, between pain and pleasure, showed a voluptuousness that was almost absent from António Ferro's motifs.

The story of *Divina* begins with a naked woman – the Divine herself – posing for a sculptor, who acts as the narrator and the chief protagonist, and of whom she is both model and lover. The story begins when they have just made love, and while her 'flesh has fallen asleep' (Portela 1923: 1) the artist cannot help feeling that his interest in her is waning. Now, after having possessed the woman, all he has eyes for is the model. But when he looks at her body to carve it, even the model is no longer there: the Divine is reduced to the raw material (the marble) works of art are made of: 'the thin, concave line of the naked back, the large parabola of the thigh, the abandoned legs; a sleeping body of a statue, in which voluptuousness had died and only the marble was left … now aroused in him only the attention of an artist before his model' (Portela 1923: 4).

The meaning of his indifference towards his lover and exclusive focus on her as a model is important for understanding how the authors used these short piece of fiction as a strategic move in the literary field. As a model, the Divine is nothing but flesh, whereas the artist, an observer of women, has grown tired of her body. Two distinct but interrelated issues are raised here. On the one hand, artistic creation is equated with work, something António Ferro or João Ameal never thought of (to write was for them like strolling down the street), but that seems particularly important to journalists – even when writing fiction – like Artur Portela. On the other hand, women are reduced to mere objects, nothing more than the raw material artists use in their work. The proletarian writer thus seemed to look at the sculptor's talent as a hard-won asset rather than as something spontaneous, while at the same time they accepted without question the – almost unconscious – hierarchy that

Figure 5.3: Cover of *Divina*, by Artur Portela. Biblioteca Nacional de Portugal.

reduced women to the status of objects of artistic and literary representation. We have already seen this in the representations of Madame Film and Mademoiselle Y, characters who were completely reduced to images of superficiality. In these stories, though, the narrator-observer becomes the narrator-sculptor (Castro's *A metamorfose* has exactly the same narrative structure and narrator) and women cease to be an image to become raw material, while superficiality is replaced by sensuality.

Once again, it was Ferreira de Castro who took the motif further. In *A metamorfose*, Afrânio, the protagonist, is another sculptor struggling with his female model. He has tried many different solutions to represent the intense beauty of his beloved (moving from clay to marble, for clay was not noble enough, but failing with marble as well) and finally ends up falling in love with the statue and forgetting the model (Castro 1924). As in Portela's *Divina*, these women are truly malleable and, as such, more than visual representations. In other words, if at first sight what really interested authors like Artur Portela or Ferreira de Castro seemed very similar to what drove Ferro in his effort to overcome the limits of text in the expression of bodies in movement, it must also be said that the choice of sculpture (and thus three-dimensionality) rather than the flat (and more abstract) pictures of cinema suggests that for Portela and Castro it was impossible to write about anything but bodies at their most carnal. In this sense, the body represented both the horizon and the limits of their literature. It was as if the journalistic imaginary of crime and violence had unconsciously been transmitted from reportage to fiction. Bodies could appear as an inescapable horizon of representation, something imposed on the journalist by the material conditions of their profession. But at the same time, these same journalists had the opportunity to enhance the impact of their fiction by filling it with the concrete materiality of the same corrupted world they had to write about in newspaper reports. What was a limitation to their journalistic work became an opportunity in their fiction. For this opportunity to become effective, however, their narratives had to show a distinction between their producers' literary status and their journalistic profession. That was the role played by both female characters and artistic creation.

The insistent use of isolated artists as protagonists was itself a concern about authorship and symbolic capital. Whereas in António Ferro women were a motif that allowed him to leap over the rhetoric of literature to the rhetoric of film, in the likes of Artur Portela and Ferreira de Castro that same motif functioned as an artistic warrant. In the frontier between the autonomous author and the anonymous reporter, this true game of *trompe l'oeil* with statues more real than the models and men living more authentically through art (creating an illusory coincidence between fiction and reality) can thus be read as a fundamental strategy of literary legitimacy.[33] It is in this sense telling that Ferreira de Castro, the reporter who achieved the greatest prominence as an author in this genre, should also be the one whose work was most reflexive and paid more attention to the correct strategies of literary success.

In fact, Ferreira de Castro would eventually become a much more successful writer than Ferro himself, especially after 1929 when a realist turn granted him a position of respect in the ranks of political literature. In the early 1920s, however, he was still trying to find his way in the field and identify the negative against whom he should be judged. Interestingly, he found it in the same literary figure chosen by Ferro: Júlio Dantas (and not in Ferro, as one would expect, given the proximity between their literary imaginaries and the distance between their social origins). Castro's critique of Dantas had two themes: literary success and sex. In his own contribution to 'Novela sucesso', *O êxito fácil* ('Easy success'), Castro told the story of a celebrated writer whose fame had been built on the same frivolous narratives about femininity that had given Dantas a prestigious position in the literary field (Castro 1923). The protagonist was obviously based on the author of *Ao ouvido de Madame X* and his career was strategically used to show how those lightweight feuilletons would necessarily fall into oblivion after the author's death. The plot is based on a flashback where the unnamed character reminisces about his whole literary life while lying on his deathbed only to realize, too late, how ephemeral literary glory is. In his first book, a collection of articles and short stories titled *Mas...* ('But ...'), Ferreira de Castro had already criticized Dantas by pointing out the latter's inability to describe bodies and his horror of sex as a creative flaw: 'copulation seemed to him like treason. The bed was like a cross. And if a woman ever laid with him, he felt so humble, so undeserving, that he didn't turn her into a book. He didn't conceive' (Castro 1921: 16).

Again, this incorporation of sexual intercourse into the literary act should be read beyond metaphor: as a reporter, Castro saw literature – or literary creation – as a bodily experience and this is where, as I have been trying to argue, we should locate his proneness to sexualize narratives. This creative process reaches a singular moment within the genre in the last pages of *Mas...*, where heterosexual penetration is explicitly depicted. Despite the near-pornographic content of the scene, what truly makes it remarkable is less its literary content than a 'formal' device where, I believe, we can identify a sharp awareness of the material quality of the printed object which only a journalist could possess: the book's last pages, where the copulation is described, were

perforated with little holes to allow for sensitive readers to easily de-
tach what might be seen as too shocking in its 'violent truth' (Castro
1921: 98). As a literary strategy against the acclaimed writer or as a
political move to provoke middle-class moralists, sex played a key role
in the making of Castro's literary legitimacy. The protagonists of the
scene were a couple of Amazonian Indians, which allowed the author
to establish a distance between the European reader and the exotic setting (but not that exotic to the writer himself, who had been an émigré
in the Amazon). The perforated pages and the analogy between writing and fecundation in his critique of Júlio Dantas, however, provided
evidence of an engagement with intellectual and bodily activities that
were not only more expected from a reporter, but also something that
in the case of Ferreira de Castro were impossible to dissociate from his
political militancy as an anarchist.

'I'm profoundly rebellious', Castro said of himself in *Mas...* (Castro
1921: 27). His specific status as a proletarian writer, however, between
the empowered intellectual and the subaltern salaried employee, produced a strange combination of creation and labour. As he explained
in the introduction to one of his stories, *A boca da esfinge* ('The mouth
of the sphinx'), the necessary effort to write the novel in just sixty-six
hours 'absorbed all his energies, just to immediately perish in the pages
of newspapers and magazines' (Castro and Frias 1924: 8). The outcome
of such effort could not but echo the product of manual production:
'the devouring work comes out of the pen as an artefact from the hands
of a prisoner' (Castro and Frias 1924: 9). This is not the image we are
used to associating with artistic and intellectual creativity. Writing here
was not just labour, but forced labour, a manual activity where the time
pressure of journalistic work resembled the working conditions on production lines. At this level, the reporter becomes a very specific symbol
of modern life, very distant from the sophistication of modernism, or
to the fascination exerted by sportsmen and aviators. He is, above all,
a proletarian. Ferreira de Castro very clearly combined this proletarian
condition with that of the writer. This combination of creation and labour put him on a particular horizon of social expectations, where the
ability to write (and publish) reinforced his political radicalism. This
was, however, a very peculiar type of proletarian, whose radicalism
was not targeted at political and economic power as such, but against
femininity as the dominant literary trope. It can thus be said that his
struggle was internal to the literary system of representation rather
than aimed at the socially privileged. In other words, female characters
as the central trope of literary fiction represented a site of contention
between writers. Women were, in this sense, and as we have already

seen in the previous chapter, a social metonym, which, in the realm of newspapers, stood as the figuration of journalism's absent cause: readership. Between the evanescent woman with which modernist journalists wrote their filmic metaphors and the sexualized female bodies of proletarian reporters, the main question was one of literary power.

This is never as clear as in the most frequent motif in Ferreira de Castro's countless short stories and novellas published in the 1920s: the artist as the unknown or misunderstood hero to whose genius women always surrender. More than the fulfilment of a secret desire, these works of fiction are about literary and social aspiration. In this sense, the ambiguous role female characters play in Castro's plots possibly works as a tool to define, negatively but rigorously, the status of the proletarian writer. These women are always given a position of social privilege, which is what makes their drive towards the unknown artist both unlikely and empowering. Although everything separated their social status from that of the artist, something in him exerts an irresistible power of attraction. Women's ambiguity thus lies in this double position, as their privileged social origins are, at the same time, exactly what empowers the socially subaltern artist to whom they submit. A complex web of social, gender and cultural relations is thus being outlined here. The content of the stories could suffer several variations, but the structure of the plot was always the same: the refusal by the young lonely artist or writer to accept the public success that would necessarily corrupt his art grants him the romantic aura that makes both his life and work irresistible to women. In the end, a female character always comes to legitimate his isolation through an urge of intellectual passion: a sportswoman that feels fatally attracted to an unattractive writer; an actress that falls in love for the anonymous playwright whose character she interprets on stage; or a female reader eager to meet the novelist 'because, after reading some of my novels, she thought I was plagiarizing her feelings' (Castro n.d.: 179). These female characters were the happy few who had somehow been granted a glimpse into the writer's realm of intimacy, thus discovering the fascinating world that was concealed by his isolation.

Ultimately, these women's love rewarded a lifestyle that refused fame and money as the two fundamental values of a society dominated by spectacle. The intransigency of creation was in this sense a piece of resistance. And yet the social isolation of these fictional writers – and the attraction women felt towards them – was filled with anxiety. The young proletarian's aspiration to literary success and personal happiness was socially and politically ambiguous. For if professional emancipation could be foreseen in the leap from journalism to literature, this came at the expense of the submission of women to their traditional representation. In fact, if these female characters were indeed the part referring to the whole of readership, it may not be too farfetched to see in their unlikely infatuation with the fictional unknown artist a wishful thinking about the ability of the proletarian writer himself to reach literary success.

As a reporter, the proletarian was sharply aware of how literary subalternity reflected his low social position. Conversely, as a proletarian, he also knew that writing for the public was an instrument of power coextensive to the impact of newspapers. In short, writing reportage and dime novels was, in this sense, both a form of class struggle and of gender domination.

Notes

1. *Diário de Lisboa*, 28 March 1922, p.2.
2. Michael Schudson situates the emergence of this interference, where 'journalism' becomes 'a kind of documentary journalism (…) frequently a documentary fiction', in the United States around 1890 (with names like Joseph Pulitzer and William Randolph Hearst): 'reporters were, for the first time, actors in the drama of the newspaper world' (Schudson 1978: 64).
3. This casual attitude towards the ethics of journalism was easier to achieve with non-political issues. The popular press emerging in the late nineteenth century equated not being 'entirely serious' with not being 'unrelentingly political' (Lee 1976: 119). On the other hand, we can relate the interview form – with its narrative dynamic and interaction with events and social actors – with the other contemporary cultural forms of mass reproduction modernist journalists were so fond of. In 1886, journalist W.T. Mead evoked journalism's ability to break the gap between the written and the oral. Interviews, according to him, were 'the phonograph of the world' (Salmon 2000: 32).
4. *O Século*, 30 March 1926, p.2.
5. *Diário de Lisboa*, 30 March 1926, p.5.
6. *Diário de Lisboa*, 2 April 1926, p.8.
7. *O Século*, 2 April 1926, p.1.
8. *O Século*, 3 April 1926, p.1; 5 April 1926, p.1.
9. *O Século*, 5 April 1926, p.1.
10. *Diário de Notícias*, 5 April 1926, p.2.
11. Quote from *Diário de Lisboa*, 5 April 1926, p.5.
12. *O Século*, 7 April 1926, p.2.
13. *O Século*, 6 April 1926, p.1.
14. *Diário de Lisboa*, 8 April 1926, p.5.
15. *Diário de Notícias*, 11 April 1926, p.1.
16. *O Século*, 12 April 1926, p.1.
17. *Diário de Notícias*, 12 April 1926, p.1.
18. *O Século*, 13 April 1926, p.1.
19. *O Século*, 13 April 1926, p.2.
20. *Diário de Notícias*, 13 April 1926, p.1.

21. Vanessa Schwartz identified a similar case, 'l'affaire Troppman', in Paris as early as 1869: 'From start to finish, this case *was* its newspaper coverage, as the press investigated alongside the police. The press, in fact, became so associated with the story that rumors circulated that one of the *Petit Journal* reporters actually helped with Troppman's execution' (Schwartz 1998: 39).
22. *O Século*, 14 April 1926, p.1.
23. *Diário de Notícias*, 14 April 1926, p.1.
24. *Diário de Notícias*, 14 April 1926, p.1.
25. On Benjamin Bentham's panopticon (an eighteenth-century apparatus of vigilance) as a model for modern forms of social control, see Foucault (1977: 195–228).
26. Tom Gunning aptly analyses the different valences of early twentieth-century press photography, and in particularly how the 'indexical aspect' is just one of its dimensions: 'photography became the ideal tool of the process of detection, the ultimate modern clue, due to three interlocking aspects: its indexical aspect, which comes from the fact that since a photograph results from exposure to a pre-existing entity, it directly bears the entity's imprint and can therefore supply evidence about the object it depicts; its iconic aspect, by which it produces a direct resemblance to its object which allows immediate recognition; and its detachable nature, which allows it to refer to an absent object separated from it in time and space. As a clue, the photograph entered into a new discourse of power and control' (Gunning 1995: 20). Reinaldo Ferreira's photos are here very close to a key social fantasy of the period of early cinema: to capture the 'instant of guilt': 'capturing the instant of guilt on film remained more the stuff of fiction-making fantasy' (Gunning 1995: 35).
27. It is doubtful whether Augusto Gomes would have been persuaded about the reporter's presence if it had not been for the photographic reconstitution of the event. Thierry Gervais shows how images, in illustrated magazines, play a decisive role in the definition of meaning: 'more difficult to handle than edited text, the publication of images constrains the issue's editing and layout. For all these different reasons, images cannot be treated as mere illustrations of the text. They contribute to the definition of the illustrated magazine's structure' (Gervais 2007: 69).
28. We should question Maria Alves's 'disappearance' from journalistic reports about the investigation, how the whole affair was handled as if it was just a question between men (the criminal, the police and journalists). Adrian Rifkin suggests that the presence of women in detective stories is particularly disturbing, as their presence in the public sphere (crimes of passion always bring the private realm into the public arena) are potentially disruptive to the social order. This danger becomes particularly threatening when it involves the display of images: 'these fated women are the vision of an imaginary freedom, whose imagination compensates for the childlike character of the repeated manipulation of the typologies of literary culture, the failure of the odyssey of man to realize the complexity of difference' (Rifkin 1993: 128).
29. Reporter X is in this sense much closer to the status of the reporter described by Dominique Kalifa than modernist journalists like António Ferro, in the way they were expected to be perceptive observers of modern life despite their lack of formal education: 'Strange conception of a profession that asked these proletarians of journalism, with no education or recognition, to be exceptional beings, bearers of the *American eye*' (Kalifa 1995: 87).
30. 'Novelists used newspapers in a variety of ways: retelling events reported by the press; reproducing journalistic voices, styles, and features; the pastiche of news items through headlines and quotations; recording the process of news production; and,

most dramatically portraying the individual reader's reaction to the news' (Rubery 2009: 11).

31. In his brilliant analysis of Manet's *Olympia*, T.J. Clark argues that what was so scandalous about the painting's depiction of a naked working-class prostitute was much less the 'prostitute' than the 'working-class' in her, and the way this was shown in her naked body: 'nakedness is a strong sign of class, a dangerous instance of it. And thus the critics' reaction in 1865 becomes more comprehensible. They were perplexed by the fact that Olympia's class was nowhere but in her body: the cat, the Negress, the orchid, the bunch of flowers, the slippers, the pearl earrings, the choker, the screen, the shawl – they were all lures, they all meant nothing, or nothing in particular. The naked body did without them in the end and did its own narrating' (Clark 1999: 146). In our case, the sexualized bodies emerge both because the naked women are working class (even Maria Alves, when it came to the description of her scandalous sexual behaviour, was socially demoted as second-class actress and chorus girl) and, more to the point, because these writers are the proletarian underground of journalism and literature.

32. The body of Maria Alves works here as the referent of what Judith Butler considers 'power's most productive effect': the constitution of 'material positivities' within which any kind of subjectivity ultimately thrives (Butler 1993: 2).

33. It is easy to imagine how the need to 'make a name for oneself' that Pierre Bourdieu refers to was particularly significant to journalists who normally did not have a chance to sign their published texts, and thus remained virtually anonymous: 'It is true that the initiative for change can be traced back, almost by definition, to new (meaning younger) entrants. These are the ones who are also the most deprived of specific capital, and who (in a universe where to exist is to be different, meaning to occupy a distinct and distinctive position) only exist in so far as – without needing to want to – they manage to assert their identity (that is, their difference) and get it known and recognized ("make a name for oneself") by imposing new modes of thought and expression which break with current modes of thought and hence are destined to disconcert by their "obscurity" and their "gratuitousness"' (Bourdieu 1996: 239).

Chapter 6

Reporters' Revolution

In this chapter I will try to define the complex status of reporters as both writers and proletarians. This complexity stems from the hybridity of their social and professional position. As writers, they were still seen as producers, the lowest rank of literature, whereas the intellectual nature of their work gave them a clearly distinct status within the proletariat. The main event this chapter refers to appeared to almost everyone as an insurmountable paradox: a strike by journalists in 1921, that is, the exercise by intellectual workers of the most powerful instrument of political struggle deployed by manual workers. The relation between the journalists and the modernist events that helped define the 1920s as a historic break and a period of dramatic changes in perception reaches a key moment here, for the sense of social disruption brought about by mixing intellectual and manual worlds could only be equated with the impact of the 1917 Russian Revolution on the political order of liberalism.

From a different perspective, but as a consequence of the contradiction between intellectual and worker, it can be said that the events were due to the ability of reporters to simultaneously constitute a political subject and represent the political subjectivity of others. This is why the representation of femininity in these reporters' narratives (in both fiction and reportage proper, as we have seen with the murder of Maria Alves) became so important to situating them. Either because men – and there were only male reporters – had a more powerful and visible social status than women, or because authors could manipulate femininity at ease, reporters found in this classical trope an appropriate way to negotiate their position in the public sphere. The dual nature of their relation to the trope of femininity – gendered and/or social – must, in any case, be disentangled. For not all men had greater social status than all women, and proletarian writers surely occupied a lower social stratum than most women who read what they published in newspapers.

So, before moving to the 1921 strike, I will make one last effort to read in a set of works of fiction how the balance of political and literary issues was negotiated through the representation of women. This time, the task may seem more straightforward, since all the narratives we will be reading are utopian episodes from literary fiction where the horizons of political expectation in the early 1920s easily become visible. My initial suggestion is that if reality was ambiguously played out between the narratives of reportage and fiction, then perhaps the ideology of reporters can be grasped more rigorously in these utopias, where the shield of overt fantasy opened the way to politics at its most doctrinaire. In this sense, a close reading of the structure of this particular genre may hopefully situate the meaning of the strike in relation to the period's dominant political perceptions, and in particular in the aftermath of the Russian Revolution as the most dramatic political break in twentieth-century history.

Utopias

Two of these utopias were written by authors we are already familiar with: 'Motivo de Aristophanes' ('Motif of Aristophanes') by Júlio Dantas was a newspaper feuilleton later published in one of his volumes about women, *Como elas amam* ('The way women love'), and *A ditadura feminista* ('The feminist dictatorship') by Ferreira de Castro was a volume in the series 'Novela contemporânea' ('Contemporary novel'), a competitor imprint to 'Novela sucesso' in the dime-novel market. The two other authors to be considered here had a very different literary profile. Both Manuel Ribeiro and João Campos Lima were renowned for their anarchism – the dominant political culture among the early twentieth-century Portuguese working class – and their novels were usually seen as a secondary dimension to their political activity, which they carried on mostly through newspapers. There are important differences between the two, however, for if Lima remained on the margins of the politically acceptable and a peripheral name in the literary milieu, Ribeiro had spectacular success when, with a trilogy of novels published from 1920 to 1923, he publicly renounced revolutionary politics and embraced Catholicism. Ribeiro's utopia involves the formation of an ideal rural community in *A ressurreição* ('The resurrection'), the trilogy's final volume. Two years later, Lima wrote another trilogy, *Via dolorosa* ('The painful road'), where an opposed utopia was staged in the first volume, *Gente devota* ('The devout people'). Whereas in *A ressurreição* the utopian community is formed by people, like Ribeiro himself, who have abandoned revolution for religion, in *Gente devota* a very similar commune is built by former priests and other Catholics who have converted to communism.

The fact that Ribeiro's immense success was not matched by Lima is very symptomatic. Apparently, at that time, readers were much happier to read about revolutionaries converting to religion than believers turning to revolutionary politics; after all, in Portugal as elsewhere, post-First World War political radicalization would lead to right-wing authoritarian solutions, rather than working-class revolutions.

In everything else, the narrative styles looked rather similar: a very conventional realism that became densely doctrinaire when narrating processes involving intellectual meditation. Moreover, both Ribeiro's and Lima's trilogies described rigorously analogous processes of conversion. In Ribeiro's *A ressurreição*, Luciano, the protagonist, is a young atheist architect who, after a close encounter with religious life in Rome, experiences a mystical transformation that ultimately leads to his conversion: some of his Catholic friends, explicitly challenging the authority of the Vatican, go back to the catacombs in order to perform religious ceremonies as primitive Christians, thus rejecting participation in worldly materialism. Two of these friends, a countess and a prince, have meanwhile given some land away where local rural workers have the opportunity to organize themselves autonomously in egalitarian communes. The results are very impressive: 'this communal regime made better men, happier, sincere. They all gave their best effort to the common tasks, working together in harmony' (Ribeiro 1923: 240). Everything happens as if the twentieth-century Italian countryside has suddenly been transformed into Jesus' Palestine, 'through the sobriety, austerity and simplicity of its life' (Ribeiro 1923: 240). Faith is the origin and cause of this success: a spiritual form of communism that works as a refusal of both modern materialism and modern ideologies.

The commune in *Gente devota* looks very similar. The narrative unfolds in Minho, a region in northern Portugal known for its conservatism and ultra-Catholicism. As in rural Italy, the same peculiar gesture triggers a similar event: a local aristocrat decides to create a rural colony to be run by workers. The result here, too, is impressive: 'the vast domains would be transformed into a centre of ceaseless activity, of life and beauty, constantly contributing to the glorious future prophesized by these new apostles' (Lima 1927: 337). From title to characters and context, Lima's novel returns to the same type of religious imaginary used in Ribeiro's *A ressurreição*. Here, however, the rhetoric of materialist detachment and spiritual virtue is used to stage an exact reversal of Ribeiro's plot. Mário, an idealist priest, refuses to participate in the system of power he is expected to form with the forces of local politics and economic interests (the traditional role of the priest in *caciquismo*) and decides to join the community. His motivations are as spiritual as those that drive Ribeiro's character Luciano to conversion. He is, after all, looking for the same 'ideal country of purified souls where the integral accomplishment of a natural destiny, made of freedom and love, dismissed all doubts and tortuous thoughts' (Lima 1927: 459). Mário's process of religious apostasy thus seems very close to Luciano's spiritual revelation. However, what triggers this change is not a conversion to faith but to revolutionary doctrines. From *A ressurreição* to *Gente devota*, the problem is thus reversed: while Ribeiro saw the corruption in revolution, Lima targeted the institutions of Catholicism. But if what counted as reality differed from one author to the other, the utopian move was identical. Reality equalled materialism and, as such, had to be refused.

Everything in these novels thus seems to be directly subsumed by the authors' political militancy. The absolute control of narrative by doctrine bound them to a very predictable worldview that undermined its utopian promise. The image of these happy communes remained all too familiar. Despite the fictionalization of non-places, their imaginary matched the most recognizable images and figures of literary realism. In this sense, it may be possible to draw distinctions around the question of genre between João Campos Lima and Manuel Ribeiro, on the one hand, and Júlio Dantas and Ferreira de Castro on the other. In fact, both Dantas and Castro used satire to distance their narratives from the most familiar tropes of the dominant form of realism and to create absurd political situations. The opposition between genres is thus what determined the opposition between the political character of both sets of fiction, to such an extent that contrary to the ideal rural communities inspired by Catholicism and anarchism in the realist model, the authoritarian regimes led by women in Dantas's 'Motivo de Aristophanes', and Castro's *A ditadura feminista* are better described as dystopias.

In his short story, Dantas rewrote Aristophanes' *Assemblywomen*. As in the classic Greek comedy, Praxagoras creates a communist regime dominated by women (Dantas n.d.b: 167–173). Unlike Aristophanes' play, however, Dantas did not use this literary convention to put forward a utopian alternative to corrupt politics, but to reduce it to an egalitarian exchange of sexual relations where communist collectivization was given an equivalent in the disappearance of all forms of sexual fidelity and emotional engagement. In both Aristophanes and Dantas, a policy of free sexual distribution was established, in which every woman – young, old, beautiful and ugly – should have intercourse with every man – young, old, beautiful and ugly. But whereas in the Greek comedy this was used to criticize male sexism, Dantas reversed the critique to mock feminist politics. In Dantas, the main cause of disruption in such a regime, which – according to the writer's conservative perspective – would be the problem of any feminization of politics, was the subversion of a golden rule of the bourgeois order: the separation between private emotions and politics and economy, with promiscuity necessarily leading to the corruption of the latter by the former (and vice-versa).

The plot of Castro's *A ditadura feminista* unfolds in 1920s Lisbon, where women also take power. In this case, Portuguese feminists, under the direct influence of an English feminist organization, establish a regime as authoritarian and absurd as that of Praxagoras. The plot and the political question it raises thus seems to replicate. However, whereas in Dantas's dystopia the regime invades the emotional life of individuals by bureaucratizing intimacy, in Castro's dictatorship, women in power misuse public institutions with their frivolous political programme: 'after dealing with the distribution of cabinet posts, the revolutionaries relaxed for a moment, cooled themselves with fans and then moved to what was really important in the revolution: should women wear trousers or skirts?' (Castro 1925: 12). The question had no true political content. The decision on what to wear did not involve any emancipatory or egalitarian move. It was sheer vanity. Female politicization thus complemented the corruption of feminized politics: women would necessarily bring frivolous materialism to politics while at the same time losing the realm of sentimentality which should supposedly distinguish their gender, in a process where privacy became purely instrumental. At this level, Ferreira de Castro seemed to have no disagreement with his nemesis Júlio Dantas. Whoever these women were, or whatever they symbolized, their political action seemed very similar to both writers. Given everything that divided them (which, as we learnt in the previous chapter, led Castro to attack Dantas in very striking terms), an analysis of their view of feminine politicization may reveal the extent to which the ideologies of such two different male writers overlapped.

Both the loss of privacy and the public invasion of intimate emotions display the same fear already at work in *A ressurreição* and *Gente devota*: from different perspectives, these works seemed to either dramatize or retreat from, but in any case react against, materialism, or, more concretely, the threat posed by modern society (*Gesellschaft*) to the notion of community (*Gemeinschaft*). Materialism, as opposed to spiritualism and its values, synthesized a set of different phenomena to produce a singular perception of what modernity was: industrialization, urbanization, democratization, to mention only the most insistent tropes of this very familiar postwar *Kulturkritik*.[1]

And yet, the role of industry, urban life or any kind of mass political participation can only be inferred from the plots of these stories. None of them addresses the phenomena directly. In a way, this was exactly the function of their utopian (or dystopian) content: to preclude any kind of indexical representation. So, in order to break down this materialism into its different manifestations, and thus identify the threats felt by these authors to their ideal notion of community, we must try to reconfigure the relation between these literary objects and their historical situation. For if, on the one hand, they explicitly stage a flight from what was most predictable in their historical circumstances, on the other hand they also engaged very clearly with the horizon of contemporary political expectations, at least in the European context. Bucolic forms of rural communal self-organization or the complete subversion of institutional politics and dominant morals by women were indeed hardly foreseeable, but as fantastic critiques of materialism they touched some very sensitive chords in the political imaginary.

In this sense, they typically exerted the kind of symbolic action Fredric Jameson identifies as 'a way of doing something to the world' by bringing 'into being that very situation to which it is also ... a reaction' (Jameson 1981: 67). The forms of this literary bringing 'into being' of what is otherwise concealed are thus problematic in their own right. Going back to *A ressurreição* and *Gente devota*, we can see how ideology worked through the weight doctrine had in the unfolding of their plots. In both cases, any contradiction within the narratives was blocked by the extreme explanatory power of the long reflections and dialogues concerning political and religious doctrines. The harmony of the communes, the perfect endings that follow the conversions of Mário and Luciano – all contradictions have been moved from society to the inner consciousness of the protagonists – were the logical corollary of the coherence of the political doctrines adopted by the writers. Realism, as a harmonious relation between reality and representation, is achieved in Ribeiro's and Lima's works by the non-contradictory nature of the political beliefs that lie at the origin of both narratives. In 'Motivo de Aristophanes' and *A ditadura feminista*, on the other hand, the complete reversal of social referent through satire produces a very similar effect: however different absurdity and harmony may be, it is remarkable how satire rendered dystopia without contradiction in exactly the same way utopia was made unproblematic by realism. In other words, historical contradictions were concealed through genre in two opposite, but equivalent, operations: whereas *Gente devota* and *A ressurreição* use realism as the positive affirmation of a positive utopia, 'Motivo de Aristophanes' and *A ditadura feminista* use satire as the negative affirmation of a negative dystopia.

In either case, the relation between genre and its referent is one of complete agreement, leaving no trace of literary contradiction.[2] It can then be said that lack of contradiction is precisely what strikes us as suspicious in these stories and moves the analysis to its historical situation not to contextualize what they said but to try to discover what they hid. For what these stories conceal is not a deception, but rather the form in which the political unconscious manifests itself ideologically.[3] Accordingly, our analysis will assume that Júlio Dantas, Ferreira de Castro, Manuel Ribeiro and Campos Lima are all, as Slavoj Žižek would put it, positing presuppositions through narrative by dealing with the world as if it were given to them in advance, when in fact the material for their fiction had already been structured by the authors' own perception of that same world.[4] Accordingly, fiction is always somehow utopian or dystopian, since it always poses a specific perception that constitutes the range of possibilities, and impossibilities, of a given set of circumstances. The relation between these works of fiction and their 1920s context can thus be reconfigured not only by assuming that the social contradictions of the plots were not the real historical contradictions faced by the authors, at least not in the way they are enacted in these narratives, but also by adding that these contradictions were what concealed 'the traumatic social division that cannot be symbolized' (Žižek 1989: 45), but which nonetheless it is our task to unveil.

Let us then assume that both the institutional forms and political processes dramatized in these works either swerved around more threatening political struggles or hid other collective forms at work in the particular historical moment. If we adopt such a position, we are immediately faced by what seems to be a major problem: the two explicit political topics here represented, feminism and religion, were far from irrelevant in 1920s Portugal. On the contrary, they are among the most dramatic ideological challenges faced by the republican regime. It is no coincidence that all the characters in *A ditadura feminista* were named after real activists in the Portuguese feminist movement (and not very subtly: Ana Castro Osório becomes Ana Costa Onofre, and Maria Veleda becomes Maria Velada). Feminism was one of the most unsettling issues faced by a political regime that proved progressive in many other areas. The exclusion of women's suffrage from the republic's list of reforms after the 1910 revolution was not just conservative atavism; it was supposedly a sign of political pragmatism in light of the persistent and pervasive influence of the Catholic Church over Portuguese society. According to this view, women would inevitably become an anti-republican, conservative, if not straightforward reactionary, segment of the electorate. This influence was in fact the reason why the regime chose the Catholic Church as the target for some of its most symbolic reforms. The separation of church and state, the legalization of divorce, the expulsion of the Jesuits from the country and the closure of religious schools were truly revolutionary acts in a society like early twentieth-century Portugal – radical moves which would eventually play a decisive role both in the fall of the regime and in the ideological priorities of the authoritarian politics that followed the nationalist revolution of 1926.

Therefore, it is obviously inaccurate, or at least insufficient, to say that the choice of religion and feminism as the political themes sidestepped the country's most pressing political issues. And yet, the particular forms in which these political themes were staged appear somehow displaced. Both *A ditadura feminista* and 'Motivo de Aristophanes' enacted forceful seizures of power whose resemblance to the occupation of the Winter Palace by the Bolsheviks in 1917 is difficult to overlook. The impact of the then very recent revolution in Russia was so powerful that it quickly became the horizon against which all political expectations were viewed, both for those who saw it as the fulfilment of old utopias, and for those who saw in it the latest form of their worst dystopian nightmares. In this sense, both satires resembled the tactics of Leninism. However, political violence was used by Ferreira de Castro in *A ditadura feminista* to emphasize how women refused to let go of any of their class privileges – for example, their fierce reaction against black women's emancipation when the revolution spread to the colonies: 'What happens now? Who will send us coffee, cocoa, all those things we need?' (Castro 1925: 25). Similarly, in Dantas's political system, feminism was made absurd precisely to the extent to which it was subsumed by a strict egalitarian structure of communist sexual intercourse. Both dystopias thus staged something like the Russian Revolution while refusing to embody its explicit class content. The same kind of displacement, where some symbolic elements of Bolshevism were displaced for different political purposes, can be seen at work in both *A ressurreição* and *Gente devota*. In this case, land was redistributed in both Minho and the Italian countryside, not through autonomous occupation but by the generosity of altruist aristocrats.

We thus seem to have reached an important non-symbolized set of contradictions. First, political processes revealed the anxiety caused by the Russian Revolution that began in 1917: a violent movement seized institutions by force and began a revolutionary process in which land, along with other forms of private property, was collectivized. Formally, these were exactly the same political processes that occurred in the Portuguese utopias and dystopias. However, a decisive change of agents took place and the presence of feminism and religion can finally unveil what remained concealed: there is no proletariat in *A ditadura feminista* and 'Motivo de Aristophanes', and no bourgeoisie in *A ressurreição* and *Gente devota*. It thus seems that the traumatic social division these authors had trouble symbolizing was the class struggle itself.

Where political struggle takes place, there is no class, and where classes are the protagonists as such, there is no struggle. If we take this line of thought to its limit and articulate these two sets of political narratives, what ultimately emerges is an apparent unwillingness to think of any form of capitalist relations. Again, this must be grasped through the problematic game of looking at what coincides with and what is displaced in relation to the Russian model. At one level, it cannot be said that production is absent or secondary in the rural utopias of Manuel Ribeiro and João Campos Lima. In fact, the moral dimension of the conversions performed by their protagonists is closely related to the harmony achieved by egalitarian labour relations. And in both female dystopias, the core of the critique is precisely the reification of relations between women and men. In both Júlio Dantas and Ferreira de Castro, the issue is not so much that women aspire to sexual emancipation – which both writers view rather nonchalantly – but the fact that they seize political power and submit the realm of social affection and intimacy – which women, from a traditionalist point of view, should normally control – to the instrumental relations of capitalism. Again, it is not that capitalist relations and the instrumental reason of bureaucracy are absent; they are simply displaced. Therefore, at a second level, where the explicit elements of plot give way to the unveiling of what is concealed by narrative, it becomes visible that where production is represented (in *A ressurreição* and *Gente devota*), social relations are pre-capitalist and political power vanishes from sight. Inversely, where power is bureaucratic and relations reified (in *A ditadura feminista* and 'Motivo de Aristophanes'), production remains carefully absent.

In a word, the war of the sexes and battles for production are ultimately there to hide class struggle in a historical moment perceived as being one of revolutionary threat. In this sense, it is fair to say that the 1921 journalists' strike, as an event traversed by class conflicts and economic implications, touched the most sensitive chord of the period's social presuppositions. The way it was publicly represented, on the other hand, as an event where the protagonists and those who wrote about it were the same people, would represent a major challenge to dominant political perceptions.

Journalists and Typographers on Strike

Labour relations under capitalism and their revolutionary potential thus seemed too real and urgent to be thought of, or represented, directly. And yet, most of the literary questions we have been dealing with, and the everyday life of journalists as such, were completely enmeshed in class relations. Moreover, the proximity and impact of the Russian Revolution turned communism into the absolute horizon of political expectations in the 1920s, either as hope, for workers and revolutionary political forces, or threat, for the bourgeoisie and its institutions. The complex ways in which our four utopias engaged with the topic show two things: that the organization of the labour force and the forms of state power were deeply rooted in the writers' unconscious, and that the Russian Revolution had been so radical and unsettling that even revolutionary journalists like Ferreira de Castro and Campos Lima had trouble facing it. The forms of class struggle, political subjectivity and labour organization specific to journalism presented their own problems. But the whole question involved in the production of newspapers began from the exact same place as any other economic activity: the role of the commodity. What was specific to this product, then, was the relation between what needed to be sold – written narratives – and the realm of intellectual values supposedly protected from the corruption of worldly materialism. In other words, the need to sell newspapers in the market meant that thought and literature could become corrupted.

According to Ferreira de Castro this could take two forms, depending on the 'seller's' social position: for writers like Júlio Dantas and Antero de Figueiredo, the press was what gave them public status, whereas for people like himself, to write in newspapers would always mean the 'betrayal of genius or the renting out of talent' (Castro 1921: 21). In other words, journalism was the insurmountable material context of literature, both because it made for the glory of opportunists and forced 'true writers' to produce for the market. Even so, the sacrifices involved in journalism could be used as an opportunity by proletarians like Ferreira de Castro to develop a heroic image of the profession. In *A epopeia do trabalho* ('The epic of labour'), a book celebrating labour by means of its most symbolic crafts, two of the professions represented were directly related to the printing of the written word. The first was typesetting, a manual trade whose practitioners manipulated letters and typefaces, and who were thus familiar with the press, which would necessarily give rise to an especially conscious kind of proletarian – 'his head is a great archive of vowels' (Castro 1926: 61) – and one already very close to the second profession: writing. As workers who manipulated the words that typesetters printed, writers were included by Ferreira de Castro in his epic on the condition that they used their literature 'to struggle for the liberation of men' (Castro 1926: 70). As in the living example of many of Ferreira de Castro's comrades in anarchist organizations and newspapers, the best of these, the writers with the strongest perception of the emancipatory power of the written word, were precisely those who had taken the leap from typesetting to journalism. This close proximity between manual and intellectual work was then the most sensitive issue in labour relations within newspapers, to such an extent that in the lower ranks of journalism – those symbolically furthest away from the 'literate-journalists' Afonso de Bragança saw as epitomized by António Ferro – the line between reporters, informers and typesetters was barely noticeable.

The whole history of the professional status of journalism from the late nineteenth century to the 1920s was, in this sense, a struggle for the autonomy of journalists in relation to writers in general. So if, on the one hand, we have seen how for many of these journalists literature came as a form of distinction (which, in rare cases like that of Ferreira de Castro, would eventually lead to a change of profession), it must also be noted that for the majority professional recognition would involve a set of technical skills that had nothing to do with the talent and inspiration required by fictional creation and intellectual reflection. The first professional associations related to the press show that before 1900 the process of distinction between writers and journalists had not yet begun: nothing in the names and structure of the Associação dos Jornalistas e Escritores Portugueses (Association of Portuguese Journalists and Writers), the Associação dos Jornalistas (Association of Journalists) and the Associação da Imprensa Portuguesa (Portuguese Press Association), founded respectively in 1880, 1896 and 1897, distinguished the different strata of workers on newspapers, and in fact only the third was supposed to include reporters and other professionals of the press, as the first two were exclusively aimed at writers who happened to write for newspapers (as most did).

A clearer differentiation had to wait until 1904, when the newly created Associação de Classe dos Trabalhadores da Imprensa de Lisboa (ACTIL, Lisbon Press Workers' Association) would state in its regulations that 'this organization will not accept as full members anyone who, despite being a writer, journalist, reporter, informant, sub-director, or person occupying any other position in the press, perform these tasks along with other professions' (ACTIL 1906: 5). In other words, any work within journalism should be specialized, and if collaboration with other professionals was acceptable, the latter should never be seen, let alone treated, as journalists. There were several reasons for this. Firstly, to consider the successful writers brought together in the prestigious, but merely symbolic, Associação dos Jornalistas e Escritores Portugueses as members of the press not only did not match their concrete professional status (as they did not live on a salary paid by newspapers),[5] but would also necessarily undermine the work of journalists making them into second-class writers. On the other hand, working journalists, especially when covering stories, required some practical perquisites (open contact with people, tickets to events and entrance to places that were hard to access) that had to be restricted to a narrow group of professionals. In short, what was mainly at stake in the struggle for the recognition of the professional status of journalists was a very practical issue: licence to hold a press card.

This issue was important and difficult enough to last until 1924, when finally the government granted the Sindicato dos Profissionais da Imprensa de Lisboa (SPIL, Lisbon Press Workers' Union), the successor to ACTIL recently created by journalists like João Campos Lima, Belo Redondo and Artur Portela, the exclusive right to issue press cards. Now, what was most remarkable about the whole process was how only a few months after the creation of the SPIL as the only association entitled to recognize someone as a journalist, writers like Júlio Dantas responded by creating the Sociedade dos Escritores e Compositores Teatrais Portugueses (Portuguese Writers' and Theatrical Composers' Society), whose aim was to protect author's rights and most especially their royalties. The identity of both groups was defined not only simultaneously but in contrast to each other. The moment when journalists secured a press card – giving them a professional status that enabled them to negotiate collectively and on equal terms with newspaper proprietors – coincided with the moment when writers realized that they also constituted a professional cadre whose interests had to be collectively protected. Thus we might say that by the 1920s there was enough room for both a journalistic market with an autonomous professional class, and a literary market (which included theatrical production) that had become profitable enough to ensure the financial independence of some authors. The specific conditions of the Portuguese public sphere (its size, to put it bluntly) were of course exiguous, and the viability of this differentiation depended on the strict separation between both activities.

These socio-professional conditions formed the background to the 1921 journalists' strike, in itself a significant episode in the wider context of the economic crisis and political radicalization that followed the First World War and whose impact cannot be understood outside the process of market competition and proletarianization I have just described.

Newspapers were frequently affected by the industrial action of typesetters. In those moments, when the machines stopped, or in the absence of
a specialist who could run them, editions would sometimes be published
anyway, but with a very basic layout and poor print quality. The very
appearance of the newspaper would make it unrecognizable, but as journalists normally did not strike, the content would then be more or less the
same as on any other day.

In 1921, however, everything would be different. An atmosphere of
political tension and economic pessimism marked the start of the year.
From early January, several editorials in *Diário de Notícias* (presumably
written by Augusto de Castro) argued that the crisis was due to the heavy
taxation imposed by the government. This position guaranteed that the
newspaper was on the side of the workers, the main victims of excessive
taxes. In one move, Castro attacked the republican government and the
influence of the state in the economy, and tried to pre-empt the rise of
a labour movement against employers such as newspaper companies.
The reason was simple: as victims of heavy taxation, the companies that
owned newspapers were themselves experiencing difficulties, which
had an inevitable impact on salaries. Apparently, the typesetters' union,
which was part of the anarchist Confederação Geral do Trabalho (CGT,
General Workers Confederation), did not think the newspapers' situation
was bad enough to justify refusing salary increases for staff in 1921. On
17 January, *Diário de Notícias* published a brief note announcing that the
workers' representatives had approved industrial action. Next day, only
two newspapers were published in Lisbon: *A Batalha* ('The Battle'), the
official organ of the CGT, and the first issue of *Imprensa de Lisboa*, a
newspaper produced exclusively by strikers and their strongest weapon
in the fight to come. Two days later, the directors of all the newspapers whose workers were on strike managed to rally a few typesetters
and produced their own title, *O Jornal*, with which they would combat
Imprensa de Lisboa on a daily basis, thus transforming a conflict *within*
newspapers into a conflict *between* newspapers.

Two things were particularly remarkable in this situation. The first
was that everyone seemed at least to agree that the struggle would be
unthinkable without a newspaper as a weapon. The second was that
the strikers had their own publication where they could publish their
views with the same level of public visibility as the organ of the newspaper companies.[6] A third element, however, must also be noted: at first
sight, both titles presented themselves as politically neutral as possible. Nothing in the names *O Jornal* or *Imprensa de Lisboa* gave any
hint of their ideological or class content. Between the workers and the
bosses, then, a third element, the readership, needed to be won round

to the cause of the individual newspapers in order for these to survive. In other words, the choice of newspaper a person bought and read had never been such a political act, and never had a political struggle depended so dramatically on journalists' ability to persuade readers what that event was about. In this sense, it is very important to see how the conflict was initially presented in the different newspapers. *O Jornal* immediately used the motivations of the CGT (and the fact that *A Batalha* continued to be published), and the choice of editor at *Imprensa de Lisboa* – none other than the 'infamous' anarchist João Campos Lima – to accuse the strikers of 'red censorship', for the suspension of the publication of the usual newspapers had made it impossible for their editors to explain their position.

This accusation was then raised to higher stakes in the first edition of *O Jornal*, where the strike was dubbed an 'incessant work of disobedience and destruction' proper to 'anarchic spirits' and 'analogous to the situation in Russia, where the most despicable tyranny had imposed itself in the name of freedom'.[7] The day before, *Imprensa de Lisboa* had reassured its readers that it would be 'a true organ of public opinion', totally independent from the 'influences' and 'unspoken consciousnesses' of all 'obscure businesses' and 'financial corruption' that controlled the press.[8] The situation seemed clear from the start. In an age of revolution, under the threat and hope of communism, the conflict between workers and bosses was ideologically defined as a struggle between communism and capitalism. Interestingly, whereas *Imprensa de Lisboa* was always very careful to protect its image against the spectre of communism – 'the public knows us well, we are those workers who have always been in close contact with that same public, and have defended and informed it',[9] the newspaper stated – *O Jornal* never spent much time dismissing the ways business and finance influenced the editorial line of newspapers.

In any case, only a few days into the strike, something else seemed to emerge as the true scandal in this 'attempt at Bolshevism', as *O Jornal* referred to the strike.[10] Let us compare two excerpts from both *Imprensa de Lisboa* and *O Jornal* to try to grasp what it was:

'Our Attitude' – For the first time in Portugal, creatures who think, men whose mission has been to lead and defend the reputation of their profession and class, abandoned the positions where they have been ignominiously imprisoned, patiently waiting for the liberating hour of redemption ... side by side with their typesetting comrades. During that decisive moment, they all hugged each other in the middle of the street and tears of joy and relief ran down those faces more used to tears of sorrow.[11]

'What we defend' – It is not just the technical, or material, fellow workers we have before us, those classes like the typesetters, printers, stereotypers, etc. – it is also the moral and intellectual part of the press represented by the writing staff who seem to want to engage with the [CGT], an openly revolutionary organization ... The unfolding of events will prove that their disgraceful gesture opens a unique and unacceptable precedent in the history of world journalism.[12]

A union between manual and intellectual workers had never been seen before. The revolutionary potential of having both in the same political struggle became immediately clear to everyone, workers and directors alike. Such a coalition transcended the division on which the whole economic and political system was based. In this sense, from a conservative point of view, the strike seemed an unnatural reversal of the established order, all the more dramatic for its resemblance to what had recently happened in Russia. The fact that journalists, the thinking – as opposed to mechanical – part of journalism, shared the same interests as manual workers could persuade people of the most absurd, and as such dangerous, political idea: that there was some kind of rationality in the cause of the proletariat, whose claims should at best be treated with compassion at times of especially despairing hardship.

The belief that the ideas were all on the one side, that is – that class struggle was in fact a conflict between rationality and irrationality – had a specific version in journalism. It was because intellectual activity, and the written word that supported it, should be kept above the pettiness of class politics that the editors of O Jornal never really felt the need to respond to the accusation that their newspapers served private interests, especially not if those accusations came from those without the right to have opinions in the first place.[13] When, on the other hand, proper journalists raised the issue, it was as if suddenly the traditional image of newspapers as the impartial champions of universal values could be questioned. The continuous attack O Jornal directed at the strikers began precisely with the idea that journalists, by siding with the typesetters, had necessarily lost their clear-sightedness. The deep conviction, or common sense, that newspapers were completely free from political ideologies was jeopardized. Accordingly, when journalists undermined their independence, they were accused of betraying freedom itself. The insistence on this theme showed how deeply the strike disturbed the order of things: 'it really is incomprehensible how an intellectual worker can join in with the claims of a typesetter or a distributor', complained O Jornal in an article repetitively titled 'Insisting'.[14] To reinforce its views, the newspaper often reprinted excerpts taken from Porto's newspapers, whose workers were not on strike. O Norte, for example, wrote in disbelief: 'we're facing an absurdity – intellectuals, men of the elite, structurally assimilated into bourgeois society, mixing with the anonymous and unconscious mob'.[15]

The distance between Porto and the strike in Lisbon seemed to allow northern editors to express views the directors in the capital tried to avoid. In fact, the very situation that *O Jornal* found 'impossible to explain' appeared rather clearly in *O Norte* as class conflict. Journalists should not engage with workers, not exactly because manual workers and intellectuals could not communicate, but insofar as the latter were, in the proper nature of their professional activities, bourgeois. In another article from *O Norte* reprinted in *O Jornal*, the conflict was reduced to a number 'of impolite attitudes by well-educated and intellectual people', 'bourgeois journalists sheltered in the enemy's field, where the plans to ruin and eliminate bourgeois society are impossible to ignore'.[16] This coincided, of course, with the kind of discourse strikers wanted to use to describe what was going on. By late January, when the strike seemed destined to last indefinitely and the different positions had firmly settled, *A Batalha* stated that 'no peace should exist between Capital and Labour' as 'Capital should be suppressed'.[17] *O Jornal*'s response to this discourse synthesized the need for an impartial – and in that sense politically invisible – press as the foundation of the bourgeois order under threat:

'In the face of danger' – Once again we feel the need to reiterate and try to fix in the spirit of all those who have the duty of defending this society under siege the fact that the current movement *against newspapers* is the most dangerous that has occurred in our country. Only a free and independent press, inspired by patriotism and reason, can resist, with its nationwide action, the subversive propaganda of indigenous Bolshevism. Its audacity knows no limits. Its agents know that the press is the guarantee of social stability, so much so that in all its strikes, their first concern is to get rid of newspapers. Watch out! If the press that still resists CGT's *mot d'ordre* surrendered, their destructive spirit wouldn't take long to light the fire of their bloody delirium in the unfortunate Portuguese land.[18]

By replacing capitalism with civilization – and thus economic interests and political power with rationality (or just common sense) – the press could be made to appear as the ultimate cement of national cohesion, and thus achieve a particularly efficient image of the process through which the constitution of any imagined community always entails the disqualification of the other – in this case the proletarian qua communist. This was particularly serious at a moment defined by a deep crisis whose origin, as we have already seen, should be traced back to the First World War and the Russian Revolution.

The impact of war and revolution on the press could be read in two ways, according to the different positions in conflict in the strike. According to Jorge de Abreu, the editor of Porto's most important newspaper, *O Primeiro de Janeiro*, and quoted in *O Jornal*, the difficulties experienced by newspapers in 1921 should be attributed to the dramatic rise of paper prices during and after the war. After 1918, the price per copy of a newspaper had more than doubled from 2 to 5 cents. As the price of paper kept going up and another rise in the price of daily newspapers proved unfeasible, the solution was either to reduce the number of pages or simply cancel the publication. This demonstrated, according to Abreu, how unreasonable the protests were, and how scandalous was the absolute lack of 'self-restraint, discipline and good sense' shown by journalists.[19]

Imprensa de Lisboa had a different view on how the war had determined the current situation. In an article published the same day as that of Abreu, João Campos Lima explained how manual workers had understood the basic rules of capitalist exploitation a long time ago. Up to the war, he continued, intellectuals, even those who depended on a salary – and journalists in particular – still believed that nothing decisive separated them from society's richer strata. Therefore, they usually viewed workers' struggles with contempt. The war, however, had changed all this, for the difficulties they were forced to experience with the crisis – 'rather than syndicalism or socialist propaganda' – gave them a new consciousness of how fragile their position really was. The result was sociological self-discovery with decisive political consequences:

> Hunger is very powerful. The intellectual rebelled, demanded, protested, positioned himself in the revolutionary field; he used proletarian tactics; when he least expected it, he saw himself side by side with the manual workers. Now, in the face of the overwhelming reality of facts, solidarity came naturally. Pride and prejudice disappeared. All that is left are the exploited, brothers fighting side by side.[20]

In the initial phase of the strike, then, whereas workers emphasized the socio-economic aspect of the question, editors dramatized its political meaning. When, by the end of January, *O Jornal* finally decided to give some space to the economic side of the conflict – 'Other Aspects of the Question' was the title of an article published on 30 January – all it did was to dismiss the fight of workers as opportunistic: 'they want more money today to be able to ask for even more money tomorrow'.[21] The article then denounced the greed of the typesetters who charged extra over and above their salaries for a number of external services, like engravings and advertisements, for which they used company equipment. The conclusion was a bold accusation: the whole point of the industrial action was to 'favour the most inept, incompetent, to the disadvantage of the most skilled, respectful and dedicated', which clearly showed how communism was in fact a form of barbarism.

This was the wrong strategy. While the strike went on and public opinion became increasingly involved, directors realized that readers would find any explanation undermining the economic dimension of the conflict unacceptable. More specifically, because manual workers also read newspapers and those who were not manual workers felt dramatically threatened by proletarianization, to dismiss the clear majority of proletarians and their demands was just suicidal. By mid February, then, *O Jornal* began carefully avoiding any generalization and focused instead on very specific targets. At first, the chosen enemy was the typesetters' union itself, and particularly its main representative, the CGT. However, this did not work either. The word *geral* ('general') in the CGT's name was not there by chance. The CGT represented too many workers for public opinion to accept it as a mere bunch of opportunists. So, if typesetters represented something universal, the weak link had to be found where the minority was. The striking journalists became an easy target. As workers, they were easily made to appear as privileged when compared with manual workers. As intellectuals, they were easily dismissed as mediocre but powerful enough to deceive with their pens the majority of hardworking honest staff in the printing trade:

'Those who profit' – The movement came from the second group (the journalists). A few reporters and informants did everything, as the great majority of typesetters knew how inconvenient the moment was for industrial action, given the hardships experienced by newspapers. But the 80 managed to persuade the 582 ... Those who are sacrificed are the proletarians who work with the machines; the distributors (newsboys) who take the newspaper where they work to every corner of the city, even when it is cold and raining. The 80 enjoy the fruits of their envy, of their resentment, their laziness, because most of them just want to profit without doing anything.[22]

The effort to divide the strikers was exposed in *Imprensa de Lisboa* on 19 February. The incoherence of *O Jornal*'s sudden shift of position in particular did not go unnoticed: after accusing typesetters of 'red censorship' and of dragging innocent journalists to perdition, now directors seemed to 'bow down before a class they can't stand' and demonize journalists.[23] Throughout February, the combat between both newspapers involved a permanent display of forces. Lists of typesetters on call were published in every edition of *Imprensa de Lisboa*, as workers divided themselves in shifts to ensure the paper could come out and so guarantee themselves some kind of income – the payment of salaries had of course been interrupted. The list showed how well organized the strike was and that workers were united and taking matters seriously, for otherwise they would not have endured the sacrifices involved in living without remuneration for – by then – more than a month.

But it also meant a provocation of the newspaper where the strikers originally worked: 'the evening edition of *Imprensa de Lisboa* is today composed by the staff of the evening edition of *Diário de Notícias*', one could read in *Imprensa de Lisboa*'s first edition.[24] On the opposite side, *O Jornal* tried to show its strength with a similar list of the names of journalists who were not on strike. It was an impressive roster of 'literate-journalists', as most of them were actually renowned writers who signed their pieces and authored books. Not surprisingly, men like Afonso de Bragança, António Ferro, João Ameal and Luiz de Oliveira Guimarães all collaborated on *O Jornal*. 'Journalistic modernism' was how *Imprensa de Lisboa* contemptuously referred to them, in response to the insulting epithet *O Jornal* used to designate the strikers: 'bricklayers'.[25] By the end of February, the tone used by directors when referring to their former employees had reached a level of absolute loathing:

> We have to admit that newspapers had visibly deteriorated with the corrupting impact of certain fake journalists, who now want to teach what journalism is to the people who generously accepted them. We are then led to believe that one of the consequences of this strike will be to sweep away all the rubbish with which these newcomers filled the newspaper columns. In fact, Lisbon's papers had never seen such a plague of mediocrity.[26]

It was difficult to see how an agreement could be reached when revolutionary strikers promised to destroy capital and the companies celebrated the strike as an opportunity to set an example of discipline and make a show of power. The radicalization of the conflict was inevitable. The daily succession of editions (two in the case of *Imprensa de Lisboa*, in the morning and in the evening) led to an escalation in the rhetorical violence used by the belligerents. The need to persuade public opinion gave way to an ever-growing need to enlarge the scope of mutual criticism and toughen rhetoric in a way that quickly reached the level of insult. This was something everyone was more or less used to, and apparently willing to accept, as we have seen in the tone taken by *O Século* and *Diário de Notícias* in their mutual diatribes when their rivalry became more acute at the time they covered the murder of Maria Alves. But the strike, and in particular the fact that the two titles had the same degree of visibility and political strength throughout the conflict, was different. For here the entire public sphere (at least in Lisbon) was dominated by class struggle for more than a month. In other words, the usual frenzy with which newspapers set the pace of everyday modern life – what I have tried to define as a modernist event – made capitalism's fundamental contradiction emerge as such: when proletarians democratized the hierarchies of journalism, by putting their opinions and interests on the same level as those of employers, the incontrovertible inequality on which the whole system stood was questioned and order was subverted. For a moment, when most newspapers were closed and circulation – the flow of news and information that put narratives in motion and constituted one of the backbones of modern life – was interrupted, it looked as though a strike of journalists and typesetters was the ideal spark for a general strike (which normally starts with the interruption of a different form of circulation, that of public transport) and thus the beginning of a revolution.

In a clear acknowledgement that the situation risked getting out of hand, the government decided that things had gone too far and mobilized army typesetters to print all the newspapers that had been closed for lack of staff. This was one of the first measures taken by a new conservative cabinet after taking power at the beginning of March 1921 and replacing the previous government that had fallen in the political crisis that marked the beginning of the year (and which the strike was both a consequence of and an active contribution to). *Imprensa de Lisboa*, which up to then had insistently protested against any political interference, immediately reassured its readers on 3 March that it would resist and warned against 'the simulacrum of newspapers put together by soldiers, whose aim is to convince the public that the newspaper strike is over'.[27] From then on, however, the position of the strikers would become more defensive. The edition of *Diário de Notícias* on the same day showed a completely different attitude. Back in the comfort of his own page, Augusto de Castro could now use a pedagogical tone and explain to his readers that tradition – 'the forms of expression celebrated by the public' – was back in place and that the time had come to 'make a strike on strikes' as public opinion was tired of turmoil and wished for political stability.[28] On the opposite side, *Imprensa de Lisboa* was now fighting against time: its daily insistence that the strike was still ongoing showed how dramatic the pressure was, with workers becoming more and more desperate after almost two months without a proper salary and showing signs that the temptation to go back to their jobs was becoming almost irresistible. This pressure had an immediate impact on the new strategy of *Imprensa de Lisboa*. From that moment on, João Campos Lima assumed the role of tribune against the interests of business monopolies in the press. Right after the most important titles had reappeared, he started a campaign discrediting the dubious political positions of influential titles like *O Século* – whose political preferences varied according to the newspaper's own interests – and *Diário de Notícias* – accused of being falsely loyal to the republic by hiding its monarchism.

Still, the attacks became more aggressive when focused on economic matters. At first, Lima tried to provoke division within the enemy – a technique directors had already used against the coalition of typesetters and journalists – by accusing *O Século* and *Diário de Notícias*, as the two newspapers with most resources (in terms of distribution, advertising and so on) of trying to ruin the competition by returning in full force whilst poorer titles were still struggling to come out every day. Towards the end of March, *Imprensa de Lisboa* focused on a violent campaign against *O Século*, suggesting that the company's legitimate proprietors had been expropriated and accusing the director of all sorts of illegalities. The campaign was aimed at postwar speculation and tried to reveal the hidden links between big business and the most influential newspapers. The result, however, was the progressive disappearance of the strike from public debate. The violence of the campaign only reinforced the perception that the strikers' cause had been doomed from the moment the government decided to intervene. *Imprensa de Lisboa* would survive until mid May, attacking all those who had abandoned the fight and accepted individual agreements with the newspaper companies, praising the ones who resisted and trying to rally the cause of journalists with other struggles and strikes. After 9 April, the anniversary of the Battle of La Lys – commemorating the most important episode of the Portuguese army's involvement in the First World War – the newspaper still joined in the wave of nationalism by promoting another campaign – this time with positive tones – on behalf of crippled veterans.

The strategy was to seize the opportunity opened by the strike and set up *Imprensa de Lisboa* as a new title aligned with leftist politics. Apparently, however, if the strike did prove to be a moment of renewal in Lisbon's journalistic milieu, this did not correspond to a demand for more politicization, let alone a move towards the left. During the strike, a group of young reporters including Norberto Lopes and Artur Portela took the initiative to create a new publication, *Última Hora*. The idea was greeted with sympathy in *Imprensa de Lisboa* on 12 February, where the paper was presented as an example of what a 'new journalism' with 'modern ideas' should look like: its audience were the new 'proletarian intellectuals', including teachers, (other) journalists, clerks, as well as artists and writers, and the content should focus on 'cultural questions' in order to 'raise the moral and intellectual level of the people'.[29] *Última Hora* matched these expectations. With an attractive layout, between newspaper and magazine, it tried to satisfy the intellectual demands of the traditionally cultivated, while taking into account how much the living conditions of some of the educated classes had deteriorated. In this sense, it focused on culture – or on a cultural approach to reality, from art and literature to economy and politics – as an alternative to the sensationalism of crime and other tragedies, and as a form of evading the radicalization of political debate and the grim conditions of material life:

This literary newspaper will be pleasant to the eye and will help you pass your time while you return from the city centre to the neighbourhood where you have decided to establish your ivory tower, thus turning your journey by tram, car or carriage into a pleasant experience where you don't have to think about the crisis or the manners of your fellow commuter … It is a newspaper for those middle-class professionals who … among us, are almost squeezed like sardines between the greed of those on top and the rise of distant claims coming from below.[30]

Despite the friendly nod to proletarian revolutionary utopias and hostility to the privileged, this new journalism would be about something other than politics and class struggle. It would, on the one hand, recognize the existence of a new social actor, those whom, speaking of this period, Siegfried Kracauer identified as the salaried masses (Kracauer 1998), while on the other hand it tried to satisfy both their intellectual routines and their right to distraction, thus transforming traditional cultural objects into the newest forms of entertainment. In this sense, the strike in general and the survival of *Imprensa de Lisboa* more specifically in the world of journalism proved unfeasible, not so much because of the actions of the authorities and employers, but because ultimately any revolution would depend on a coalition that proved too short lived.

Despite the brief lifespan of *Última Hora*, this type of publication would prove very influential in 1920s journalism. The same group of young reporters was soon invited to set up another project. In April 1921, under the direction of a prestigious intellectual, Joaquim Manso, the whole generation of modernist journalists – including strikers like Norberto Lopes and Artur Portela and non-strikers like António Ferro and Afonso de Bragança – got together in the most innovative newspaper of the period: *Diário de Lisboa*, described by António Ferro as a newspaper-magazine, thus emphasizing not only the paper's power to produce written images but also its ability to refashion the modern world through the exciting narratives – reportage – that made it so much more interesting to readers. This was the history of journalism that began in April 1921, and that in part has constituted our own history of modernist journalism throughout this book. Behind the glamour of modernist journalists and their reports, however, some issues still had to be settled. On 27 April, *Imprensa de Lisboa* marked one hundred days of the strike. It was not a celebration. The duration of the conflict proved too long to endure without a salary, and workers had already started negotiating with the newspapers. The paper's last words proudly emphasized the meaning of the struggle, how it had scared the powerful and demonstrated the strength and resistance of united proletarians. On the other hand, it also recognized that when bonds weakened and some abandoned the strike, the ones who stayed were doomed to defeat and unemployment.

On 8 May, *Imprensa de Lisboa* still refused to admit defeat: 'Will we be alone? That's fine. Abandoned? Better still'.[31] A few days earlier, however, *A Batalha* started a campaign pointing out that the harsh reality of unemployment demanded a contribution from everyone: 'WORKERS: the time has come to help those men who have been fighting the bosses for the last 104 days!'[32] Those 104 days had not only rendered the position of strikers more fragile, it had also reinforced the legitimacy of the bourgeois public sphere. In between the display of power by conservative politics (in newspapers like *Diário de Notícias*) and the emergence of a new middle-class way of life (epitomized by *Diário de Lisboa* and its modernist journalism), the defeat of the proletarian struggle in 1921 seemed to anticipate the strong counter-revolutionary reaction – in itself a combination of conservatism and modernity – that was about to take place in Portugal and beyond with the emergence of fascism in the period between the two world wars.

Notes

1. As we will see in the next chapter, the new notion of culture that emerged in the period between the two world wars was one of the most decisive responses to these modern phenomena. Our authors' spiritual retrieval may, in this sense, be better understood in the light of what Herbert Marcuse called, only a few years later, 'the culture of souls': 'the culture of souls absorbed in a false form those forces and wants which could find no place in everyday life. The cultural ideal assimilated men's longing for a happier life: for humanity, goodness, joy, truth, and solidarity. Only, in this ideal, they are all furnished with the affirmative accent of belonging to a higher, purer, nonprosaic world' (Marcuse 2007: 100).
2. Literary contradiction is defined by Jacques Rancière as a kind of disagreement between a certain referent and its representation. In Proust, for instance, the contradiction assumes the form of a gap between the 'gravity of the expression' and 'frivolity of the subject' (Rancière 2011: 155).
3. Ideology is here 'in its basic dimension', which, according to Slavoj Žižek, works as 'a fantasy-construction which serves as support for … "reality" itself: an illusion which structures our effective, real social relations and thereby masks some insupportable, real, impossible kernel', that is, antagonism: 'a traumatic social division which cannot be symbolized' (Žižek 1989: 45).
4. '[I]n his particular-empirical activity, the subject of course presupposes the "world", the objectivity on which he performs his activity, as something given in advance, as a positive condition of his activity; but this positive-empirical activity is possible only if he structures his perception of the world in advance in a way that opens the space for his intervention'. (Žižek 1989: 218).
5. According to Christophe Charle, salaries were a decisive feature in defining the status of journalists in France, especially after the First World War. This was the moment of a clear separation between the journalist and the writer, when journalists found themselves sharing the same set of problems, and struggles, as manual professionals within the press: 'the end of the war did not put an end to this unrest: in fact, salaries, especially those of typesetters, due to their strong trade union movement, put strong pressure on the newspaper companies. The latter tried to make up for the advantages given to manual workers by cutting expenses in newspaper offices. Journalists thus

experienced a feeling of demotion: the gap between the better-paid typesetter and the lower ranks of journalists was sometimes reversed. To the latter, given the symbolic hierarchy that places intellectual work above other kinds, this is the world upside down. The debate around "intellectual workers" comes from here' (Charle 2004: 271). In Portugal during the same period the issues were very similar.

6. A strike where workers could fight on equal terms with the bosses was surely a rare moment in the working-class movement. Moreover, the fact that this particular strike occurred in the realm of newspapers constituted a unique opportunity for workers to show what a proletarian public sphere could look like. The creation of a newspaper to counter the position of the companies resembles what Oskar Negt and Alexander Kluge have defined as the best strategy for the proletariat for acting within the bourgeois public sphere: 'it is essential that proletarian counter-publicity confront these public spheres permeated by the interests of capital, and does not merely regard itself as the antithesis of the classical bourgeois public sphere. Practical experience is the crux. The working class must know how to deal with the bourgeois public sphere, the threats the latter poses, without allowing its own experiences to be defined by the latter's narrow horizons' (Negt and Kluge 1988: 63).

7. *O Jornal*, 20 January 1921, p.1.

8. *Imprensa de Lisboa*, 19 January 1921, p.1.

9. *Imprensa de Lisboa*, 19 January 1921, p.1.

10. *O Jornal*, 25 January 1921, p.1.

11. *Imprensa de Lisboa*, 18 January 1921, p.1.

12. *O Jornal*, 21 January 1921, p.1.

13. The strike thus constitutes a perfect example of those rare opportunities in which people break with the order that ascribes them to fixed places and allows them to go where they are not supposed to be, moments of 'disagreement' in which Jacques Rancière identifies the emergence of true politics. Rancière illustrates a particular political moment, the 'secession of the Roman plebeians on Aventine Hill', from the perspective of speech. Here, a political event occurred precisely when those who were not supposed to speak suddenly assumed the right to have their own say: 'the position of the intransigent patricians is straightforward: there is no place for discussion with the plebs for the simple reason that plebs do not speak. They do not speak because they are beings without a name, deprived of logos – meaning, of symbolic enrollment in the city. Plebs live a purely individual life that passes on nothing to posterity except for life itself, reduced to its reproductive function. Whoever is nameless *cannot* speak. Consul Menenius made a fatal mistake in imagining that *words* were issuing from the mouths of the plebs when logically the only thing that could issue forth was noise' (Rancière 2004: 23–24).

14. *O Jornal*, 23 January 1921, p.1.

15. *O Jornal*, 24 January 1921, p.2.

16. *O Jornal*, 24 January 1921, p.2.

17. *A Batalha*, 22 January 1921, p.1.

18. *O Jornal*, 29 January 1921, p.1.

19. *O Jornal*, 21 January 1921, p.1.

20. *Imprensa de Lisboa*, 21 January 1921, p.1.

21. *O Jornal*, 30 January 1921, p.1.

22. *O Jornal*, 12 February 1921, p.1.

23. *Imprensa de Lisboa*, 19 February 1921, p.1.

24. *Imprensa de Lisboa*, 19 January 1921, p.1.

25. Cf. the evening's edition of *Imprensa de Lisboa*, 12 February 1921, p.1.
26. *O Jornal*, 26 February 1921, p.1.
27. *Imprensa de Lisboa*, 3 March 1921, p.1.
28. *Diário de Notícias*, 3 March 1921, p.1.
29. *Imprensa de Lisboa*, 12 February 1921, p.1.
30. *Última Hora*, 16 February 1921, p.2.
31. *Imprensa de Lisboa*, 8 May 1921, p.1.
32. *A Batalha*, 30 April 1921, p.1.

Chapter 7

Storing Information

Take a newspaper / Take some scissors / Choose from this paper an article of the length you want to make your poem / Cut out the article / Next carefully cut out each of the words that makes up this article and put them all in a bag / Shake gently / Next take out each cutting one after the other / Copy conscientiously in the order in which they left the bag / The poem will resemble you / And there you are – an infinitely original author of charming sensibility, even though unappreciated by the vulgar herd!

—Tristan Tzara, 'To Make a Dadaist Poem'

Archive

I suggest we start this final chapter by going back to the front page of *Diário de Notícias* of 13 January 1890 which we analysed in Chapter 1. One of this book's initial theses was that the page's political meaning should be looked for at the level of its layout, rather than just in its content, particularly of the British Ultimatum, where historians usually identify the birth of Portuguese twentieth-century political history. In fact, as I tried to argue, that edition already staged the structure with which newspapers would organize public perceptions over the following decades. This point was illustrated through the analysis of the day's main stories, not only the intense circulation of information around the Ultimatum but also the complex set of visibilities at work in the report of the suicide of Júlio César Machado.

These were shocking events to readers of *Diário de Notícias* in 1890. And yet, our own comprehensive reading of that same front page is bound to surprise us for a different set of reasons. To start with, because after the news of the Ultimatum and the suicide readers who continued all the way to the end of the last column would embark on a journey that took them not only to many different places (the telegraphic communication of the Ultimatum had already done that) but also to the most disparate types of information: religious events, historical celebrations, the movement of ships, a homage to a journalist, a robbery in a military barracks, the illness of the king of Spain, administrative problems in Angola, the question of electric lightening in Leiria, the illness of Lord Hartington in London, troubles in Haiti (relayed from New York through Havas), the activities of several associations, the last will of the German empress, updates on the epidemic of influenza in Guimarães, riots in Barcelos, the case of a corrupt politician in Ponte de Lima, a *Te Deum* in Cascais with the royal family, the death of a colonial functionary in Macao, several arrests and military promotions, the nomination of a new judge, a new portrait of the king, information on the spread of influenza in London, Berlin, Geneva and Pest, a train accident, the death of the aunt of a famous aristocrat, some lost telegrams, some advertising, and shows that could be seen in Lisbon, with special reference to a spectacular programme at the Coliseum.

The list's length highlights the randomness of the news, a direct consequence of newspaper dependence on the contingency of occasional sources of information: we can assume that the news from different places in Africa had been brought by a ship just arrived in Lisbon, while all the different news from Minho – the troubles in neighbouring Guimarães, Barcelos and Ponte de Lima – had surely been sent by the same source in the region, and presumably information regarding influenza throughout central and northern Europe were taken from a foreign source (a newspaper or press agency). But the length of the list also invites us to quantify the content: the entire page amounts to about 6,500 words text (this was of the front page alone, as the rest of the newspaper was filled with ads). What at first sight seems just a single page one can glance over thus becomes, when closely read, a much more significant collection of information.

Quantity, as in the number of words and in the diversity of pieces and sections, constitutes a decisive element in characterizing newspapers as a form of industrial production. In thirty years, from the 1890s when the Ultimatum took place to the 1920s of the reports we have analysed, newspapers spread out in different directions. They practically reached the entire national territory and beyond, but they also claimed to be able to incorporate – and this is what our list of news suggests – events of all kinds happening anywhere in the world. Better still, with longer editions, more text, more journalists and sections and a better structured layout, newspapers had evolved from a 'messy' set of fragmented stories, 'a bombardment of undigested stuff' (Barnhurst and Nerone 2001: 251) into more ordered narratives.[1] Moreover, during those decades, titles created in the nineteenth century like *Diário de Notícias* and *O Século* extended their claim to representing a total coverage of reality by being able to present themselves with a history of their own and, as such, as an archive containing information about the preceding half century. In this sense, it is interesting to notice how this historicization of newspaper titles was less the result of the accumulation of symbolic prestige than of the more literal accumulation, year after year, of daily editions.[2]

The full impact of this temporal accumulation, the quantity of days and years covered by the paper, could only be assessed with some sense of another kind of quantity: that of the number of copies of each daily edition, which would correspond to the size of a newspaper's readership. Only a week after the end of the 1921 strike analysed in the previous chapter (and *Imprensa de Lisboa*'s last edition), *O Século* tried to get back to business as usual with a challenge to its readers: 'How many people read *O Século*?' it asked.[3] The idea was to show advertisers – on whom the newspaper depended financially – that its readership matched almost exactly the number of literate citizens among Portugal's population, and thus approximately the total number of consumers in the national market. Considering that at least three different people read each copy of the daily edition, *O Século* explained, the total number of readers would be around 400,000 (unless the people who only read the ads was also considered, which would double those figures: six readers per copy, totalling 800,000). Furthermore, considering the overwhelming extent of illiteracy in 1920s Portugal (about 80 per cent, according to the newspaper, which is not far from the real figure), the number of readers had to be calculated in relation to the restricted number of the literate: about 1.2 million people. This meant, according to the forceful argument put forward by *O Século*, that the newspaper was read 'by almost every Portuguese who can read', or at least, I would add, two thirds of the total number of potential readers. One should also mention all those who listened while the newspaper was being read aloud by someone else, still a common habit in both rural and urban areas at the time.

Another attempt to show the impact of the industrial scale of the press was undertaken by *Diário de Notícias* on the paper's sixtieth anniversary, on 29 December 1924. In a written version of what would be shown on screen four years later in *Como se Faz um Número do Diário de Notícias*, an article titled '*Diário de Notícias* Today' tried to stress the key idea also put forward in the dispute with *O Século* after the murder of Maria Alves: the newspaper was a form of industrial mass production not only because it printed hundreds of thousands of copies every day, but above all for its capacity to produce news on everything within reach on a daily basis:

> *Diário de Notícias* must know everything, must always be vigilant – its information ser-
> vices cover, in an enormous net, the whole life of the capital … Minutes after an occur-
> rence, the reporter must know all of its details and must also have it written and ready to
> become public: for the newspaper is either done on time, without losing a single moment,
> vertiginously thought out and vertiginously made, or else it will have no use but to become
> wrapping paper … Readers must imagine an important event – a revolution, for example.
> Multiply reporters: put ten men, or more, as many as necessary, running throughout the
> city, searching for any clarification that may reconstitute the event's plot; tell them not to
> overlook what apparently seems most insignificant in any circumstance.[4]

In sum, more than just an order of discourse, the overwhelming presence
of newspapers in the world (the spatio-temporal ubiquity of *Diário de
Notícias*'s 'enormous net') seems to evoke, as I already suggested, the
way Michel Foucault describes the panopticon as the instrument of biopolitics (Foucault 1977: 195–228). In our case, it should be stressed how
journalism acted at the level of social perception. In other words, it was
not enough for newspapers to employ their mechanisms of vigilance.
Readers, that is, society, not only felt their presence, they also had to act
as accomplices by looking through the apparatus (that is, reading and
giving a sense to narratives published in newspapers) and thus taking
part in the system of control.[5]

However, to represent the weight of this presence was a problem. For
if newspapers were able to continuously publish everything for decades
(and be individually read on a daily basis throughout one's entire lifetime), the quantitative results of this would become hard to imagine, let
alone represent, in words. To say, for instance, that each day *Diário de
Notícias* printed more than 100,000 copies, totalling over 36 million a
year, was impressive but still rather abstract. The solution was to show
what that meant in pictures (once again, the newspaper could still be
essentially a written form, but its self-representation had to be rendered
through images). Readers were thus shown that the height of a pile made
of all the paper used by *Diário de Notícias* in a year would more than
double that of the Eiffel Tower; spreading out the print run of one edition of the paper would cover the distance from Lisbon to Porto, all editions over a month would reach the North Pole, and all editions in a year
would circumnavigate the planet three times; finally, if we were to cut
the paper up and lay its columns end to end, these would reach the moon.

The visual aspect of this quantification was very striking. Not by
chance, both *Como se Faz um Número do Diário de Notícias* and another
shorter documentary film about the making of *O Século* made in 1924
also tried to illustrate these large quantities. Whereas in the latter we can
see a huge roll of paper unfolding down one of Lisbon's longest avenues,
Como se Faz um Número do Diário de Notícias took the motif further by
allegorically equating the exhaustive presence of the newspaper with life

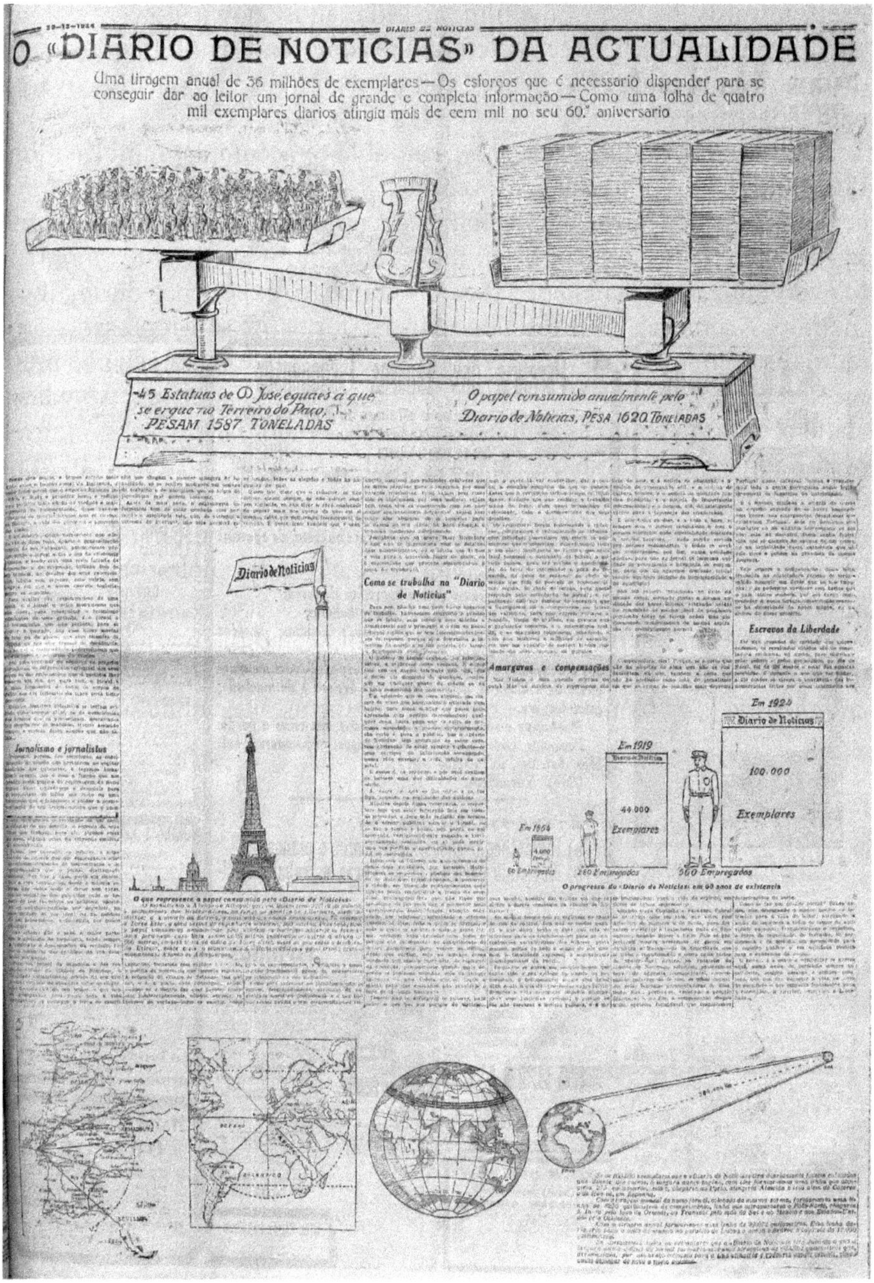

O «DIARIO DE NOTICIAS» DA ACTUALIDADE

Uma tiragem anual de 36 milhões de exemplares—Os esforços que é necessario dispender para se conseguir dar ao leitor um jornal de grande e completa informação—Como uma folha de quatro mil exemplares diarios atingiu mais de cem mil no seu 60.º aniversario

Jornalismo e jornalistas

Como se trabalha no "Diario de Noticias"

Amarguras e compensações

Escravos da Liberdade

Figure 7.1: *Diário de Notícias*, 29 December 1924. Archive of *Diário de Notícias*.

itself: towards the end of the film, an old man is shown slowly walking down what should be interpreted as the long road of life, an ordinary road which, on closer inspection, can be seen to be completely covered with newspapers.

So it was not just that the press was able to accumulate information. If the procedures of journalism were really that efficient in their comprehensiveness, then it was life itself they accumulated.[6] Newspapers, in this sense, were both a deposit of all things and, more importantly, a mirror of everything each person had the opportunity to experience during their lifetime. According to these newspapers' forms of self-representation, journalism, more than a lifelong companion to modern women and men, was a record of their lives. The idea that everything happening anywhere could become news gives us the quantifiable version of the two syntheses performed by the newspaper we analysed in Chapter 1. There, I tried to conceptually render those syntheses – the circulation of disparate news assembled on the page on the one hand; and the production of meaning by readers on the other – by deploying 'glance' as the appropriate gesture to think about the role of readership. Now, I will need to come to terms with not only a description of the process of accumulation, but also with the meaning of all this quantity of information. In this case, the images and rhetoric used by newspapers to situate themselves in the world seem

Figure 7.2: Still from *Como se Faz um Número do Diário de Notícias*. ANIM/Cinemateca Portuguesa.

to match Friedrich Kittler's historical definition of the discourse network in 1900 as the evolution from 'alphabetization made flesh' (the discourse network in 1800) to 'technological media' (Kittler 1990: 178), a historical process where words became material, and ideas, as a consequence, were materialized in pure quantity – which represented both a challenge to modern literature as well as a game, as Kittler illustrates with the work of Stephan Mallarmé, and as Tristan Tzara's poem used as the epigraph to this chapter also suggests.

On the one hand, the involvement of these material words in the development of capitalism, according to Kittler, was mainly achieved through the different mechanisms of modern writing: the telegraph putting words in circulation, the typewriter mechanically producing those same words, and daily newspapers storing them. On the other hand, 'writing ceased to wait, quiet and dead, on patient paper for its consumer' (Kittler 1990: 223), for now it became a participant in, rather than a mere representation of, the thing represented, in a way that resembles our own definition of reportage as narrative in motion. Words, in the discourse network of 1900, were turned into things, signifiers whose circulation allowed them to become signifieds in their own right, as if meaning gave way to the material presence of words produced by machines (typewriters, rotary printers) just as the gramophone had done with sounds and film with images.[7] This could not fail to provoke a major disruption in established cultural hierarchies, especially in the literary field. For, among other things, it represented a blow to the ownership of discourses as one of the practical as well as symbolic foundations of the previous discourse network.

Discourses were thus circulating, rather than waiting quietly on the page (or the book, itself quietly waiting for the reader in the study), but they were also accumulating, producing data, rather than knowledge, and demanding memorization rather than understanding.[8] Newspapers, once again, seemed more than just fit a model created for other media. As in Cézanne's pictorial challenge to the attention of the modern (film) spectator, according to Jonathan Crary (or in Walter Benjamin's idea that Dadaism anticipated cinematic techniques), so too the archival quality of the discourse network described by Kittler seems to find in journalism a predecessor to all other forms.[9] From the circulation of information to its storage, newspapers closed a circle. In fact, it is hard to imagine any other mechanism of reproducibility with the same circulating dynamic, as we have seen, but also with the same capacity to match the ultimate ambition of Kittler's network: to store the world on a 1:1 scale – where 'writing become[s] ... an exhaustion that endlessly refuses to end' (Kittler 1990: 326) – or, even more to the point, to store and exhibit, just like a modern museum, everything and all kinds of things that happened anywhere in a state of permanent accumulation.[10]

And yet, newspapers surely exaggerated. Even as late as the 1920s, the services of reportage and telecommunication did not completely manage to cover the entirety of life and only rarely were they able to grasp what happened beyond the limits of the public sphere. On the other hand, not only did a lot in people's lives go on regardless of what newspapers said, but there were also large segments of the population left outside the journalistic network (starting with the three-quarters of Portugal's population that were illiterate). The discourse produced by journalists on their own mobility and on their newspapers' capacity to contain the whole world should thus be read as a strategy. For with all its exaggerations, the metaphor of filmic reportage and the hyperbolic image of accumulated newspapers unveiled struggles and anxieties felt by reporters and newspapers at the exact moment when cameras and other machines were becoming dominant in a new age of mechanical reproduction.

Culture

In this book we have looked at newspapers as near visual objects readers could glance over and as archives storing written information. In both cases, the news they could show, the information they could store, depended on the material form through which they existed: as paper folios circulating every day and, after a few decades, as a mass of accumulated paper. It is almost as if the quality of what they said, the inner value of their narratives (say, of a daring flight or a violent crime) was less important than those forms of material existence. Meaning, in this sense, depended on the speed of their circulation or on the sheer quantity of information stored. In both cases, the newspaper seemed remarkably close to, one could almost say contaminated by, the form of capital: fleeting in permanent circulation, endlessly accumulating. This is, one might add, what makes newspapers such an interesting object in the study of modernity. But there is also another reason: if it is possible to establish a historical narrative from the moment readers could glance over newspapers to the moment newspapers constituted themselves as the archive of the world, then it becomes obvious that this is a narrative about the normative role of the press. In other words, from narratives in motion whose meaning depended to a large extent on the contingencies of reading, newspapers increasingly became the most authoritative discourses of modernity. Modernity, in these circumstances, ceased to be that historical process based on progress and constant transformation to become a heightened form of social discipline.

This historical process can be seen as the media, or cultural, counterpart to the master social and political narratives of instrumental reason and biopolitics. It is, however, difficult to give it a date, to submit it to a chronology. In fact, it could be said that newspapers never ceased to be both things, a tension between the contingencies of circulation and the uncontrollable appropriations of reading on the one hand, and the crystallization of social norms, political truths and historical memory on the other. However, in the case of Portuguese newspapers at least – but give or take a decade or two, this is a common process in all more or less industrialized countries – the passage from the 1920s to the 1930s seems to be a key moment in the normalization of journalistic narrative and in the normative power of newspapers. Two things already familiar in this book contribute to this. First, the most important titles were already old enough to become well-established institutions, which, in the realm of the press, meant that the daily content published throughout more than half a century could now be seen as a form of patrimony. Second, with the popularization of talkies and radio broadcasts in the 1930s, the anxious frenzy we saw in the press of the 1920s to put narratives in motion and simulate the simultaneity of telecommunication could finally abate. This, I believe, reinforces the legitimacy of using modernism as a historical category and literary genre to situate newspapers in the 1920s. For if, following Fredric Jameson, modernism was the cultural logic of a period of modernization, rather than that of an already fully modernized historical moment, it could be suggested that, with the full emergence of the age of mechanical reproduction in the 1930s, modernist journalism fulfilled its historical role (Jameson 2002: 141).

But we are still left with one last question to answer of the time when film became the new familiar narrative in motion and readers finally experienced full simultaneity and immediacy via the radio: what historical meaning can we attribute to the quantity of newspapers accumulated (and stored) day after day, year after year? I started this chapter by suggesting that this almost accidental archive constituted a new normative narrative in which information was set in stone as the archival memory of modern societies. And yet, the sheer size of all this stored information made it unmanageable as a new form of social regulation. A new figure thus had to emerge to maintain the power of accumulation without being mistaken for any form of industrial production. This was, as I will now try to demonstrate, the role of a particularly authoritative form of archive: culture.

Before concluding this book I would like to look at the ways in which the press coped with what by the 1920s was still just a prospect – although a rather concrete one – of permanent circulation and incessant accumulation. To answer this, it may be necessary to return some historicity to this narrative. The trajectories of some of our reporters in the 1930s will show us how they experienced, from the perspective of journalism, the moment when the formation of Kittler's 1900 discourse network – set in motion with the invention of film and the gramophone – finally reached the point when some of the tasks performed by newspapers became obsolete: the industrialization of film with sound took charge of popular fiction while the national broadcast of radio became the new instrument for the experience of imagined communities. It was a rather ironic process that allows us to retrospectively set the limits of the journalistic rhetoric of filmic metaphors and narratives in motion that has filled this book: while the written press still had more impact on its readers than film on its viewers – and radio on its listeners – the new world of images was enthusiastically embraced and the press constantly shown as being on the front line – metaphorically and otherwise – of an emerging visual culture; now, in the 1930s, when the age already was that of its own technological reproducibility (Benjamin 2008), newspapers functioned as the last defence of a written civilization under threat.

Interestingly, all our protagonists, the reporters and writers we have become acquainted with, will actively work against what was seen as the chaotic world of fleeting images left in movement without any kind of control. The most famous 'literate-journalists', the elite of journalism, invariably embraced fascism. João Ameal suddenly abandoned both modernism and journalism in the mid 1920s after a religious 'revelation'. Afterwards, he became one of the most important champions and doctrinarians of fascism in Portugal and a leading nationalist historian. In 1929, he received an invitation from José Leitão de Barros, film-maker and editor of *Notícias Ilustrado* – the magazine of *Diário de Notícias* – to collaborate in the magazine's effort to 'invent' a new country through images. Barros was deeply involved – with the likes of António Ferro, as we will see – in the shift from modernism towards nationalism. The project of inventing a new country was in this sense closely related to the national revolution initiated in 1926, which would become institutionalized with the creation of António de Oliveira Salazar's Estado Novo in 1933.

In a letter sent to Ameal, Barros argued that writers were under pressure from the new world of aeroplanes, gramophones and cinema, and that radio and television would inevitably take over the written word in the near future. Revolution, according to Barros, thus meant a violent replacement of the forms of perception: 'reading is no longer necessary: it is enough to see and listen'.[11] Ameal was of course close to the content of that revolution, but not to its form. In his response, in an article published in *Notícias Ilustrado* on 3 March 1929, he declared his horror of a world reduced to its mechanics, as only the written word could be proficient in the expression of thought and imagination. In sum, he reiterated the absolute superiority – expressive, civilizing and even religious – of the word:

> 'reading is no longer necessary: it is enough to see and listen'. It would be easy to reply with a slightly poetic sophism: couldn't we say that *to see* and *to listen* are, to a certain extent, *reading*, *reading* in the sounds and images arriving to us through space and life? But I don't like to think through sophisms … That's why I'd rather use another, entirely legitimate, argument: the word is superior, as an expression and index, to both image and sound – and it is still something else, namely the mental synthesis, the epitome of all science and all consciousness … Word is sound, is image, and is even colour, temperature, shape – and, most of all, it is intention, reflection, judgment … 'In the beginning was the word'… – the scriptures say. And it is from the verb that everything flows, that everything runs and spreads, beings and horizons, universes and civilizations. (Ameal 1929: 18)

The word should be seen as the organizing principle of everything else. Only through the word could images and sounds be given sense by consciousness and thought. Ameal thus seemed at odds with that part of his generation who stuck to images and their disruptive power. For him, very clearly, the struggle between words and images (and sounds) could be rigorously equated with a struggle between order and disorder. And yet, the involvement of men like Barros and Ferro in the making of the dictatorship's propaganda would soon show that it did not necessarily have to be like that. On the contrary, all the modernist images of new nationalism would fit perfectly into the world of order and tradition João Ameal wrote about in his books on fascism and Portuguese history.

António Ferro became, in 1933, the director of the newly created Secretariado de Propaganda Nacional (SPN, Secretariat of National Propaganda) and, in 1934, of the Sindicato Nacional dos Jornalistas (National Union of Journalists), which replaced the Sindicato dos Profissionais da Imprensa de Lisboa under the Estado Novo's corporatist structure. These were privileged positions from which to manage the institutionalization of authoritarianism on the one hand, but also the period of transition from a public sphere still organized around the press to a new system in which the new culture industries of image and sound were becoming hegemonic. Ferro's activity as head of the SPN in this context was very impressive. With the collaboration of some of the most important modernist visual artists – painters, illustrators, film-makers and architects – the SPN came up with a carefully balanced renewal of the nation's image. On the one hand, the representation of the people and of national symbols radically modernized the image of the country (thus abandoning the mild imagery of naturalism). On the other hand, however, any disturbance to order and tradition was immediately tempered by a very strict sense of belonging and distribution: workers at work, women at home, all regions – both metropolitan and colonial – clearly identified and distinguished through its unique landscape, architecture, cuisine, clothes, folklore and so on (Sapega 2008). More than political propaganda in the strict sense, Ferro's 'policy of the spirit' can be seen as a monumental synthesis of what Portugal and its people should look like.

Authority and political repression were, in this sense, directly translatable into the stabilization of those moving narratives and fleeting images from the by now already distant age of the 'jazz-band'. But this did not just represent a conservative political turn in the 1930s by the most modernist reporters of the 1920s. To start with, not all reporters analysed in this book became fascists. Artur Portela and Norberto Lopes – the famous reporters of Coutinho and Cabral's flight to Brazil and the Augusto Gomes trial – for instance, would live their entire journalistic carriers struggling against state censorship. Eventually, they would become figures of the anti-fascist resistance, if not for explicitly political reasons, then at least as journalists skilful in the use of double meanings and creating messages between the lines to circumvent censorship. The relationship between journalists and readers thus became defensive. Unlike big public events where both sides of journalistic communication shared the same public space – the streets of the city where events took place and newspapers circulated – with dictatorship and its hostility to crowds, the relation between journalists and readers changed into an almost secret dialogue of murmurs and half-truths.

But something else also changed in the public status of the press between the 1920s and the 1930s. For reasons that were not strictly political, newspapers seemed to have lost their power to mobilize narratives as images and disturb given perceptions. Somehow, the press also became more conservative in a sense that went beyond the political actions and opinions of journalists. In fact, the normative distribution of the different sections in the newspaper may be seen as the journalistic counterpart of the synthesis of Portugal created by the dictatorship's propaganda. As in the distribution of the country's different components – from landscape to regional lifestyles – within the same nationalist narrative, so too newspapers like *O Século* and *Diário de Notícias* made an important contribution to a generalized systematization of reality. The way newspapers contributed to this was less as vehicles of nationalism – which they often were as well – but mostly by breaking down the everyday into different sections and categorizing readers around new thematic magazines and supplements – on sports for men, cooking and fashion for women, cinema for the youth and comics for children – where everything and everyone was distributed according to pre-established places within a well-defined social hierarchy.

In this sense, the 1930s can be seen, at different levels, as a decisive moment in the history of journalism, when the press had to rethink its own position in relation to modernization in two different but interrelated historical processes. On the one hand, the world and its forms of representation seemed increasingly submitted to mechanisms of control and rationalization. Whereas nationalist propaganda standardized the nation, the structure of daily newspapers systematized the everyday. On the other hand, the press itself was losing its position as the dominant producer of images and information to more efficient forms of cinema and radio broadcasting. Some 1920s modernist journalists adapted to the new situation by following António Ferro as managers of the nationalist culture industry. Others kept within the limits of written journalism, but now in a situation where the position of newspapers was under threat. Those same reporters, like Artur Portela and Norberto Lopes, who used reportage as the narrative of modernity in the 1920s would soon become tragic heroes tirelessly pushing for freedom of speech.

Having said this, the struggle to circumvent censorship was not the only form of resistance that emerged in the 1930s. For if threats against the press came from two different places – fascist politics and audiovisual forms – then the most politicized journalists had to find a way to resist both. In other words, when authoritarianism got hold of the state and controlled the mechanisms of sounds and images at the exact same moment when these became hegemonic (and noting this coincidence is surely a good way to situate fascism historically), resistance was all the written word was left to do. In these circumstances, writers and journalists had to resist not only political silencing but also the overwhelming 'noise' of the culture industries. This is where we will meet, one last time, our most militant journalists. From the mid 1920s into the 1930s, it became very clear to proletarian writers like João Campos Lima and Ferreira de Castro that the most decisive political cause in the realm of culture was the defence of language and ideas. This would grant them a prominent place in Portuguese anti-fascist culture. More specifically, the definition of a new idea of culture as written language and its mobilization as the refuge of intellectual rationality and political consciousness against both fascist nationalism and the audiovisual forms of mass politics and mass entertainment would become a cornerstone of 1930s politics.

We can see how this political culture was founded on a paradox: not only were these progressive, revolutionary writers, forced to take a defensive position in a moment of political setback, the internal circumstances of the cultural field also alienated them from any contact with emergent cultural forms (the culture industries), thus restricting their practice to what was by then becoming residual: the press.[12] But the paradox does not stop here, because the press as a refuge against mass culture – at a moment when, through the audiovisual, cultural forms seemed finally able to overcome the obstacles posed by illiteracy – reproduced the most conservative traits of highbrow culture. Those same words that had only recently circulated through the streets of the city and metaphorically engaged with the everyday were now treated as cultural heritage. In the 1930s, those proletarian reporters that had so intensely participated in journalistic events were becoming proper intellectuals, observing the world from afar. As always, the press not only followed but helped organizing the whole process: gradually, these reporters abandoned the newsrooms of daily newspapers to found weekly or monthly cultural magazines and gave up on reportage to dedicate themselves to a form of culture now defined as the literary patrimony of leftist revolutionary traditions.

Again, we need to historicize what happened. The process started as early as 1925, when the anarchist newspaper *A Batalha* created its own magazine, *Renovação* ('Renewal'), a 'Fortnightly magazine of art, literature and novelties'. *Renovação* was, of course, very different from those other magazines where António Ferro and João Ameal had planned to invent reality through a coextensive movement of images and reporters. For one, it did not contain reportage. Its role was rather to give its proletarian readers a clear and systematic corpus of ideas. Culture, in this sense, still stood for the process of self-education traditionally referred to as *Bildung*. But now it had to readjust in order to fulfil two urgent tasks: to think of itself collectively, as a proletarian culture in a world of masses, and resist the specific forms of mass culture gaining terrain through the mechanical reproduction of images – and which nationalism appropriated so easily.[13] Accordingly, a journalist like Ferreira de Castro (later to become one of the leading intellectuals of anti-fascism) contributed to the magazine by guiding readers through complex ideological and aesthetic questions. More than a journalist, or even a writer, he was already acting as a proper intellectual – and even writing a series of articles theorizing about the role of intellectuals in the defence of freedom. This meant shifting away from being the reporter he had been, thereby distancing himself from the everyday, to engage in talk about reality through the mediation of concepts. As the 1920s came to a close, this tendency would become more evident. In 1929, João Campos Lima edited a magazine whose title, *Cultura*, already assumed that the public would easily recognize the word as a reference to the defence of a threatened civilization based on ideas and literacy. A year later, this same group of anarchist journalists and intellectuals created *O Globo*, presented as 'an anticipation of the journalism of the future',[14] whose content combined some information and politics with doctrine and, above all, a pedagogical corpus to educate readers.

The genre found its ultimate realization in 1934 with still another weekly magazine, *O Diabo*, or 'The Devil'. For six years – up until it was forcibly closed down by censorship – all the disparate groups of journalists, intellectuals and writers marginalized by the dictatorship used the magazine as a cultural 'popular front' against nationalism (Trindade 2004). *O Diabo* would constitute, in this sense, one of the most symbolic bulwarks of the opposition to the Estado Novo. The magazine launched a comprehensive critique of the industrialization of the press, sports, cinema, radio and all other mass phenomenon controlled by the market and/or nationalism. Contrary to the twin threats of the Secretariado de Propaganda Nacional and popular films and songs, it would become a site of intense ideological work and, as such, the place where culture was more strongly systematized as a tool to be used to read the world. More specifically, culture in *O Diabo* became a language of critique and, consequently, the last sphere of social life where political and historical transformation still seemed imaginable.

Under the rule of nationalist authoritarianism and traditionalism, this truly looked like the last haven of freedom. Despite their political differences, all movements, from anarchists – Ferreira de Castro was one of the magazine's directors – to republicans and socialists, used it to perpetuate their own traditions of struggle and would later evoke it as part of their memory. It was, however, as the setting for the emergence of Marxism and of a new generation of Marxist writers and intellectuals in the Portuguese public sphere that *O Diabo* would be most remembered. This new generation had its roots in the different traditions circulating through the magazine – the last director, a young communist, was Lima's son – but their impact would radically change the landscape of both Portuguese culture and the country's leftist politics. On the one hand the magazine laid the grounds for neo-realism, the most important cultural movement resisting fascism during the dictatorship and whose literary manifestations would become dominant in the imaginary of the opposition. On the other, with Marxism, *O Diabo* became a site of an intense negotiation between two inseparable but contradictory interpretations of culture: as the language of critique I have just mentioned (of capitalism, nationalism and its culture industries) and as the disciplinary systematization of an all-encompassing ideology.

I must insist on this last point as it will allow me to situate the role of 1930s culture in the reconstitution of the public sphere, and in particular its role in the development of journalistic readership, as the new readers of *O Diabo* should look very different from the crowds of modernist journalism discussed in Chapters 2 and 3. While reading *O Diabo*, or as the addressees of culture in general, these new readers were supposed not only to acquire the necessary intellectual tools to understand the world around them, but also, and as one would expect of Marxist political culture, to participate in its transformation. Readers, in other words, were encouraged to become cultivated, and this was seen as a truly emancipatory move when compared to the supposedly passive, even when passionate, relationship promoted by newspapers.

José Rodrigues Miguéis – probably the first intellectual to use historical materialism in a public discussion in Portugal – tried to articulate this difference by highlighting the differences between a weekly magazine like *O Diabo* and the daily press. According to him, newspapers were too ephemeral to constitute a proper form of knowledge. The habit of Portuguese readers of using libraries not to search for knowledge but to look at old newspapers seemed to him sterile, almost mournful: 'we can feel, in libraries, the love of the Portuguese for fossils'.[15] Miguéis's point brings us back to the question of the archive, for what he was suggesting was that stored newspapers were culturally pointless. Information was a commodity to be quickly consumed and the news became obsolete in just twenty-four hours. Old newspapers would in this sense constitute a dead, passive, archive.

Reading old newspapers in libraries was the exact opposite of the critical attitude required by culture as a dynamic form of interaction with the present. Accordingly, the subjects of cultural production, the readers of the cultural magazine, should assume a completely different role from previous forms of reading. This new reader was, then, very distant from the passive reader of newspapers in libraries, but also from the more active participants in sensational events like the public manifestations around the flight to Rio de Janeiro or the football match where they cheered for Portugal against Spain. The reader of the cultural magazine was not to be mistaken for the crowds of mass events. In the context of 1930s Marxism, deeply marked by Leninist productivism, readers were automatically equated with the proletariat, and proletarians were necessarily treated as fellow travellers in the same political cause: 'your duty is to set *O Diabo* in motion in your village and in your club, among your friends and amidst your family', the newspaper extolled.[16] The image of the reader as consumer and, to a certain extent, distributor of the magazine, may at first sight not seem very different from that of readers of 1920s modernist journalism. After all, in both cases, the newspaper would only reach its full meaning when the process of circulation took it to the realm of its readership. The difference, then, was in the meaning produced by modernist newspapers and cultural magazines. Whereas the former were animated by emotions (feelings of nationalism, or fear, as in the murder of Maria Alves), *O Diabo* was based on political ideas. The magazine reader, in this sense, was somehow also an intellectual. In short, given the political meaning of the magazine, and of culture in this context, readers qua proletarians should be seen as the true agents of the political struggles cultural journalism was supposed to trigger.

The way in which *O Diabo* defined its relation with readers can in this sense be said to invert the forms of engagement of modernist reporters with the world. While, in the 1920s, António Ferro and João Ameal presented themselves and their magazines as machines inventing reality, *O Diabo* defined itself as the expression – almost the reflection – of intellectually autonomous readers: 'you, reader, you; intellectual or worker, are our brain, our heart, our hands'.[17] The authority in these magazines was then apparently transferred from the dynamism of modernist reporters to a completely different type of modernity, that of labour as the embodiment of historical transformation. From this perspective, culture's legitimacy would depend on its ability to be proletarian, that is, the cultural form of the most dynamic agent in the ultimate modernist event: revolution. As workers, or, with the revolutionary legitimacy of the working class, these readers opened the space for the emergence of a new political subjectivity. But this, the magazine incessantly insisted, would only happen if they ceased to be passive readers and became active forces in the making of the newspaper. Ultimately, the magazine should take the activism of proletarian writers further and radicalize the struggle embodied in the 1921 strike of journalists and typesetters into a truly egalitarian situation where the distinction between writers and proletarians would disappear altogether.[18] Only in these circumstances could the magazine become the voice of the people and, as such, constitute an enhanced version of the 1:1 scale relation between the press and the world.

Unfortunately, the history of these new dynamic narratives, not only circulating in printed form, but in fact being constantly produced and reproduced between writers and readers in an egalitarian mass movement of historical transformation, cannot end on this utopian note. For when we move from well-intentioned appeals to the proletariat to the concrete forms of interaction between the magazine and its readers, the former's tone seems to drastically change. *O Diabo*, despite its rhetorical radicalism, still seemed to find it difficult to grant readers full intellectual autonomy. On 20 September 1936, for example, the magazine admonished one reader who had contacted the magazine looking for some guidance or clarification:

> we can infer, by your letter, that you don't keep the paper's past editions. My dear friend, you're not supposed to throw *O Diabo* away after reading it. For it already constitutes a corpus of culture that is unusual in our milieu, and so you need to read the past numbers in your spare time. There is something to learn in all of them.[19]

The professorial tone of the reprimand illustrates how, after all, the magazine did not manage to eliminate the old privileges of the cultural relationship. The letter had been sent to a section called 'consultation room', which suggests that the magazine should still be seen as a place of experts, specialized in forms of knowledge that it was difficult for non-professional intellectuals to access. Conversely, it was still impossible for the reader to be a writer or a full-time intellectual because, as a worker, they only had their 'spare time' to read the magazine and its 'past numbers'.[20]

More importantly, the 'corpus of culture' was proof of the authority of the archive, inescapable even in the most revolutionary setting. Culture was still treated as a form of accumulation, a patrimony perpetuating old forms of legitimacy. Contrary to the daily information of old newspapers, it was not perishable. But this only contributed to make its accumulation more authoritative. Readers were invited to engage with cultural objects for their self-fulfilment and political self-consciousness. But only as long as they remained readers, that is, the receivers of accumulated cultural goods. This sets a final limit on our narratives in motion. For, according to whoever wrote the above unsigned note, narratives were not supposed to circulate at all. As that reader was soon to find out, after being patronizingly admonished by their magazine, cultural narratives too were stably deposited in the archive. The cultural authority of the proletarian as the force of historical transformation seemed unable to overcome the power of those who managed the accumulation of knowledge.

It may seem ironic, not to say dramatic, that this short but sharp reproach came in those same pages that were supposedly fighting for freedom of speech and intellectual autonomy. It was as if the hierarchical roles of the cultural field, and the mechanisms for the production and circulation of words, obeyed a higher rationality, above political divisions. This is surely in part true, and an important aspect of modernity as a process of rationalization. However, the historical context with which this book finishes has another and even more dramatic irony in store for us. For such a display of intellectual authority came in a moment when a cultural system based on writing and reading was itself becoming undermined by other forms. True power was shifting to images and sounds, and these were all on the side of authoritarianism. As for the Marxist intellectuals responsible for the creation of an emergent working-class culture, all they were left with to fight fascism were newspapers, a residual cultural form made of an already weakened version of the written word.

Notes

1. Kevin Barnhurst and John Nerone describe this evolution from 'the primitive Victorian newspaper', seen as 'messy' but also 'weird and dramatic' and 'copious and busy', to a more 'rational, functional, and premeditated' set of narratives organized by 'modern design' in terms of an ordering of the world that would make it more perceptible; they add, 'the streamlining of the front page helped readers navigate their world with more confidence and efficiency' (Barnhurst and Nerone 2001: 251).
2. An initial manifestation of this historicization was the habit of collecting periodicals in volumes. According to Margaret Beetham, 'this is a paradox. A periodical, by definition, appears in single numbers separated by time. Putting several numbers into one bound volume changes all this, not least by suggesting that *really* the periodical is a kind of book and the numbers are incomplete sections of the whole' (Beetham 1990: 23).
3. *O Século*, 16 May 1921, p.1.
4. *Diário de Notícias*, 29 December 1924, p.9.
5. I thus believe that the press, in particular, and the circulation of information in general, can be seen as a key site of modern social control, especially when we consider the participation of readers in the making of journalistic meaning. It is not very difficult to see how the logic of 'access to information', the relation between 'masses', 'samples' and 'data', the 'floating rates of exchange' and particularly the image of the 'serpent' mentioned by Gilles Deleuze can help us think about the production of information as a commodity and its circulation through reading: 'the numerical language of control is made of codes that mark access to information, or reject it ... Perhaps it is money that expresses the distinction between the two societies best, since discipline always referred back to minted money that locks gold as numerical standard, while control relates to floating rates of exchange, modulated according to a rate established by a set of standard currencies. The old monetary mole is the animal of the space of enclosure, but the serpent is that of the societies of control' (Deleuze 1992: 5).
6. If the newspaper was at all able to structure the perception of lived experience, then life itself had to become organized around the time unit of the daily newspaper: the everyday. Richard Terdiman, following Henri Lefebvre, draws a straight line between the development of daily newspapers (*le quotidien*) and the emergence of a modern notion of everyday life (*quotidien*): 'daily life and the daily paper grew up together, in response to the same determinants: [Henri Lefebvre] "until the nineteenth century, until the advent of competitive capitalism and the expansion of the world trade, the quotidian as such did not exist". Lefebvre's assertion could as well describe the transformations by which the newspaper became an indispensable element of emerging

everyday life … As such the newspaper becomes a characteristic metonym of modern life itself' (Terdiman 1985: 119–20).

7. Kittler refers to Freud's psychoanalysis and Saussure's linguistics as parallel (and as such coextensive) phenomena of the discourse network, as in both cases the signifier – the unconscious, the sign – also determined the signified. However, it is through the realm of the new machines enabling the reproducibility of sounds and images (the gramophone and film, to which, as before, I will add the newspaper as a machine that transformed words into circulating things, thus enabling them to be seen and heard) that he takes his argument further: 'as technological media, the gramophone and film store acoustical and optical data serially with superhuman precision. Invented at the same time by the same engineers, they launched a two-pronged attack on a monopoly that had been granted to the book until the time of universal alphabetization: a monopoly on the storage of serial data. Circa 1900, the ersatz sensuality of Poetry could be replaced, not by Nature, but by technologies. The gramophone empties out words by bypassing their imaginary aspect (signifieds) for their real aspects (the physiology of the voice)' (Kittler 1990: 246).

8. Richard Terdiman described this paradox between evanescence and durability, the accumulating power of daily information, rather competently: 'in the image of the daily paper, gone in twenty-four hours, the media participates in a paradox. Each number of a daily may be fleeting. But its power to form social consciousness and practice extends far beyond its ephemeral existence. This power has proven astonishingly durable. It arises uncannily through evanescence. News publications are not just consumed. We read them; they form us. We discard yesterday's paper, but our habit of doing so only reinforces our practice of reaching for this morning's delivery. It deepens our quotidian anticipation of the *quotidien*, our daily expectation of the 'news'. (Terdiman 1985: 372).

9. Jonathan Crary already seemed to suggest that there was no contradiction between glancing over and storing, as brevity was the time unit of the discourse network. In other words, the capacity to permanently absorb new things was not incompatible with the work of storing them: 'the plural composition of *Pines and Rocks* [Paul Cézanne, 1897], its particular "jumble", is relevant to one of the crucial hypotheses of Freud's "Project". Jacques Derrida emphasizes that already in 1895, Freud had defined the paradoxical operation of the psyche as "a potential for indefinite preservation and an unlimited capacity for reception". That is, Freud tried to conceptualize how we simultaneously have the facility for *storage* of memories and the ability to receive new images free of the residue of earlier "traces". Of interest here is Freud's imaginary solution which Derrida describes as "a double system contained in a single differentiated apparatus: a perpetually available innocence and an infinite reserve of traces"' (Crary 2000: 338).

10. The ability to reproduce the world at the exact same scale thus seems to grant the newspaper a museological, rather than just archival, role. Vanessa Schwartz compares the Grévin Museum in Paris with journalism's encyclopaedic account of modern life: 'modeling itself on the newspaper reinforced, rather than opposed, the Musée Grévin's status as a museum. In the same way that the universal survey museum such as the Louvre functioned as a summary of all knowledge, the press claimed to represent all of contemporary life. The museum's insistent classificatory schemes matched the newspaper's rubrics: the *feuilletons*, the *échos* and the *fait divers*. In addition, both the component parts of the museum and the newspaper did not consist of a developmental narrative in which one section followed the next in any particular logic: rather their parts combined instead to create a summary whole' (Schwartz 1998: 109).

11. Letter from José Leitão de Barros to João Ameal, 31 January 1929. João Ameal archive (E37), Portuguese National Library, Lisbon.
12. If it is possible to use Raymond Williams's notion of the *residual* to speak of cultural apparatuses, then newspapers in the 1930s could be seen as cultural objects 'effectively formed in the past, but ... still active in the cultural process, not only and often not at all as an element of the past, but as an effective element of the present' (Williams 1977: 122).
13. Kittler sees the discourse network of the 1900s as what broke *Bildung* apart. Culture, in the context I am trying to locate it, could then be seen as either a reaction against the period's historical transformations or as the retrieval of a past unity: 'Culture [*Bildung*], the great unity in which speaking, hearing, writing, and reading would achieve a mutual transparency and relation to meaning, breaks apart' (Kittler 1990: 222).
14. *O Globo*, 9 March 1930, p.8.
15. *O Diabo*, 13 September 1934, p.4.
16. *O Diabo*, 11 May 1940, p.4.
17. *O Diabo*, 24 June 1939, p.1.
18. The proletarian reader *O Diabo* had in mind does not seem very different from Jacques Rancière's emancipated spectator as the one who is able 'to challenge the opposition between viewing and acting', as surely between writing and reading (Rancière 2009: 13).
19. *O Diabo*, 20 September 1936, p.4.
20. In Rancière's terms, it can be said that here *O Diabo* failed to become a true 'ignorant schoolmaster' – i.e., the one who only teaches his ignorance as every person is equally intelligent – and free itself from the traditional methods of 'public instruction: 'the instruction of the ignorant by the learned, of men buried in egotistical material concerns by men of devotion, of individuals enclosed in their particularities by the universality of reason and public power. This is called public instruction' (Rancière 1991: 131).

References

ACTIL (Associação de Classe dos Trabalhadores da Imprensa de Lisboa). 1906. 'Regulamento interno da Associação de Classe dos Trabalhadores da Imprensa de Lisboa'. Lisbon: ACTIL.

Adorno, T.W. 2001 [1991]. *The Culture Industry: Selected Essays on Mass Culture*, ed. J.M. Bernstein. London: Routledge.

Ameal, J. 1922. *A religião do espaço*. Lisbon: 'Lumen' Empresa Internacional Editora.

—— 1929. 'A palavra, a imagem e o som (carta ao director do *Notícias Ilustrado*)', *Notícias Ilustrado*, 3 March, p.18.

Ameal, J., and L. de O. Guimarães. 1924. 'Entre nós', *O Chiado* 1 (Summer): 2–3.

Anderson, B. 1991 [1983]. *Imagined Communities. Reflections on the Origin and Spread of Nationalism*, rev. edn. London: Verso.

Anderson, P. 1984. 'Modernity and Revolution', *New Left Review* 144: 96–113.

Araújo, N. de. 1923. *O crime da carne branca*. Lisbon: Francisco A. Direitinho.

Auerbach, E. 1953. *Mimesis: The Representation of Reality in Western Literature*, trans. W.R. Trask. Princeton: Princeton University Press.

Avellar, F. 1888. 'O Dandy', *A Ginástica* 1: 1–6.

Bakhtin, M. 1984 [1929]. *Problems of Dostoevsky's Poetics*, trans. and ed. C. Emerson. Minneapolis: University of Minnesota Press.

Barnhurst, K., and J. Nerone. 2001. *The Form of the News*. New York: Guildford Press.

Beegan, G. 2008. *The Mass Image: A Social History of Photomechanical Reproduction in Victorian London*. New York: Palgrave Macmillan.

Beetham, M. 1990. 'Towards a Theory of the Periodical as a Publishing Genre', in L. Brake, A. Jones and L. Madden (eds), *Investigating Victorian Journalism*. London: Macmillan, pp.19–32.

Benjamin, W. 1983. *Charles Baudelaire. A Lyric Poet in the Era of High Capitalism*, trans. H. Zohn. London: Verso.

—— 2002 [1982]. *The Arcades Project*, trans. H. Eiland and K. McLaughlin. Cambridge, MA: Harvard University Press.

—— 2008. *The Work of Art in the Age of Its Technological Reproducibility, and Other Writings on Media*, ed. M.W. Jennings, B. Doherty and T.Y. Levin. Cambridge, MA: Harvard University Press.

Bergson, H. 2007 [1911]. *Creative Evolution*, trans. A. Mitchell. New York: Cosimo.

Bourdieu, P. 1996 [1992]. *The Rules of Art: Genesis and Structure of the Literary Field*, trans. S. Emanuel. Stanford: Stanford University Press.

Bourke, J. 1996. *Dismembering the Male: Men's Bodies, Britain, and the Great War*. London: Reaktion Press.

Bouveresse, J. 2001. *Schmock ou le triomphe du journalisme. La grande bataille de Karl Kraus*. Paris: Seuil.

Bragança, A. de. 1922. 'Crónica', *Contemporânea*, May, pp.1–3.

—— 1922. 'Crónica de Livros', *Diário de Lisboa*, 28 March, p.2.

Butler, J. 1993. *Bodies that Matter: On the Discursive Limits of 'Sex'*. New York: Routledge.
Campbell, K. 2000. 'Journalistic Discourses and Constructions of Modern Knowledge', in L. Brake, B. Bell and D. Finkelstein (eds), *Nineteenth-century Media and the Construction of Identities*. New York: Palgrave, pp.40–53.
Casetti, F. 2008 [2005]. *Eye of the Century: Film, Experience, Modernity*, trans. E. Larkin and J. Pranolo. New York: Columbia University Press.
Castro, A. de. 1916. *Fumo do meu cigarro*. Lisbon: Empresa Literária Fluminense.
––––––– 1917. *Fantoches e manequins*. Lisbon: Editora Literária Fluminense.
––––––– 1933. *Sexo 33 ou a revolução da mulher (ídilios e ironias)*. Lisbon: Emprêsa Nacional de Publicidade.
Castro, F. de. 1921. *Mas...* Lisbon: Tipografia Boente and Silva.
––––––– 1922. 'Os paramos do desejo', *A Hora. Arte, Atualidades, Questões Sociais* 1: n.p.
––––––– 1923. *O êxito fácil*. Lisbon: Francisco A. Direitinho.
––––––– 1924. *A metamorfose*. Lisbon: Jayme Lança.
––––––– 1925. *A ditadura feminista*. Lisbon: Jayme Lança.
––––––– 1926. *A epopeia do trabalho*. Lisbon: Livraria Renascença.
––––––– n.d. *O êxito fácil e outras novelas*. Lisbon: Sociedade Contemporânea de Autores.
Castro, F. de, and E. Frias. 1924. *A boca da esfinge*. Lisbon: Livrarias Aillaud and Bertrand.
Catroga, F. 2010 [1991]. *O republicanismo em Portugal. Da formação ao 5 de Outubro de 1910*. Lisbon: Casa das Letras.
Charle, C. 2004. *Le siècle de la presse (1830–1939)*. Paris: Seuil.
Charney, L., and V. Schwartz (eds). 1995. *Cinema and the Invention of Modern Life*. Berkeley: University of California Press.
Clark, T.J. 1999 [1984]. *The Painting of Modern Life: Paris in the Art of Manet and His Followers*. London: Thames and Hudson.
Coelho, T.P. 1990. '"Pérfida Albion" and "Little Portugal": The Role of the Press in British and Portuguese National Perceptions of the 1890 Ultimatum', *Portuguese Studies* 6: 173–90.
Collier, P. 2006. *Modernism in Fleet Street*. London: Ashgate.
Conceição, A.P. da. 1929. *Tragédias do ar. Crónicas dos desastres mortais da aviação portuguesa*. Lisbon: Paulo Guedes.
Crary, J. 2000. *Suspensions of Perception: Attention, Spectacle, and Modern Culture*. Cambridge, MA: MIT Press.
Dantas, J. 1915. *Ao ouvido de Madame X*. Porto: Livraria Chardron.
––––––– 1916. *Mulheres*. Porto: Livraria Chardron.
––––––– n.d. *Como elas amam*. Lisboa: Sociedade Editora Portugal-Brasil.
Debord, G. 1994 [1967]. *The Society of the Spectacle*, trans. D. Nicholson-Smith. New York: Zone Books.
Deleuze, G. 2005 [1983]. *Cinema 1: The Movement-Image*, trans. H. Tomlinson and B. Habberjam. London: Continuum.
––––––– 1992. 'Postscript on the Societies of Control', *October* 59: 3–7.
De Marchis, G. 2009. *E Quem é o autor desse crime? Il romanzo d'appendice in Portogallo dall'ultimatum alla repubblica (1890–1910)*. Milan: Edizioni Universitarie di Lettere Economia Diritto.
Didi-Huberman, G. 2009. *Quand les images prennent position. L'oeil de l'histoire*. Paris: Minuit.
Domingues, M. 1923. *Delicioso pecado*. Lisbon: Francisco A. Direitinho.
Dos Passos, J. 2001 [1938]. *USA*. London: Penguin.
Eagleton, T. 2003. *Figures of Dissent*. London: Verso.

Eksteins, M. 1989. *Rites of Spring: The Great War and the Birth of the Modern Age.* Boston: Mariner Books.

Elias, N., and E. Dunning. 1986. *Quest of Excitement: Sport and Leisure in the Civilizing Process.* Oxford: Blackwell.

Elsaesser, T. 1990. 'Introduction', in T. Elsaesser and A. Barker (eds), *Early Cinema: Space, Frame, Narrative.* London: BFI Publishing, pp.11–30.

Feio, M. 1924. *A alma de Sacadura Cabral.* Lisbon: Imprensa Beleza.

Ferreira, R. 1923. *O presidente da república.* Lisbon: Francisco A. Direitinho.

———— 1926a. 'As 2 hipoteses do crime de Maria Alves', *ABC*, 8 April, pp.4–5.

———— 1926b. 'A tragédia da actriz Maria Alves', *ABC*, 15 April, pp.4–5.

———— 1926c. 'Reporter X e Augusto Gomes', *ABC*, 13 May, pp.4–5.

———— 1926d. *Memórias do Repórter X. Homens de dia, mulheres de noite. Lenine, Mussolini, Raquel Meller, Rasputine, Mata-Hari.* Porto: Albatroz Editora.

Ferro, A. 1921a. 'Crónica literária', *Diário de Lisboa*, 25 June, p.2.

———— 1921b. 'A *Ilustração Portuguesa* entrevista a *Ilustração Portuguesa*', *Ilustração Portuguesa*, 8 October, p.232.

———— 1923a. *Batalha das flores.* Rio de Janeiro: H. Antunes.

———— 1923b. *A idade do jazz-band.* São Paulo: Monteiro Lobato.

———— 1924. *Mar alto.* Lisbon: Livraria Portugália Editora.

———— 1987. *Obras de António Ferro*, vol. 1. *Intervenção modernista, teoria do gosto.* Lisbon: Verbo.

Foucault, M. 1977 [1975]. *Discipline and Punish: The Birth of the Prison*, trans. A Sheridan. New York: Pantheon.

Fritzsche, P. 1992. *A Nation of Fliers: German Aviation and the Popular Imagination.* Cambridge, MA: Harvard University Press.

———— 1996. *Reading Berlin 1900.* Cambridge, MA: Harvard University Press.

Garcez, A. 1924. 'Um film desportivo', *Sport Ilustrado. Publicação quinzenal de fotografias e sport*, 30 April, p.1.

Gervais, T. 2007. 'L'illustration photographique. Naissance du spectacle de l'information', Ph.D. diss. Paris: École des Hautes Études en Sciences Sociales.

Ginzburg, C. 1980. 'Clues: Morelli, Freud, and Sherlock Holmes', *History Workshop* 9: 5–36.

Gramsci, A. 1971. *Selections from the Prison Notebooks*, trans. Q. Hoare and G.N. Smith. London: Lawrence and Wishart.

Gumbrecht, H.U. 1997. *In 1926: Living at the Edge of Time.* Cambridge, MA: Harvard University Press.

Gunning, T. 1990a. 'The Cinema of Attractions: Early Film, Its Spectator and the Avant-Garde', in T. Elsaesser and A. Barker (eds), *Early Cinema: Space, Frame, Narrative.* London: BFI Publishing, pp.56–62.

———— 1990b. 'Non-Continuity, Continuity, Discontinuity: A Theory of Genres in Early Film', in T. Elsaesser A. Barker (eds), *Early Cinema. Space, Frame, Narrative.* London: BFI Publishing, pp. 86-94.

———— 1995. 'Tracing the Individual Body: photography, detectives, and early cinema', in L. Charney and V. Schwartz (eds), *Cinema and the Invention of Modern Life.* Berkeley: University of California Press, pp. 15-45.

Gunthert, A. 1999. 'La conquête de l'instantané. Archéologie de l'imaginaire photographique en France (1841–1895)', Ph.D. diss. Paris: École des Hautes Études en Sciences Sociales.

Jameson, F. 1981. *The Political Unconscious: Narrative as a Socially Symbolic Act*. Ithaca, NY: Cornell University Press.

—— 2002. *A Singular Modernity: An Essay on the Ontology of the Present*. London: Verso.

—— 2009. *Valences of the Dialectic*. London: Verso.

Jauss, H.R. 1982. *Towards an Aesthetic of Reception*, trans. T. Bahti. Minneapolis: University of Minnesota Press.

Jilani, S. 2013. 'Urban Modernity and Fluctuating Time: "Catching the Tempo" of the 1920s City Symphony Films', *Senses of Cinema* 68. Retrieved from http://sensesofcinema.com/2013/feature-articles/urban-modernity-and-fluctuating-time-catching-the-tempo-of-the-1920s-city-symphony-films/

Kalifa, D. 1995. *L'encre et la sang. Récits de crimes et société à la Belle Époque*. Paris: Fayard.

Kittler, F. 1990 [1985]. *Discourse networks 1800/1900*, trans. M. Metteer and C. Cullens. Stanford: Stanford University Press.

Kracauer, S. 1995 [1963]. *The Mass Ornament: Weimar Essays*, ed. and trans. T.Y. Levin. Cambridge, Mass.: Harvard University Press.

—— 1998 [1930]. *The Salaried Masses: Duty and Distraction in Weimar Germany*, trans. Q. Hoare. London: Verso.

Kraus, K. 2013 [1919]. *The Last Days of Mankind*, trans. M. Russell. Retrieved 11 February 2015 from: http://thelastdaysofmankind.com/act-i-scene-14.html.

Kraus, R. 1999. *The Picasso Papers*. Cambridge, MA: MIT Press.

Lee, A.J. 1976. *The Origins of the Popular Press in England, 1855–1914*. London: Croom Helm.

Lewis, P. 2007. *Cambridge Introduction to Modernism*. Cambridge: Cambridge University Press.

Lima, J.C. 1927. *Via dolorosa – gente devota*. Coimbra: 'Atlântida' Livraria Editora.

Lopes, N. 1923. *Cruzeiro do sul*. Porto: Renascença.

Machado, J.C., and A. Hogan. 1861. *A vida em Lisboa*. Lisbon: Typographia do Panorama.

Mallarmé, S. 1998. *Oeuvres complétes*. Paris: La Pléiade.

Marcuse, H. 2007. *Art and Liberation: Collected Papers of Herbert Marcuse*, vol. 4, ed. D. Kellner. London: Routledge.

Maria, A. n.d. *O grande e horrível crime de Maria Alves esganada pelo seu próprio amigo*. Lisbon: Humberto Peres.

Melo, A. de. 2004. *Cinco escudos azuis. A história da selecção nacional de futebol de 1921 até aos nossos dias*. Lisbon: D. Quixote.

Mitchell, W.J.T. 1994. *Picture Theory*. Chicago: University of Chicago Press.

Morin, E. 1978. *Le cinéma, ou l'homme imaginaire*. Paris: Minuit.

Mulvey, L. 1975. 'Visual Pleasure and Narrative Cinema', *Screen* 16(3): 6–18.

Musil, R. 1995 [1943]. *The Man Without Qualities*, trans. S. Wilkins and B. Pike. London: Picador.

Negt, O., and A. Kluge. 1988. 'The Public Sphere and Experience', *October* 46: 61–82.

Osborne, P. 1995. *The Politics of Time: Modernity and the Avant-Garde*. London: Verso.

Pessoa, F. 2001. *The Selected Prose of Fernando Pessoa*, trans. and ed. R. Zenith. New York: Grove Press.

—— 2002 [1984]. *The Book of Disquiet*, trans. R. Zenith. London: Penguin.

—— 2006. *A Little Larger Than the Entire Universe: Selected Poems*, trans. and ed. R. Zenith. London: Penguin.

Portela, A. 1921. 'Jornais e jornalistas – Como se faz uma entrevista moderna', *Diário de Lisboa*, 30 November, p.5.

———— 1923. *Divina*. Lisbon: Francisco A. Direitinho.

———— n.d. *Tudo amor. Prosas e tanagras*. Lisbon: Ottosgrafica.

Portela, A., and N. de Araújo. 1927. *O crime de Augusto Gomes. Notas de reportagem colhidas por dois jornalistas*. Lisbon: Tip. da Emprêsa do Anuário Comercial.

Proust, M. 2000 [1921]. *In Search of Lost Time*, vol. 3: *The Guermantes Way*, trans. C.K.S. Moncrieff and D.J. Enright. London: Vintage.

Rancière, J. 1991 [1987]. *The Ignorant Schoolmaster: Five Lessons in Intellectual Emancipation*, trans. K. Ross. Stanford: Stanford University Press.

———— 1994 [1992]. *The Names of History: On the Poetics of Knowledge*, trans. H. Melehy. Minneapolis: University of Minnesota Press.

———— 2004 [1995]. *Disagreement: Politics and Philosophy*, trans. J. Rose. Minneapolis: University of Minnesota Press.

———— 2009 [2008]. *The Emancipated Spectator*, trans. G. Elliott. London: Verso.

———— 2011 [1998]. *Mute Speech: Literature, Critical Theory and Politics*, trans. J. Swenson. New York: Columbia University Press.

Redondo, B. n.d. *O crime de Augusto Gomes*. Lisbon: Colecção Os Grandes Criminosos, Livraria Barateira.

Reitter, P. 2008. *The Anti-Journalist: Karl Kraus and Jewish Self-fashioning in Fin-de-Siècle Europe*. Chicago: University of Chicago Press.

Ribeiro, M. 1923. *A ressurreição*. Lisbon: Livraria Editora Guimarães.

Rifkin, A. 1993. *Street Noises: Parisian Pleasure, 1900–1940*. Manchester: Manchester University Press.

Rodrigues, D. 1910. 'Factos são provas', *Tiro e Sport* 453: 2.

Rubery, M. 2009. *The Novelty of Newspapers: Victorian Fiction after the Invention of the News*. Oxford: Oxford University Press.

Salmon, R. 2000. 'A Simulacrum of Power: Intimacy and Abstraction in the Rhetoric of the New Journalism', in L. Brake, B. Bell and D. Finkelstein (eds), *Nineteenth-Century Media and the Construction of Identities*. New York: Palgrave, pp.27–39.

Sapega, E. 2008. *Consensus and Debate in Salazar's Portugal: Visual and Literary Negotiations of the National Text, 1933–1948*. Philadelphia: Penn State University Press.

Schivelbusch, W. 1986 [1977]. *The Railway Journey: The Industrialization of Time and Space in the Nineteenth Century*. Berkeley: University of California Press.

Schudson, M. 1978. *Discovering the News: A Social History of American Newspapers*. New York: Basic Books.

Schwartz, V. 1998. *Spectacular Realities. Early Mass Culture in Fin-de-Siècle Paris*. Berkeley: University of California Press.

Sherry, V. 2003. *The Great War and the Language of Modernism*. Oxford: Oxford University Press.

Starr, P. 2004. *The Creation of the Media: Political Origins of Modern Communications*. New York: Basic Books.

Stein, G. 1998. *Writings, 1932–1946*. New York: Library of America.

Terdiman, R. 1985. *Discourse/Counter-Discourse: The Theory and Practice of Symbolic Resistance in Nineteenth-Century France*. Ithaca, NY: Cornell University Press.

Thiesse, A.-M. 1984. *Le roman du quotidien. Lecteurs et lectures populaires à la Belle Époque*. Paris: Le Chemin Vert.

Trindade, L. 2004. *O espírito do diabo. Discursos e posições intelectuais no semanário O Diabo, 1934–1940*. Porto: Campo das Letras.

—— 2008. *O estranho caso do nacionalismo português. O Salazarismo entre a literatura e a política*. Lisbon: Imprensa das Ciências Sociais.

Vasconcelos, A. 1909. *A aviação*. Porto: Actualidades Científicas, Livraria Portuense de Lopes & Cᵃ.

Williams, R. 1977. *Marxism and Literature*. Oxford: Oxford University Press.

White, H. 1987. *The Content of the Form: Narrative Discourse and Historical Representation*. Baltimore: Johns Hopkins University Press.

—— 1999. *Figural Realism: Studies in the Mimesis Effect*. Baltimore: Johns Hopkins University Press.

Žižek, S. 1989. *The Sublime Object of Ideology*. London: Verso.

Zweig, S. 1964 [1943]. *The World of Yesterday*, trans. H. Zohn. Lincoln: University of Nebraska Press.

Index

www.ingramcontent.com/pod-product-compliance
Lightning Source LLC
Chambersburg PA
CBHW070925030426
42336CB00014BA/2544